New England
COOKING

SEASONS & CELEBRATIONS

Also from Berkshire House Publishers

The New Red Lion Inn Cookbook
Suzi Forbes Chase

The Kripalu Cookbook: Gourmet Vegetarian Recipes
Atma Jo Ann Levitt

Soups & Stews for Fall and Winter Days
Liza Fosburgh

Apple Orchard Cookbook
Janet Christensen & Betty Bergman Levin

New England COOKING

SEASONS & CELEBRATIONS

CLAIRE HOPLEY

Principal photography by
Peter Johannes

BERKSHIRE HOUSE PUBLISHERS
Lee, Massachusetts

New England Cooking: Seasons & Celebrations
Copyright © 2001 by Berkshire House Publishers

Photographs © Peter Johannes, except where noted.

Library of Congress Cataloging-in-Publication Data

Hopley, Claire.

New England cooking : seasons & celebrations / Claire Hopley ; photography by Peter Johannes.
    p.   cm.
Includes bibliographical references and indexes.
ISBN 1-58157-052-X (alk. paper)
    1. Cookery, American—New England style. I. Title.

TX715-2.N48 H664 2001
641.5974—dc21

                                                                    2001025427

_____

ISBN 1-58157-052-X (alk. paper)

Edited by Constance Lee Oxley
Cover, book design, and typesetting by Jane McWhorter, Blue Sky Productions
Index by Elizabeth T. Parson

Berkshire House books are available at substantial discounts for bulk purchases by corporations and other organizations' promotions and premiums. Special personalized editions can also be produced in large quantities. For more information, contact:

Berkshire House Publishers
480 Pleasant Street, Suite 5
Lee, Massachusetts 01238
800-321-8526
E-mail: info@berkshirehouse.com
Web: www.berkshirehouse.com

Manufactured in Singapore
10 9 8 7 6 5 4 3 2 1

To Bob, with love

ACKNOWLEDGMENTS

Nothing can be achieved without help, and this book has benefited from the work and kindness of numerous people. Many food companies have assisted with information. In particular, thanks go to the staff of King Arthur Flour in Norwich, Vermont, and to Vermont cheese makers, including Jedd Davies of Cabot Cheese, Cynthia Major of Vermont Shepherd, Cynthia Dawley of Crowley, and Bob Reese and Richard Chalmers of Vermont Butter and Cheese Company. Ray McNeill of Brattleboro was a fount of information about microbrewing. In Massachusetts, I would like to thank Marie and Henry Lukasik of Lukasik Game Farm in South Hadley, Michael Miller, who makes Berkshire Blue cheese, and Bob and Carol Russell and Kerry Downey Romaniello of Westport Rivers Winery. Dr. Joseph Zaientz and George Bernard of the Shad Museum in Haddam, Connecticut, shared their encyclopedic knowledge of shad. In Walpole, New Hampshire, I benefited from the generosity of Paula Burdick of Burdick Chocolate and the folks at Fannie Mason Cheese, who returned a missing notebook to me. Thanks also to Jeff Kaelin of Stinson Foods in Bath, Maine, who told me about sardine canning.

Several cooks have allowed me to use their recipes: Rob Chirico, Dorothy Johnson, Kristine Elison, Tamara Hopley, James M. Flaherty, Muirreann Glenmullen, Donald Francis, Julia Melchionda, Jim Dodge, formerly Executive Chef of the Museum of Fine Arts in Boston and now of the Getty Museum in California, Christopher Freeman, Executive Chef of the Wauwinet on Nantucket, and Jeffrey Paige, Executive Chef of the Creamery Restaurant at Canterbury Shaker Village in New Hampshire. Sister Frances A. Carr of the Sabbathday Lake Shakers in Maine allowed me to adapt recipes from her book, *Shaker Your Plate: Of Shaker Cooks and Cooking.* Tom Jane of Prospect Books allowed me to use the chowder recipe on page 56. Many people have discussed ethnic foods with me: Janet Teng, Jennifer Veshia, Camella Peace, Rich Alpert, Onawumi Jean Moss, and Micheline Coen. Melinda McIntosh and other reference librarians at the W.E.B. Dubois Library at the University of Massachusetts answered my questions. Five Colleges, Inc. have supported my work. I thank them all.

The photo shoot was made easier by the help of Frank Lattuca and Linda Kinney of the Hotel, Restaurant and Travel Administration Department of the University of Massachusetts at Amherst, who provided a location and props. Members of Linda Kinney's catering class prepared many of the dishes in the photographs. Many thanks to her and her students, Jill De Cisero, Nancy Roux, Stacy Nichols, Dionne Stennett, Kevin Raposo, and most especially Cindie Nielson, who did a power of work and was lots of fun. Similarly, Michael Madeira of the Lord Jeffery Inn in Amherst put up with major disruption while dishes were photographed at the Inn. At Yankee Candle in South Deerfield, Jim Ovitt made it possible to photograph Christmas scenes and Lynn Drobnik provided candles. I would also like to thank Lunt's of Greenfield, Massachusetts, who lent the Revere bowl in which the Trifle with Jelley & Flowers is pictured; Simon Pearce of Windsor, Vermont, for the dish used for the Floating Island and the plate displaying the Duck Breasts with Blueberry-Lavender Sauce, and Bennington Potters for the blue-and-yellow dishes used to picture pasta recipes. Thanks also to Unity Pond Pottery of Unity, Maine, for use of the blue bowl in which the Clam Chowder is pictured; Gricus Pottery of Houlton, Maine, for use of the bowl in which the mussels and lobsters are shown; Whitney's Blueberries of Machias, Maine, for the boxed blueberries shown in a field; Strawberry Hill Farms of Skowhegan, Maine, for their maple syrups and other products; and Heritage Seafoods of Eastport, Maine, for the salmon which appear on page 21. Thanks to Nick Hopley for lending his marathon medals. Thanks also to photographer Peter Johannes and his sons Adrian and Jordan for their hard work.

I owe a special debt to Michele Melchionda for research and translation help and for her support, especially at the photo shoot, where her artistry with the food, flowers, and props made all the difference.

My work as a writer would not have been possible without the collaboration of many editors including Fiona Luis, Louise Kennedy, Bonnie Wells, Margot Cleary, Linda J. Forristal, and Bruce Heydt. My publishers, Berkshire House, have been a delight to work with: a special thanks to Editorial & Production Director Philip Rich, Marketing & Sales Director Carol Bosco Baumann, and Editor Constance Lee Oxley for their kind and professional help.

My agent Jeanne Fredericks has been optimistic when I was not. I appreciate all her work. Most importantly, I want to thank my family and especially my husband Bob for his confidence in me, his research help, and for doing everything and eating everything while I was working on the book. I couldn't have done it otherwise.

CONTENTS

*Asterisks denote main or side dishes with no meat or fish.

All of the recipes in this cookbook
are for 4 servings, except where noted.

INTRODUCTION

In the spring, ardent householders take arms against the mob of dandelions invading their lawns. Not Phil Tonks of Grand View Winery in East Calais, Vermont. On the third weekend in May, he organizes a Dandelion Festival to gather the flowers and to demonstrate such dandelion dishes as dandelion salad, dandelion pesto, and dandelion-kiwi sorbet — and of course, dandelion wine.

That's typical of New England, as I discovered when I arrived here in the 1970s. New Englanders are always celebrating food and drink because the changing seasons are always bringing something new. Living in the fertile Pioneer Valley of Massachusetts, I soon joined my neighbors in waiting for the bundles of asparagus that appeared at local farms in May, the strawberries in June, and then the corn of high summer.

Further south, Connecticut River towns have shad bakes where they feast on the shad that return each spring. In the summer, churches host strawberry teas and blueberry breakfasts. Seaports put on seafood festivals to highlight their clams, lobsters, and oysters, while Fort Fairfield, Maine, celebrates the potato at its Potato Blossom Festival. Fall brings chowder festivals, apple pie contests, Oktoberfests, and the Franklin County, Massachusetts, Cider Day, where visitors sample cider and cider vinegar, stock up on apples and pears, and watch demonstrations of cooking and cheese making. Even in the snows of February, the year's first maple syrup lures New Englanders out to breakfast at sugarhouses, where stacks of pancakes, streams of syrup, and bowls of sugar-on-snow with pickles are the order of the day.

Maple syrup stores well, but until the mid-twentieth century, many of New England's other foods could be enjoyed only in their brief seasons. If you did not eat asparagus in May, then you had missed it for a year. There were no tomatoes in December, no apples or parsnips in June. And while homemakers canned and pickled to preserve the harvest, their products did not match the flavors of just-picked new-season crops or just-caught fish from the sea. After a winter of eating preserved foods — and a limited range of them at that — the first greens to push their way through the earth must have been wonderfully welcome. Here is the source of New Englanders' celebratory attitude toward food.

Today, of course, supermarkets stock almost everything throughout the year. Still, affection for local foods remains. Families love to get out to pick-your-own farms and orchards. Shoppers throng weekend farmers' markets to buy local crops and delicacies from artisanal producers, who make crusty breads, fine cheeses, and tangy sauces and condiments. Respected locally, these producers do not go unacknowledged in the wider world. Cabot Cheese of Vermont regularly wins awards for the best Cheddar in the country, while smaller cheese makers, such as the Vermont Butter and Cheese Company and Vermont Shepherd, win national accolades and ribbons. Salsa is not traditional New England fare, but in a competition with 900 brands, Uncle Mike's Salsa of Belchertown, Massachusetts, came out tops.

Enjoying foods from afar is just as typical of New England as celebrating local products. Many of the foods that were to become regional staples arrived with the English settlers of the seventeenth and eighteenth centuries. They brought apples, cheese, puddings, pies, beer, and an enthu-siasm for large roasts. Once here, the settlers delighted in the plentiful fish and wildfowl and adopted native fare, such as cranberries, squash, and corn. But since at least the beginning of the nineteenth century, New Englanders have been enjoying the foods of other nations. All early cook-books have recipes for making "a mango." This was a homemade chutney intended to reproduce the effect of Indian mango chutney by using small unripe muskmelons instead of the unobtain-able mangos. Curry powder was around before 1833, when Lydia Maria Child published a recipe for curried fowl. The pineapple-topped gateways of the eighteenth-century merchant mansions of seaports like Salem and Portsmouth attest that tropical fruits fascinated seafarers, and they brought home those that would survive the journey. Coconuts were putting in a regular appear-ance by the middle of the nineteenth century, and cooks were shredding them for special occasion desserts. Emily Dickinson wrote one of her poems on the back of a coconut cake recipe given by a neighbor. By the end of the century, oranges had become a must for Christmas.

By this time, immigrants from Ireland, Poland, Portugal, Greece, and Italy had brought new foods and recipes with them. At first, their favorite dishes did not appear beyond the communities where they lived, but gradually they have been shared by all. Supermarkets stock Polish kielbasa and Portuguese linguica and chourico alongside Italian sausage and the breakfast sausage links that trace back to England. Bakeries stack poppy seed kolaches from central Europe near loaves of Portuguese bread, Jewish challah, and French baguettes. At Christmas, Italian panettone, German stollen, and French Yule logs rival Christmas cookies. Italian pasta and pizza have long been fam-ily favorites. More recently, Japanese sushi, Indian curries, and Vietnamese spring rolls have lost their mystery and now appear in supermarket delicatessens.

As for seafood, so many people of Italian heritage live on the coast that much of New England's fish is cooked in dishes that owe more to Mediterranean traditions than to those of the Atlantic. Indeed, one chef working in the hills of Vermont claims that New England food today is basically Mediterranean food. That does less than justice to the Anglo-American base of New England cooking and to the vivid Asian dishes that have brightened the culinary repertoire. But it does get at the great changes that have taken place since the beginning of the twentieth century, when John Collins Bossidy called Boston "The home of the bean and the cod." Beans and cod now play minor roles in a dramatic cuisine that has become the most varied in the nation.

This makes everyday eating fun. But in New England, the significance of food shines out most brightly on holidays. At the great national holiday Thanksgiving, the loaded table is an emblem for the accumulation of good things — a role it repeats at Christmas. Equally, at the many ethnic holidays of the year — Chinese New Year, St. Patrick's Day, Passover, Kwanzaa -- food is more than nourishment: it affirms a shared ancestry and history. Similarly, Boston recalls New England's history at the annual running of the Marathon on Patriot's Day, while Rhode Islanders hold May breakfasts as a reminder that Rhode Island, though the smallest colony, was the first to declare its independence on May 4, 1776.

In these ways, food becomes a metaphor for the work and effort, the lives and history that distinguish a region and make its people a community. This book aims to capture the array of foods created by the farmers, manufacturers, and cooks of New England, with recipes rooted in the last four centuries of the region's history and in the seasonal events that commemorate it.

NOTES ON INGREDIENTS

EGGS

Extra-large eggs were used in testing all of the recipes in this book. A few recipes contain eggs that are only partially cooked. The American Egg Board estimates that there is a minute chance — 0.005 percent (five one thousandths of one percent) that uncooked eggs may cause salmonellosis, so such dishes should not be served to young children, the elderly, or those with impaired immune systems. All eggs should be refrigerated. If you beat eggs for use in a later stage of a recipe, return them to the fridge until you need them.

FLOUR

New Englanders rarely use self-rising flour. Recipes in this book were tested with King Arthur's All-Purpose Flour or King Arthur's Flour for Bread Machines. This flour is produced for King Arthur's of Norwich, Vermont, and can be purchased in supermarkets in New England and many other states, or by mail order. When cake flour is specified, Softasilk was used.

HERBS

New Englanders have always used herbs for flavoring, but their favorites have changed over time. Amelia Simmons's American Cookery, published in Hartford, Connecticut, in 1796, listed thyme, sweet marjoram, summer savory, sage, parsley, and pennyroyal as "useful in cookery." All would have been familiar to the English settlers who landed in Massachusetts in 1620, and they remained staples into the nineteenth century, when Shaker herb catalogues still specified them as "kitchen herbs," though they listed dozens of herbs for medicinal use. Today, sage is common only in stuffings, but marjoram (oregano) and thyme remain essential. Bay leaves and basil, introduced by immigrants from the Mediterranean, have become staples. Basil is a popular garden herb in the summer; it dies at the first murmur of frost, but hydroponic growers have made it available all year. Rosemary is a contemporary favorite with roasted and grilled meats and vegetables. Dill, which arrived with immigrants from Poland and northern Europe, appears in many pickle and vegetable recipes. Most herbs taste best when grown in sunlight and picked just before they blossom.

MAPLE SYRUP

Maple syrup is the condensed sap of the sugar maple, *Acer saccharum*. It takes 35-40 gallons of sap to make 1 gallon of syrup, so it is expensive. Grading systems vary from state to state, but the paler the syrup the higher its grade and cost. Pale amber-colored syrups are delicate and should not be used in cooking because their flavor disappears. The cheaper dark syrups taste more dramatic and stand up better to other ingredients. Supermarket brands of pancake syrup are sugar and corn syrup with added colorings and flavorings. They are unsuitable for use in the recipes in this book.

PEPPER

Black, white, and green peppercorns come from the same plant, *Piper nigrum*. Black peppercorns are dried, barely ripe seeds; white peppercorns are dried ripe seeds with the skins removed; and green peppercorns are unripe seeds that are dried or brined. Freshly ground black pepper is the most aromatic, but once ground its flavor disappears quite quickly, so ground black pepper is a poor purchase; grind it as needed. White pepper is hotter. Green peppercorns are milder but aromatic. While freshly ground black pepper is best for many seasoning purposes, use white pepper for most fish and egg dishes or for pale sauces, whose appearance would be marred by black specks. White pepper brings out the flavor in cheese dishes. Green peppercorns taste delicious with steak and other meat and fish dishes; they are relatively new on the market, so experimenting with them is interesting.

SPICES

The European discoverers of America were hunting for a quicker route to the spice islands of the East. Success would have brought them riches because despite their high cost, spices were essential for seasoning food in Europe. The first English settlers in New England commonly used mace, nutmeg, cinnamon, ginger, coriander, and pepper to flavor their foods, often combining them to create highly flavored dishes. The only spices found in the Americas were chili pepper and allspice, often called Jamaica pepper in old recipes because it comes from the Caribbean. Eighteenth- and nineteenth-century New Englanders used allspice in meat dishes, as well as in some baked goods. Conveniently, it combines the flavors of cinnamon, cloves, and pepper. Today, New Englanders invariably add cinnamon, sometimes in excess, to apple dishes and many baked goods. Chili is a recent favorite, especially in salsas and dishes adopted from Southeast Asia, the Caribbean and Mexico, and the Southwest.

CHAPTER 1

FIRST HARVESTS

Spring comes to New England on a February day when the sky is blue, and the ground is white with snow. Winter is getting tiresome by then, but it's not just the bright weather that promises a new season; it's the sap drip, dripping into buckets clustered around maple trees. The sap is colorless and tasteless, and it takes thirty-five to forty gallons to make one gallon of syrup, so producers watch for those brilliant days of early spring. The daytime sun makes the sap run; clear nights with freezing temperatures halt its flow.

A day or two after the first buckets have appeared, steam billows from sugarhouses, where evaporators bubble the sap down into syrup. If you stop to buy a jug, you'll often find two or three neighbors gathered there, enjoying the warmth and the chat, but keeping sharp eyes on the seething mass as its color develops. As it moves from yellowy to gold, the sugar maker matches its hue to a shade card with the colors of the various grades. The earliest syrup, called "first run," is pale topaz. Its flavor is delicate, and its price is high. Later in the season, the color darkens, moving through shades of amber to agate brown. These darker Grade B syrups cost less though they taste more robust, more "mapley." This syrup is the best for cooking because its flavor stands up to other ingredients in the recipe.

Even for pouring on pancakes, many New Englanders enjoy the darker syrups most. One of the rites of spring is to drive to a farm that serves breakfast during the maple season. The menu is always simple: dark rivers of maple syrup poured over waffles and berries or pancakes with bacon and sausage. Or, if snow conditions are right, as they usually are in Vermont, New Hampshire, and Maine, there may be "sugar on snow": boiling syrup poured onto bowls of clean snow. As the hot syrup hits the cold snow, it turns into sweet toffeelike strands. "Too sweet," some might think, so it always comes with a bracing dish of dill pickles.

By April, the snow is melting and nighttime temperatures stay above freezing, so the sap flows up the trees constantly, doing its job of swelling the buds into leaves. By then, it has a "buddy" flavor that spells an end to making maple syrup — the first harvest of New England's agricultural year.

But as soon as spring loosens winter's grasp on the ground, rhubarb pushes its pink fists through the soil and stretches out its leafy stalks. Mint makes the first steps towards summer's rampageous growth, and purple pom-pom flowers dance on pillows of chives. Morel mushrooms sometimes peep out in old orchards. Fern shoots unfurl on riverbanks — "fiddleheads" they are called, and foragers pick them to partner the shad that run upriver in May.

By then, there's asparagus. One morning the tips have nudged away the soil; a couple of days later the whole stem has shot up: a hear-ye announcing that spring is now. No more buds and little shoots; no more faint whispers and first twitters. The leaves are out, the flowers are blooming, the birds are feeding chicks, and gardeners are watching their radish, spinach, and lettuce grow.

Many villages in the rich land of the Connecticut River valley in Massachusetts specialize in growing vegetables, and in spring, asparagus is their pride. It is not simply the taste that everyone appreciates so much, though it is the very essence of spring. It's the arrival of the asparagus — so early and so dramatic. Churches and fire districts celebrate with asparagus and ham suppers; they are usually raising money for a good cause, but the impetus seems less utilitarian, more joyous. Like the pancake and maple syrup breakfasts of March and the ice-cream socials and strawberry teas that follow in June, asparagus suppers are harvest festivals, a celebration of having come through another winter.

THE MOTHER OF LEVEL MEASUREMENTS

"A tablespoonful is measured level. A teaspoonful is measured level." This instruction appears in all Fannie Farmer's cookbooks. She explained, "To measure tea or tablespoonfuls, dip the spoon in the ingredient, fill, lift, and level with a knife, the sharp edge of the knife being towards the spoon."

Fannie Merritt Farmer was born in Boston in 1857 and grew up in Medford, Massachusetts. Lamed by a childhood illness, she did not enroll in the Boston Cooking School until she was 31. She was a star pupil, and by 1893, she was the principal. She believed that cooking was drudgery "if one does not put heart and soul into the work." Similarly, she threw herself into teaching and writing, and she excelled at both. Nonetheless, when she proposed her classic The Boston Cooking-School Cookbook, the publisher doubted its viability and insisted that she finance its production costs; it was an instant success. When she died in 1915, by this time head of her own establishment, Miss Farmer's School of Cookery, her book had sold 360,000 copies, and the Mother of Level Measurements, as she was called, was and long remained, America's authority on cooking.

Fannie Farmer's Maple Parfait with Glazed Walnuts

Fannie Merritt Farmer's *The Boston Cooking-School Cookbook* dominated American kitchens from when it was published in 1896 to the 1930s and beyond. Today, her fondness for finicky garnishes and absurd combinations of ingredients make many of her recipes unappealing. Nonetheless, her book, constantly updated for years after her death, has some gems, including this maple ice cream, which is simplicity itself. The parfait on its own is an experience in velvet. But if you want a contrasting crunch, add the glazed walnuts.

MAPLE PARFAIT
4 egg yolks
1 cup Grade B or other dark maple syrup
2 cups heavy cream

GLAZED WALNUTS
²/₃ cup walnut pieces
Butter
4 tablespoons dark maple syrup

1. To make the parfait, beat the egg yolks in the top part of a double boiler or in a bowl that you can set over a saucepan of simmering water.

2. In a small saucepan over moderate heat, heat the 1 cup syrup until hot but not boiling. Pour the syrup into the egg yolks. Place the double boiler with water in the bottom part over moderate heat. (If using a bowl, set over a saucepan of simmering water.) Stir the mixture until it thickens into a custard. To test for consistency, pour some of the mixture from a spoon back into the saucepan; when the last few drops lengthen before slowly dripping down, the custard is ready. (If the mixture develops little scrappy bits, immediately remove from heat and beat vigorously, ideally with an electric mixer.) Set aside to cool.

3. Meanwhile, pour the cream into a large bowl and whip into billowy clouds. When the maple mixture has cooled to room temperature, fold the mixture into the whipped cream and pour into a deep bowl or plastic container. Cover and place in the freezer for 2 hours.

4. Remove the mixture from the freezer and whip energetically with an electric mixer, making sure to stir in the semifrozen portion from the sides of the bowl. Repeat this step 2–3 hours later, then again in about 2 hours after that. (This breaks up the ice crystals so you end up with a smooth mixture.)

5. To make the walnuts, discard any blackish walnut pieces and bits of walnut skin. Lightly grease a plate with the butter.

6. Bring the syrup to a boil over high heat in a small saucepan. Add the walnut pieces and boil briskly, stirring constantly, until the syrup has evaporated and the walnuts look shiny, about 3–4 minutes. Quickly, tip the walnuts onto the prepared plate. Separate with a fork and let cool. Sprinkle the walnuts on top of servings of the parfait and serve immediately.

Gingerbread Pancakes with Lemon Sauce

Bintliff's American Cafe on Congress Street in Portland, Maine, serves an array of imaginative pancakes. These gingerbread pancakes are modeled on theirs, and serving them with maple syrup, as well as lemon sauce, gilds the lily but tastes delicious on a Sunday morning.

LEMON SAUCE
1 egg, beaten
$^1/_2$ teaspoon grated lemon zest
Juice of 1 large lemon
3 tablespoons granulated sugar
$^1/_4$ cup water

GINGERBREAD PANCAKES
1 cup all-purpose flour
1 teaspoon baking powder
2 teaspoons ground ginger
$^1/_2$ teaspoon ground cinnamon
$^1/_4$ teaspoon ground nutmeg or mace
1 egg
1 cup buttermilk
1–2 tablespoons confectioners' sugar

1. To make the lemon sauce, combine all of the lemon sauce ingredients in a small saucepan and cook over moderate heat, stirring frequently, until the sauce has thickened. Keep warm.

2. To make the pancakes, mix together the flour, baking powder, ginger, cinnamon, and nutmeg in a large bowl. Make a well in the center. In another bowl, beat together the egg and buttermilk and pour into the well. Mix thoroughly.

3. Grease a large cast-iron skillet or nonstick griddle. Place over moderately high heat and pour on enough batter to form 3-inch diameter pancakes. Cook until the top surface has lots of tiny holes. Flip and cook the other side. Repeat with remaining batter. Keep prepared pancakes in a warm oven until ready to serve.

4. Sift a dusting of the confectioners' sugar on top of each serving and serve the lemon sauce and hot maple syrup on the side. Makes 10–12 pancakes.

Sugary Crunch Rhubarb Tart

If you made a list of all the recipes you ever found for rhubarb, you would find that most of them were for pies. No wonder nineteenth-century New Englanders often called it pieplant. Lydia Maria Child, who wrote *American Frugal Housewife* in 1833, also called it the Persian apple. Despite this pretty name, she didn't approve of rhubarb pies, complaining that "These are dear pies, for they take an enormous quantity of sugar." Presumably she would have disapproved of this free-form tart with its sugar-crusted pastry, which is especially good because it is sweet and rich enough to balance the sour rhubarb. Both the pastry and the filling can be made a day or two before you assemble the tart.

PASTRY
2 cups all-purpose flour
1 stick (4 ounces) frozen butter
One 3-ounce package cold cream cheese
$^1/_3$ cup granulated sugar
$^1/_3$ cup ice water
15 sugar cubes
1 egg beaten with 1 tablespoon milk

FILLING
3 – 4 stalks rhubarb (about 12 ounces)
$^1/_2$ cup granulated sugar
1 teaspoon ground ginger

1. To make the pastry, put the flour into a large bowl. Cut the butter and cream cheese into bits about the size of a grape. Add the bits to the flour and toss to cover. Add the sugar and transfer the mixture to a food processor. Process until the pieces of butter and cheese are the size of small peas. Add the ice water and pulse 5 – 6 times, or until the mixture clumps without forming a solid mass. (If you don't have a food processor, make this pastry by rubbing the butter and cream cheese into the flour with your hands, but don't attempt this on a hot day — make sure your hands are cold.)

2. Turn the mixture out onto a sheet of plastic wrap or baking parchment and pull it together with your hands, forming an 8-inch disk. Fold the plastic wrap over the disk and chill for 2 hours or longer if that is easier.

3. To make the filling, wash the rhubarb, cut off both ends of each stalk, and strip off any stringy skin. Cut the rhubarb on the diagonal into 1-inch pieces. Put the pieces into a saucepan with only the water that clings to them. Cover and cook over low heat without stirring until some juice begins to run from the rhubarb. Add the sugar and ginger. Do not stir; simply shake the pan gently, then cover and cook until the sugar has just dissolved. Do not let the rhubarb cook through. Let cool.

4. Preheat the oven to 450° F. Lightly grease a baking sheet.

5. To assemble the tart, put the sugar cubes into a plastic bag and crush with a rolling pin until the cubes are in little chunks. Set the sugar bits and the egg and milk mixture aside.

6. Flour a pastry board and a rolling pin. Place the disk of pastry on the board and sprinkle lightly with flour. Quickly roll the disk into a 12-inch circle. Don't worry about raggy edges. Place

the pastry over the rolling pin then roll so that the pastry lies over the pin and can be easily placed onto the prepared baking sheet.

7. Using a slotted spoon, lift the rhubarb pieces from their juice and pile in the center of the pastry, leaving about 2 inches all around. If you have an especially wide border of pastry at one side, trim a little. Lift up the edges of the pastry and fold them over the rhubarb so that it is only partly enclosed.

8. Working quickly, brush the pastry with the egg and milk mixture, then scatter on the crushed sugar cubes. Place the baking sheet on the top rack in the oven and bake for 10–15 minutes or until golden. Reduce the temperature to 375º and bake for 10 minutes more or until nicely browned. Let cool for 10 minutes.

9. Transfer the tart to a serving dish with a large spatula. If you like, you can reheat the juice and pour it over the center before serving. Serve warm.

RHUBARB

The Zoroastrians of ancient Persia believed that the first human beings sprang from a rhubarb plant. The Persians thought that eating rhubarb purified the system. Rhubarb also features in traditional Chinese medicine, and when it arrived in Europe in the sixteenth century it was in its Chinese role as a purgative. You can see why the Renaissance poet John Skelton wrote of "the rhubarb of repentance," and Shakespeare's Macbeth longed for some "rhubarb . . . to drive these English hence." In Elizabethan times, the root was the crucial part, and it was not until later that the juicy stalks suggested themselves as a filling for pies — a convenient springtime substitute for the berries of summer and the apples of fall. New Englanders probably did not grow rhubarb in their gardens until the nineteenth century, when reports of the culinary uses of its stalks were received from Canada and Europe. Most traditional recipes call for it in pies and baked goods, but the occasional recipe for chutney, jam, and drinks made from rhubarb shows that once it was perceived as a substitute for fruit, it was used in other fruitlike ways. Botanically, it's a stalk like asparagus and celery.

Rhubarb & Raisin Chutney

By late May, rhubarb is growing in hedgelike stands, and growers sell it cheaply or even give it away. Here is an excellent way to preserve the abundance. You can double the recipe if you'd like extra jars to give to friends.

9–10 large stalks rhubarb (about 2–2 $^1/_2$ pounds)
1 tablespoon water
2 cups chopped onion
2 large cloves garlic, chopped
2 tablespoons peeled and chopped fresh gingerroot
1 teaspoon salt or to taste
1 tablespoon ground allspice
$^1/_4$ teaspoon cayenne pepper
1 cup raisins
3 tablespoons Worcestershire sauce
$^1/_3$ cup white vinegar
1 $^1/_2$–2 cups firmly packed dark brown sugar

1. Wash the rhubarb, cut off both ends of each stalk, and strip off any stringy skin. Cut the rhubarb on the diagonal into 1-inch pieces. Combine the rhubarb, water, onion, garlic, and ginger in a large shallow pan, cover, and cook over low heat for 5 minutes, or until the juice begins to run from the rhubarb.

2. Stir in the salt, allspice, cayenne pepper, raisins, and Worcestershire sauce. Cover and simmer for 8–10 minutes, or until the rhubarb and raisins are soft and juicy.

3. Add the vinegar and 1 $^1/_2$ cups of the sugar. Stir until the sugar has dissolved, then take a small spoonful of the chutney, let it cool, and taste it. Add the remaining sugar and more salt if you would like, then bring to a vigorous boil. Boil uncovered, stirring frequently, until the chutney is as thick as jam, about 5 minutes, depending on the juiciness of the rhubarb. Let cool.

4. Pour the cooled chutney into clean jars and keep in the fridge if you plan to store for longer than a few days. Makes about 4 cups of chutney.

Scarlet Rhubarb Compote

Rhubarb does not always get the love that it deserves. It is undeniably sour. It also quickly falls apart into a stringy mass. You need to work against these qualities. Sugar alone does not solve the sourness problem, but sugar combined with dairy foods, such as yogurt, cream, or butter, does seem to help. A couple of dabs of butter added to a rhubarb pie or cobbler makes all the difference and so does a dollop of yogurt or whipped cream. Avoid the stringy effect by never cooking rhubarb with any liquid other than that clinging to the stalks after you have washed it. And, most important, don't stir it, unless you are making chutney or jam where you actually want it to fall apart. This rhubarb compote is simplicity itself and looks quite ravishing in its glowing scarlet syrup.

8 long stalks rhubarb (about 1 $^1/_2$–2 pounds)
$^2/_3$ cup strawberry, raspberry, or red currant jelly
$^1/_3$ cup granulated sugar
1 $^1/_2$ cups vanilla-flavored custard-style yogurt

1. Preheat the oven to 350° F. Wash the rhubarb, cut off both ends of each stalk, and strip off any stringy skin. Cut the rhubarb on the diagonal into 1-inch pieces.

2. Pour about half of the jelly into a baking dish and spread over the bottom. Add the rhubarb, dotting it with the remaining jelly. Sprinkle the sugar on top. Cover the dish and bake without stirring for 25 minutes or until tender. Cool to room temperature. Serve with scoops of the yogurt.

Ginger Scones

Scones now rival muffins at breakfast or a coffee break. Like muffins, they are easy to make and lend themselves to all types of flavors and add-ins. These ginger scones are addictive. Serve them with ginger marmalade or preserves, or use them as shortcakes with servings of Scarlet Rhubarb Compote (see recipe on page 8). In Britain, their native country, scones, often topped with jam and cream, are eaten with tea. How do you pronounce the word? In Scotland and northern England, it is "scon" to rhyme with "gone"; in the south of England, it is "scone" to rhyme with "stone." Since scones originated in the north, I go for the northern pronunciation.

3 cups all-purpose flour
1 tablespoon baking powder
1 tablespoon ground ginger
$^1/_2$ teaspoon salt
$^1/_2$ cup granulated sugar
1 stick (4 ounces) cold butter
$^1/_2$ cup golden raisins
$^2/_3$ cup buttermilk, or $^2/_3$ cup milk plus 1 teaspoon fresh lemon juice
$^1/_2$ cup ginger preserves or marmalade, or $^1/_4$ cup chopped crystallized ginger

1. Preheat the oven to 425° F. Lightly grease a baking sheet.
2. Mix together the flour, baking powder, ginger, salt, and sugar in a large bowl. Cut the butter into several bits and rub them into the flour mixture until it looks like coarse crumbs. Stir in the raisins.
3. Make a well in the center of the flour mixture. In a small bowl, mix together the buttermilk and ginger preserves and pour into the well. Working quickly, combine with the dry ingredients until you have a lumpy dough. Turn onto a board and knead just a couple of times.
4. Divide into 8–12 portions (depending on whether you want smaller or larger scones) and shape into patties. Place them on the prepared baking sheet. (To make triangular scones, form the mixture into one or two round cakes and score into wedges. Separate into triangles after cooking.) Bake for 15 minutes or until golden and a toothpick inserted in the center comes out clean. Cool on a wire rack.

Mint, Cucumber & Cheese Bread

Most herb breads feature summer herbs such as thyme or rosemary, but mint, one of the first herbs to appear each year, is excellent in bread, tinting it pale green as well as flavoring it. Changing the variety of cheese in this recipe changes the flavor, but it is always good, especially with vegetable soups.

3 cups all-purpose flour
1 tablespoon granulated sugar
1 tablespoon baking powder
$^1/_2$ teaspoon salt
4-inch piece English cucumber, washed and unpeeled
2 eggs
$^2/_3$ cup milk
1 tablespoon light vegetable oil
2 tablespoons chopped fresh mint
$^3/_4$ cup crumbled Vermont feta cheese, or 1 cup grated Vermont Cheddar cheese

1. Preheat the oven to 350° F. Grease a 9 x 5-inch loaf pan.

2. Mix together the flour, sugar, baking powder, and salt in a large bowl. Make a well in the center of the flour mixture.

3. Grate the cucumber into a small bowl. (You should have about $^2/_3$ cup grated cucumber.) Lightly beat together the eggs and milk and set aside 2 tablespoons for brushing the bread.

4. Stir the cucumber, oil, and mint into the egg and milk mixture and pour the whole lot into the well of the dry ingredients. Mix quickly but thoroughly until you have a soft dough.

5. Fold in the cheese. Put the bread in the prepared pan and brush the surface with the reserved milk mixture and bake for 25–30 minutes, or until the crust is golden and a toothpick inserted in the center comes out clean. Cool on a wire rack.

Chicken with Mushrooms

Most mushrooms appear in the fall, but morels are an exception; their season is April and May. Another of their oddities is that their pointed and deeply pitted caps are hollow, so large ones can be split and stuffed. Though morels are among the most prized of edible mushrooms, New Englanders are not avid morel hunters like the people of Michigan and the Northwest, but enthusiasts can find them in sandy soil, often near old apple or hickory trees. Identifying wild mushrooms is a risky business for all except experts. If you do not have mushroom expertise, use dried morels, which can be purchased from specialty groceries and some supermarkets. If you can't find them, try this recipe using any flavorful variety of mushroom.

$^1/_3$ cup dried morels or other dried mushrooms, if available
2 cups water
$^1/_2$ pound crimini or button mushrooms, washed and thickly sliced
1 bay leaf
8 chicken thighs
Salt and black pepper
$^1/_4$ cup chopped onion
$^1/_2$ cup diced green bell pepper
$^1/_2$ cup white wine
1–2 teaspoons soy sauce

1. If you are using dried morels or other mushrooms, put them into a bowl and cover with the water. Let sit for 1 hour (or longer if more convenient). Scoop out and chop the mushrooms. Save the liquid.

2. Put the sliced crimini or button mushrooms into a small saucepan with the reserved liquid and the chopped soaked mushrooms. Add the bay leaf, cover, and simmer for 15 minutes.

3. Meanwhile, season the chicken pieces with the salt and black pepper, then heat a large non-stick skillet over high heat. Put the chicken pieces skin-side down into the skillet and cook quite briskly for 6–7 minutes, or until the skin has turned an appetizing golden color. Turn, reduce the heat, and continue cooking for 10 minutes more. Remove the pieces from the skillet and set aside. Discard all but 1 tablespoon of fat.

4. Add the onion and bell pepper to the skillet and soften over moderate heat for 2 minutes, stirring to scrape up any browned bits on the pan. Add the wine and let sizzle for 1 minute, then add the simmering mushroom mixture. If you did not use dried morels or other dried mushrooms, add 1 teaspoon of soy sauce. Bring to a moderate boil, return the reserved chicken to the skillet, and simmer for 10 minutes. Taste for seasonings and add more salt, black pepper, or soy sauce if necessary.

Fiddleheads Tossed with Lemon & Spring Herbs

It's easy to see how fiddleheads got their name. The baby ferns look exactly like the scroll of a violin. While young ferns are eaten in many parts of the world, some species are inedible. The fiddleheads eaten in New England are the ostrich fern, *Matteuccia struthiopteris,* and the cinnamon fern, *Osmunda cinnamomea.* If you can't recognize them in the wild, look for fiddleheads during their brief season in supermarkets and specialty food stores. In Maine, you can find canned and pickled fiddleheads. They taste a little like spinach and a little like asparagus. Asparagus and fiddleheads are interchangeable in most recipes. This recipe celebrates both fiddleheads and early herbs.

³/₄ pound fiddleheads
1 teaspoon salt
1 sprig fresh mint with 8–10 leaves
2 teaspoons light vegetable oil
2 teaspoons snipped fresh chives
1 teaspoon finely chopped fresh parsley
1 teaspoon chopped fresh mint
1–2 teaspoons fresh lemon juice or wine vinegar or to taste
Sprigs fresh mint or chive blossoms for garnish

1. Prepare the fiddleheads by cutting off the browned end of the stem and brushing away any flaky bits of brown skin with a damp paper towel.

2. Bring a saucepan of water to a boil. Add the salt and mint sprig, then drop in the fiddleheads. Simmer for 6 minutes or until tender. Drain and discard the mint sprig.

3. In the last minute of cooking, warm the oil in a skillet over low heat. Stir in the chives, parsley, and mint, then immediately add the drained but still hot fiddleheads. Toss gently with the oil and herbs for a few seconds. Stir in the lemon juice to taste. Transfer the fiddleheads to a warmed serving dish and garnish with the mint sprigs or chive blossoms or some of each. Serve immediately.

Asparagus & Ham Wraps

The New England tradition of serving ham with asparagus probably comes from the days when farmers were using up the last hams of the old year just as the first vegetables of the new year came in. It survives because the complex taste of ham pairs well with the vigorous green taste of asparagus. If you are cooking a whole ham, such as in Baked Ham with Cider Sauce (see recipe on page 37), simply steam asparagus and serve as a side dish. If you want a smaller meal, try wrapping sliced ham around asparagus and baking the little bundles in a cheese sauce as in this recipe.

24 thick stalks asparagus
1 teaspoon salt
8 slices boiled or baked ham
2 tablespoons butter
2 tablespoons all-purpose flour
1 ¹/₂ cups milk
1 loosely packed cup grated Vermont Cheddar cheese
¹/₂ cup freshly grated Parmesan cheese
¹/₂ cup fresh bread crumbs
Pinch cayenne pepper or white pepper

1. Preheat the oven to 375° F. Lightly grease a 9-inch square shallow baking dish.
2. Wash the asparagus and snap off and discard the woody ends. Bring a skillet of water to a boil. Add the salt and asparagus and cook for 3–4 minutes only. (The asparagus should remain quite crisp because it will be cooked again.) Drain the asparagus in a colander and cool under cold running water. Set aside 8 of the thinner stalks for garnish.
3. Divide the remaining 16 stalks into 8 pairs and wrap each pair in 1 slice of the ham. Place the wrapped asparagus in a single layer in the prepared dish.
4. For a cheese sauce, melt the butter in a small saucepan over medium heat. Off the heat, stir in the flour, and when you have a smooth mixture, stir in ¹/₂ cup of the milk. Return the saucepan to the heat and add the remaining milk in 2–3 batches, stirring constantly until the sauce thickens. Mix together 1 tablespoon of the Cheddar, 1 tablespoon of the Parmesan, and the bread crumbs in a small bowl and set aside. Stir all the remaining cheeses into the sauce, along with a light seasoning of the cayenne pepper. When everything is thoroughly blended, taste and add more salt and white pepper if you think it is necessary.
5. Pour the sauce over the ham and asparagus, making sure to cover all. Sprinkle the reserved bread crumb mixture on top and bake for 10–12 minutes, or until the sauce is bubbly and the top is gold. During the last few minutes of cooking, add the reserved asparagus stalks to the dish, arranging them attractively. Serve when they are heated through.

Asparagus Pesto & Pine Nuts with Penne

Sometime in the early 1980s, New Englanders fell in love with pesto, a mixture of pounded basil, pine nuts, garlic, and Parmesan cheese from northern Italy. Now pesto is a new New England tradition. Parsley and mint sometimes replace basil for riffs on the pesto theme, and the Italians make a pesto rosso with sun-dried tomatoes. But the most elegant variation is this version inspired by the asparagus grown in the Connecticut River valley of Massachusetts. Like the classic Italian pesto, it's perfect on pasta but good on lots of other things, too. You can spread it on bread, dollop it on baked potatoes, or serve it as a dip. This meatless recipe is a favorite, especially as a vegetarian main dish. The garnish of asparagus tips, toasted pine nuts, and Parmesan cheese highlights the main ingredients of the pesto.

ASPARAGUS PESTO
2 pounds medium-thick stalks asparagus
1 teaspoon salt
3 tablespoons olive oil
1 small clove garlic, cut into 2–3 pieces
2 teaspoons fresh lemon juice or more to taste
¹/₃ cup pine nuts
¹/₃ cup grated Parmesan cheese
Salt to taste

PENNE
¹/₃ cup pine nuts
1 teaspoon salt
1 pound penne pasta
¹/₄ cup grated Parmesan cheese

1. To make the pesto, wash the asparagus and snap off and discard the woody ends. Cut off the tips and set the tips aside.

2. Bring a skillet of water to a boil and add the 1 teaspoon salt. Drop in the asparagus stalks and half of the reserved tips. Boil for 5–6 minutes or until completely tender. Place a colander on top of the pot that you will use for cooking the pasta and drain the asparagus in the colander, thus capturing its cooking broth, which will be used to flavor the pasta cooking water. Set aside the stalks and tips.

3. Heat the oil in a small saucepan over moderate heat and soften the garlic for 2–3 minutes without browning. Pour the mixture into a blender, add 6 of the asparagus stalks, and blend until fairly smooth. Add the lemon juice and more stalks, a few at a time, blending after each batch. Add the pine nuts and the ¹/₃ cup Parmesan and blend until smooth. Taste and add salt or more lemon juice if you would like.

4. Preheat the oven to 300º F. To make the penne, put the pine nuts into a shallow baking pan and toast for 7 minutes or until golden brown.

5. While the pine nuts are toasting, add enough water to the reserved asparagus broth to make 3 quarts. Add the salt and bring to a full boil. Tip in the pasta and stir vigorously. Boil for 7 minutes (or according to package directions) until tender but toothsome. Drain and return to the pot. Toss with ³/₄ cup of the asparagus pesto.

6. While the pasta is cooking, bring a small saucepan half-filled with water to a boil. Season lightly with salt and add the reserved asparagus tips. Boil until crisp-tender only, about 2–3 minutes. Drain.

7. Tip the hot pasta onto a large, warmed serving dish. Scatter the asparagus tips and the $^1/_4$ cup Parmesan on top and sprinkle with the toasted pine nuts. Serve more pesto and Parmesan at the table.

JANE MCWHORTER

Asparagus in Rolls

You can eat asparagus on its own with just a dab of butter or a shard or two of Parmesan cheese to keep it company. Lemons and eggs also enhance its flavor. The recipe for asparagus in a lemony sauce served inside hollowed rolls appeared in Hannah Glasse's *The Art of Cookery* published in 1747 and well known to eighteenth-century New Englanders. In her recipe, the rolls are deep-fried, and the asparagus stalks are stuck in holes cut into the top crust, so, she explained, "it may look as if it was growing." All this is tricky. But the recipe is appealing, and many nineteenth-century New England cookbooks offered versions of it, sometimes calling it "ambushed asparagus," presumably because the asparagus is hidden in the rolls, lying in wait for the eater, as it were. The following interpretation is easy and delicious. The rolls are lightly baked, not fried. Eat them for lunch or a light supper, or as a vegetarian alternative to hamburgers.

4 bread rolls
2–3 tablespoons butter, melted
1 teaspoon salt
20–24 medium-thick stalks asparagus
4 egg yolks

2–3 tablespoons fresh lemon juice
Zest of half a lemon
4 tablespoons milk
Salt and white pepper to taste
1–2 tablespoons cream (optional)

1. Preheat the oven to 300° F. Cut a slice from the top of each roll. (This slice will become a lid.) Scoop out the bread from the center of each roll and lightly brush the resulting cavity with the melted butter. Also lightly butter the underside of the lid. Replace the lids and wrap each roll in aluminum foil. Place in the oven and let warm for 10–15 minutes.

2. Wash the asparagus and snap off and discard the woody ends. Bring a skillet of water to a boil. Add the 1 teaspoon salt and drop in the asparagus. Boil for 3 minutes or until crisp-tender. Remove the asparagus with a slotted spoon and set aside. Reserve the cooking liquid and let simmer while you make the sauce.

3. In the top part of a double boiler or a small bowl poised over a saucepan of simmering water, whisk the egg yolks with the lemon juice and zest. In about 2–3 minutes, the egg yolks will begin to thicken. At this point, stir in the milk, a little at a time. Season with the salt and a little pepper. Continue whisking as the sauce thickens, watching it hawkeyed for signs of it developing a scrambled egg texture. If this happens, remove from the heat and whisk rapidly to smooth it out. Add the cream at the end if you want a richer consistency. Remove the sauce from above the simmering water, but keep warm.

4. To assemble the dish, cut 2–3 inch tips from the asparagus and reserve. Cut the stems into $1/2$-inch pieces. Bring the reserved asparagus liquid back to a boil and toss the asparagus stem pieces into it to reheat for 1 minute. Remove them with a slotted spoon and stir them into the lemon sauce. Spoon this mixture into the rolls, cover with the "lids," and keep warm in the oven. Now put the reserved asparagus tips in the simmering liquid to reheat for about 30 seconds. Remove them with a slotted spoon, drain, and arrange them in the rolls with the tips protruding from one side. Position the lids at an angle. Serve immediately.

Spinach & Radish Salad with Maple-Mustard Dressing

A salad of early greens used to be a tradition in New England, and indeed in many other places where winter is harsh enough to have made it impossible to eat greens at any time other than the warmer months. Greens were supposed to cleanse the blood and be generally good for you, and they certainly provided a tonic supply of vitamins missing in the traditional winter diet. Colonists included violet, dandelion, and sorrel leaves in their salads. With the year-round availability of lettuce and other green vegetables, the passion for spring greens has been lost. Nonetheless, the first local greens — usually spinach — taste wonderful. This salad lends itself to many variations. You could add arugula or some sliced mushrooms or bacon cut into half-inch bits. Black olives are another possibility. Dry mustard powder, such as Colman's or a Chinese brand, is what you need to give the dressing its edge; Dijon doesn't do it.

SALAD

8–10 loosely packed cups baby spinach leaves
2 hard-boiled eggs, shelled
12 medium radishes, thinly sliced
2 tablespoons snipped fresh chives

DRESSING

2 tablespoons pure maple syrup
1/2 teaspoon ground mustard
1 teaspoon grated lemon zest
1 tablespoon fresh lemon juice
2 tablespoons light vegetable oil
Salt to taste

1. To make the salad, wash the spinach well, then pick it over, discarding tough stalks and leaves. Dry the leaves on paper towels.

2. Chop the eggs, keeping the whites and yolks separate if you like.

3. To make the dressing, put the syrup into a small bowl and stir in the mustard until you have a smooth mixture. Add the zest, lemon juice, oil, and a little salt. Whisk lightly then taste. Add more salt if necessary.

4. Put the radish slices into a salad bowl with 1 tablespoon of the chives and turn the radishes in 1 tablespoon of the dressing. Add the spinach and the remaining dressing and toss. Sprinkle on the chopped eggs and scatter the remaining chives on the top.

Trout Stuffed with Leeks & Bacon

Bacon is the classic angler's accompaniment to trout, and just-caught fish fried with bacon eaten on the banks of a river big with waters from melting snow must be a rare delight. Most trout, however, is farm-raised and it cries out for flavorful accompaniments, so the traditional bacon still has a role to fill, as do leeks, which are oniony without being overpowering. This recipe makes a convenient one-dish meal. You can make the stuffing up to a day ahead of time. Stuffing the fish and placing them on their bed of sliced potatoes is then only the work of minutes.

STUFFING
6 strips lean bacon
1 medium leek
2 tomatoes, peeled, seeded, and coarsely chopped
2 cups dried bread crumbs
1 teaspoon dried thyme
1 tablespoon snipped fresh chives
Salt and black pepper to taste

TROUT
4 large potatoes, peeled and cut into $^1/_4$-inch slices
1 teaspoon salt
4 fresh butterflied trout
Salt and black pepper
4 slices lean bacon
1 bunch watercress, washed

1. To make the stuffing, broil the bacon until golden brown, then cut into 1-inch pieces and put into a bowl. Discard all but 1 tablespoon of the fat left in the skillet.

2. Clean the leek, discarding coarse outer layers and the top tuft, then thinly slice. Add both leek and tomatoes to the bacon fat left in the skillet and stir-fry for 2–3 minutes, or until the leek has wilted.

3. Add the leek and tomato mixture to the bacon in the bowl. Stir in the bread crumbs, thyme, and chives and season with the salt and black pepper. Form into a compact stuffing and divide into 4 portions. (If you are making the stuffing ahead of time, simply cover the bowl and store in the fridge for up to 1 day.)

4. When you are ready to make the meal, preheat the oven to 375º F. Grease a large shallow baking dish into which the trout will just fit.

5. To make the trout, put the potatoes into a large saucepan, cover with water, add the salt, and bring to a boil. Boil for 15 minutes or until tender but not falling apart or mushy. Drain and arrange the potatoes in a single layer of overlapping slices in the prepared dish.

6. Preheat the oven to 375º F. Wash and dry the trout. Season the inside with a little salt and black pepper. Lay a portion of the stuffing on one-half of each trout. Fold the other half over. Place the prepared trout on the potato bed, then place 1 strip of bacon on each trout.

7. Place in the center of the oven and bake for 15 minutes. If the bacon does not brown in this time, turn on the broiler and place the trout under the broiler until the bacon is golden. Garnish with the watercress and serve from the baking dish.

CHAPTER 2

THE WANDERERS' RETURN

Shad is get-it-while-you-can food. If you don't eat it in the spring when it swims up the Connecticut and other New England rivers, you will have missed your chance until another year. Salmon used to be that way, too.

Salmon and shad are anadromous fish: They are born in rivers, stay there for a couple of years, then, as the fish equivalent of teenagers, they head off to the Atlantic. Apparently, they live it up in the ocean because when family responsibility strikes them a couple of years later, they are big and fat. Anxious to get to a gravelly bed where they can spawn, they swim back to the rivers where they were born.

The wanderers' return has always signaled a feast. In pre-Colonial times, Native Americans moved from their winter woodland homes down to the river valleys so they could enjoy the salmon and shad runs. In 1796, *American Cookery,* the first cookbook written and published in America, called salmon "the noblest and richest fish taken in fresh water." As for shad, nineteenth-century newspapers from riverside towns noted its return so readers could

be sure to buy some at their local markets. Writing in *The Pocumtuc Housewife* in 1897, the ladies of the Deerfield Parish Guild in Deerfield, Massachusetts, advised novice housewives to serve salt shad for breakfast, suggesting, "When the Shad catch comes, buy a Barrel of them and slat them yourself. They are very nice." Deerfield remains a good shad-fishing spot, while Haddam, Connecticut still has a shad shack that sells locally caught shad in the spring. It also has a Shad Museum, where visitors can see traditional shad fishing equipment and listen to recordings of shad fishermen recounting the days when the shad fishery was a major business. Today, only about twenty boats fish commercially, but that is enough to provide the shad for the annual shad bakes of Connecticut towns, such as Essex, where a thousand people sit down to eat at the annual event.

The treat at these spring festivities is planked shad. To make this, fillets are nailed to hardwood boards and strips of bacon are fastened across the fillets. They are then brushed with sauce, often a secret recipe, and dusted with paprika. Finally the boards, each with several fillets, are poised on edge around an open fire, which roasts the fish, automatically basting it with the fat that runs from the bacon. Thirty to forty minutes later, it is ready to eat.

Shad roe — the egg-filled sacs of the female — is a particular delicacy. Haddam's Shad Museum has a giant long-handled frying pan used for cooking over an open flame. Butter is the canonical ingredient with shad roe, and slow cooking is the rule because high temperatures make the tiny eggs sputter and explode. Of course, male shad lack the delicious bonus of the roe, so nineteenth-century fishermen often threw them back into the water, knowing few customers would want them.

How fish find their way back to their native rivers used to be a mystery. Now biologists believe that as the two-year-olds undergo the blood chemistry changes that adapt them for life in the salt water of the ocean, they are imprinted with the chemical scent of their river. When it is time to return, they unfailingly nose out the right estuary as evidenced by the fish that researchers have tagged: none has ever been found in any river other than that which gave it birth.

Water temperature determines the time of their return. Shad spawn when the water reaches seventy degrees. Thus they appear in southern rivers in late winter, but don't come to the mouth of the Connecticut River until late April. Days later, you can spot the shad from the underwater windows of the public observation room at the Holyoke Dam, eighty-six miles to the north. Here, two elevators literally lift fish over the dam, sending over 200,000 fish a year on their way upstream to Turner's Falls, where a ladder lets at least some of them get as far north as Bellows Falls in Vermont. One of the most dramatic sights of New England's spring, this stream of returning fish triumphs over the pollution that killed them off in earlier years.

Salmon, a more finicky fish than shad, disappeared from the Connecticut River nearly 200 years ago, when dams and pollution stopped them from getting to the tributaries where they bred. With the cleanup of the river and the development of fish elevators, salmon now make their way as far as the Holyoke Dam. Most are then taken to the Cronin National Salmon Station in Sunderland, Massachusetts, where they live until ready to spawn in the fall. Scientists then use DNA testing to make sure that the eggs are fertilized by genetically diverse milt. Placed in river beds, the fertilized eggs hatch in the spring, producing tiny salmon that eventually begin the seaward cycle all over again.

The journey south is full of risks, however. One threat is another anadromous fish, the striped bass. Impelled by a voracious appetite, it snaps up young shad and salmon before they reach the sea, and many returning salmon are scarred from encounters with them. Despite this seeming ability to take care of themselves, stripers, as they are often called, were so imperiled that in the 1980s, the government placed a ten-year moratorium on fishing for striped bass. With this protection, New England's coast now has rich supplies, and over one million of them throng the lower Connecticut River.

Striped bass often appear in fish markets. So, too, do salmon — not the wild salmon who fare forth into the Atlantic, but salmon from fish farms on the Maine coast, where salmon are raised throughout the year. This creates a regular supply for both supermarkets and businesses that smoke salmon. As these businesses have thrived, smoked salmon has become less expensive, as have other smoked delicacies, including trout, bluefish, haddock, mackerel, tuna, whitefish, sturgeon, eel, scallops, mussels, and shrimp.

Smoked fish and seafood are not entirely

new to New England. In earlier centuries, coastal dwellers sometimes dealt with a glut of fish by smoking it in their chimneys. This did not dry the fish as thoroughly as salting it, which was the typical New England preserving method, so smoked fish had to be eaten within a shorter time. Its advantage was that it had an interesting flavor that appealed especially to late nineteenth-century immigrants from the British Isles, where smoked fish, especially herring and haddock, was traditional fare. A few New England businesses catered to their taste; they even exported smoked haddock to Canada. Nonetheless, today's New Englanders can buy far more varieties of smoked fish and seafood than ever before.

Dr. Joseph Zaientz of the Haddam Shad Museum says that smoked shad is excellent. Pasta and quiches, even pizzas, with smoked salmon appear on menus — much to the horror of purists who insist that smoked salmon should be eaten just as it comes, with perhaps, a few chives or capers and brown bread. Newer products, such as smoked scallops or mussels and smoked fish pâté, carry no such weight of tradition. They need no cooking, so they make perfect nibbles with drinks, yet their potent flavors can inspire innovative main dishes, too.

Baked Shad with Creamed Roe

The backbone of the shad has lateral V-shaped bones branching from it, making the fish notoriously difficult to fillet for all except experts. Luckily, the shad that you buy in the supermarkets is already filleted, so you don't have to worry about this task. Look for shad as early as March, when it is available from southern rivers, but generally expect it no later than June, when New England's supplies are finished. This recipe derives from one in Fannie Merritt Farmer's *The Boston Cooking-School Cookbook,* which suggests boiling the roe for 20 minutes. This is much too long. Boiling makes the eggs gritty, but shad roe poached in barely trembling water for a few minutes emerges smooth and soft, very delicious and very filling.

4–6 ounces fresh shad roe	*1 teaspoon all-purpose flour*
1 tablespoon fresh lemon juice	*5–6 tablespoons half-and-half*
Salt and white pepper	*1 egg, beaten*
1–1 1/2 pounds fresh shad fillet	*Salt and black pepper to taste*
1 tablespoon light olive oil	*Fresh lemon juice to taste*
1 tablespoon butter	*3–4 tablespoons fresh bread crumbs*
2 teaspoons chopped shallot or onion	*Sprigs fresh parsley and lemon wedges for garnish*

1. Wash the shad roe gently and pat dry. Place in a small saucepan and add the 1 tablespoon lemon juice. Cover with cold water and simmer for 5 minutes. Drain. As soon as the roe is cool enough to handle, cut through the membrane and remove the eggs. Mash the eggs in a bowl and season with the salt and white pepper. Set aside.

2. Preheat the broiler. Season the shad fillet with the salt and pepper and brush the top surface with the oil. Place the fish on an oiled griddle pan or baking sheet and broil for 5–6 minutes.

3. While the shad is broiling, melt the butter in a medium saucepan over moderate heat. Add the shallot and soften for 2 minutes. Stir in the reserved roe, sprinkle with the flour, and stir in 5 tablespoons of the half-and-half. Cook over moderate heat, stirring constantly, for 1–2 minutes or until hot and thickened. Stir in the egg and season with the salt, black pepper, and lemon juice. The black pepper and lemon juice flavors should be quite strong, and the consistency should be like oatmeal. If thicker, stir in the remaining half-and-half.

4. Remove the shad from the broiler. Spread the roe mixture on top and sprinkle with the bread crumbs. (The exact amount depends on the length of the fish.) Replace the shad under the broiler for 2 minutes, or until the bread crumbs are golden and crisp. Garnish with the parsley sprigs and serve with the lemon wedges.

Shad Escabeche

Shad is the largest member of the herring family, and like herring and other oily fish, it is good pickled or cooked in vinegar. Here it is lightly fried then marinated in a pungent souse. In effect, it is a form of ceviche, the South American fish dish marinated in citrus juice. The vinegar, which should be a flavorful wine or herb vinegar, preserves the fish, so this is an excellent do-ahead recipe, usable also with salmon and salt cod.

1 ¹/₂ pounds fresh shad, cut into 4–6 pieces
¹/₄ cup all-purpose flour
1 teaspoon ground paprika
4 tablespoons olive oil
¹/₄ teaspoon cayenne pepper (optional)
1 small onion, thinly sliced
2 cloves garlic, thinly sliced
¹/₂ teaspoon black peppercorns
2 large bay leaves
1 ¹/₂ cups red or white wine vinegar

1. Place the shad pieces on a plate and sift the flour over both sides. Sprinkle the upper surface with the paprika. Heat 3 tablespoons of the oil in a skillet and cook the fish for 4 minutes on each side. Drain on paper towels.

2. Place the cooked fish in a single layer in a shallow dish. If you want a slightly fiery taste, sprinkle with the cayenne pepper. Scatter the onion, garlic, and peppercorns on top. Break each bay leaf into 2 or 3 pieces and place here and there over the fish. Whisk together the remaining oil and the vinegar and pour over the top.

3. Cover with plastic wrap and place in the fridge for at least 12 hours or up to 3 days. Turn the fish several times in the marinade.

4. To serve, remove any bits of onion or bay leaf on the surface. Serve cold with a potato salad (see recipe on page 45).

Phyllo Pillows of Salmon with Tarragon

Try this dish when you have guests or for some other reason where you cannot pay full attention to the fish. The phyllo wrappings protect the salmon so that if you leave it for a minute or two longer, it comes to no harm. Use as few sheets of phyllo as possible to wrap the salmon, so it stays crisp.

1 ¹/₂ pounds center-cut fresh salmon fillet, cut into 4 pieces
Salt
6 tablespoons butter at room temperature
1 tablespoon finely chopped fresh parsley
2 tablespoons chopped fresh tarragon
1 teaspoon Worcestershire sauce
9 sheets (half of a 1-pound package) phyllo pastry, thawed
Sprigs fresh tarragon for garnish

1. Preheat the oven to 400° F. Lightly grease a shallow baking dish or tray.

2. Lightly season the salmon pieces with the salt. Make a pocket in each piece by cutting almost all the way through the thickest part.

3. Mix together 3 tablespoons of the butter, the parsley, tarragon, and Worcestershire sauce in a small bowl. Divide the mixture into 4 parts and fill the salmon pockets.

4. Take half of the pastry from the package and immediately cover the sheets with plastic wrap and a damp kitchen towel. Melt the remaining butter in a small saucepan.

5. Take 2 or 3 sheets of the pastry from under its wraps and brush lightly with the melted butter. Place 2 or 3 more sheets on top and brush very lightly with the butter again. Estimate its dimensions and those of your pieces of salmon. You are going to wrap the salmon in the pastry, and depending on its size, these sheets may be big enough to be halved and used for two salmon pieces. If possible, use the halved sheets. If you have to use full sheets for each piece of salmon, you will probably have excess pastry, which you should trim away after you have the salmon securely parceled. Wrap all of the salmon appropriately, then place seam-side down in the prepared dish. Lightly brush the exterior of the pastry with more melted butter.

6. Place the salmon in the center of the oven and bake for 15–18 minutes, or until the pastry is golden. Remove from the oven and let stand for 1–2 minutes before serving. Garnish with the tarragon sprigs and serve.

Pasta with Smoked Salmon, Lime & Chives

Some purists scorn the idea of cooking smoked salmon, and they have a good point. Few things are more delightful than an unadorned plate of its translucent, coral-colored slices with whole wheat bread on the side. For many years, few would have thought of eating smoked salmon in any other way because it was such a rarity. But now that salmon farming has made salmon and smoked salmon widely available, other options have a place. Any time you have a slice of smoked salmon left in a package, use it to give a new flavor layer to fish cakes or fish stews. This recipe calls for more than a few morsels. Its virtue is that it is a quick and easy dish made almost entirely of ready-to-eat ingredients — an excellent choice when you want something special but don't have much time to put it together. The smoked salmon is added at the end and is "cooked" only by the hot pasta.

1–2 limes
1 tablespoon butter
²/₃ cup cream
Salt and black pepper
1 tablespoon salt
¹/₂ pound fettuccine pasta
2 tablespoons grated Parmesan cheese
4 teaspoons capers
¹/₂ pound smoked salmon, cut into ¹/₂-inch strips
2 tablespoons snipped fresh chives

1. Using a zester, grate long strips of peel from 1 lime. If some strips curl, set aside for garnish. Finely chop the remaining peel to make 1 tablespoon. Squeeze the limes and reserve the juice.

2. Melt the butter in a large skillet. Stir in the chopped lime zest and ¹/₄ cup of the lime juice, then immediately add the cream and season with the salt and black pepper. Simmer for 3 minutes, or until the cream has thickened. Set aside.

3. Bring 3 quarts of water to a rolling boil in a large saucepan. Add the 1 tablespoon salt and drop in the pasta. Cook for 6-7 minutes or just until al dente. During the last minute of cooking, reheat the reserved lime sauce. Drain the pasta and return immediately to its pan. Quickly add the lime sauce, Parmesan, and 2 teaspoons of the capers, and toss with the pasta.

4. While everything is still very hot, add the smoked salmon and 1 tablespoon of the chives. Stir over low heat for a few seconds, then tip onto a warmed serving platter. Sprinkle with the remaining capers and chives and a few drops of lime juice and serve. Makes 4 first-course servings or 2 main dish servings.

Smoky Salmon Rosti Cakes

Good fish cakes, made with plenty of brightly seasoned fish or seafood, are delicious and come in seemingly endless variety. This recipe differs from the usual potato-based cake in that the potatoes are parboiled then grated rather than mashed, and the salmon is chopped raw rather than cooked then flaked. The result is more crumbly but has more texture and more flavor because neither of the two main ingredients has been cooked ahead of time.

1 pound fresh salmon fillet
2 slices smoked salmon (optional)
2 tablespoons finely chopped fresh parsley
3 medium potatoes (about 1 pound)
Salt and black pepper
1 egg white
Light olive or vegetable oil
Lemon wedges, capers, and chopped fresh parsley for garnish

1. Discard any skin or bones from the salmon and cut the salmon into $1/4$-inch pieces. (If you are using the smoked salmon, cut into $1/4$-inch pieces and toss with the fresh salmon.) Place in a large bowl and mix in the parsley.

2. Wash the potatoes and place, unpeeled, in a medium saucepan of water. Bring to a boil and boil for 10 minutes or just until you can stick a knife blade into the potatoes. Drain and cool under cold running water. When you can handle them, peel and grate the potatoes into the salmon mixture, mixing in as you grate. (Grated potatoes tend to clump together, so this is best accomplished with your hands.) Season well with the salt and black pepper.

3. Beat the egg white only until it looks sudsy. No need to let it bulk up into a foam. Stir the egg white into the salmon mixture.

4. Preheat the oven to 200º F. Heat $1/4$ inch of the oil in a large skillet until it is just trembly. Wet your hands and form the salmon mixture into 8 large or 12 small cakes. Cook the cakes, a few at a time, for 3–4 minutes on each side, turning only once. Lift the cakes onto a plate and place in the oven to keep warm, while you cook the remaining cakes.

5. Garnish with the lemon wedges, capers, and parsley and serve. For a first course, serve with an arugula, watercress, or romaine salad lightly dressed with vinaigrette. For a main course, serve with vegetables.

Rough-cut Smoked Salmon & Seafood Pâté

Today, fish pâtés, especially smoked fish pâtés, are almost as common as traditional meat pâtés, but usually they have a smooth texture. This rough-cut version is modeled on coarse, country-style meat pâtés. I find the identifiable little chunks of fish and seafood toothsome, and since the proportion of fish and seafood to cream cheese is greater than in smooth pâtés, it is more flavorful, too. Serve it with crackers.

³/₄ cup mascarpone or other cream cheese at room temperature
1 tablespoon fresh lemon juice or more to taste
¹/₄ teaspoon grated lemon zest
2 teaspoons snipped fresh dill
1 teaspoon crushed capers
Black pepper to taste
2 slices smoked salmon, chopped (about 2 ounces)
¹/₂ cup smoked or cooked fresh scallops or shrimp, thinly sliced (about 2 ounces)

1. Mix together the mascarpone, lemon juice, and lemon zest in a medium bowl until smooth.

2. Stir in the dill, capers, and black pepper. Gently fold in the salmon and scallops. Taste for flavor and seasonings and add more lemon juice or black pepper if needed. (Salt probably won't be necessary because the smoked ingredients are already salty.)

3. Press the mixture into a small dish and serve with crackers. Makes about 1 ¹/₃ cups.

Salmon, Leek & Corn Chowder

This chowder captures the full flavors and pastel colors of early summer. It's an easy recipe to double or triple. Exact amounts don't really matter here, though each of the major ingredients should be plentiful.

3 medium–large leeks
³/₄ pound fresh salmon fillet
2 tablespoons butter or light vegetable oil
3 medium potatoes, peeled and cut into ¹/₂-inch pieces (about 1 pound)
Salt and white pepper
2 cups water or fish stock
2 ears fresh corn, shucked
3 cups milk
2 tablespoons snipped fresh chives, chopped fresh parsley, or some of each

1. Cut off the coarse top leaves and outer layers of the leeks, leaving any tender green part. Make a 4–5-inch slit from the top of the leeks downward, then open out the layers and run cold water through the layers to remove any grit. Cut the leeks into ¹/₂-inch slices.

2. Discard any skin or bones from the salmon and cut the salmon into ¹/₂-inch pieces.

3. In a large pot over moderate heat, melt the butter and add the leeks. Stir in half of the potatoes and season with the salt and white pepper. Put half of the salmon on top, then the remaining potatoes, then the remaining salmon. Season again. Add the 2 cups water, cover, and simmer for 10 minutes.

4. Strip the kernels from the ears of corn. Add the kernels and milk to the pot and simmer for 4–5 minutes more, or until the potatoes are tender. Check the seasonings. Stir in 1 tablespoon of the chives. Ladle the chowder into soup bowls and garnish with the remaining chives. Serve hot.

New England Salmon Salad

In her account of foodways among nineteenth-century coastal New Englanders, *Saltwater Foodways*, Sandra L. Oliver explains that salmon, often served in a salad, was always highly esteemed, but by the end of the century, overfishing and the industrial damming and pollution of rivers had made the Atlantic salmon relatively rare. Pacific salmon abounded, however, and from 1866, they were being canned in California. Soon canned Pacific salmon was taking the place of fresh Atlantic salmon in salmon salads, no doubt appealing because it was easy to use, highly flavored, and relatively inexpensive.

Though tuna is caught off New England, it had little appeal until the twentieth century, except among immigrants from southern Europe. But in the 1920s canned tuna arrived from California, and since then it has replaced salmon salad — at least as a sandwich filling. Americans now eat three and one-half pounds of canned tuna each per year — enough to make about twenty-two tuna salad sandwiches. And a good thing, too; for many years, fresh Atlantic salmon was virtually unobtainable. Fish farming has brought it back, so if you want a cool dish for a summer lunch or supper, a traditional salmon salad is again an option. In this recipe, the salmon is paired with spring herbs and greens.

1 pound cooked salmon
2 tablespoons chopped fresh parsley
1 tablespoon snipped fresh chives
Salt and black pepper to taste
$^1/_3$ cup mayonnaise
Fresh baby lettuce or spinach leaves, washed
2 hard-boiled eggs, sliced or chopped
8 radishes, washed, trimmed, and sliced

1. Flake the salmon into medium-large pieces. Combine the salmon, parsley, and chives in a medium bowl and season with the salt and black pepper. Add the mayonnaise and toss gently to combine all of the ingredients.

2. Line a platter or individual plates with the lettuce. Add the salmon salad in a mound and garnish with the eggs and radishes. Serve. If you use the salad as a sandwich filling, chop the eggs and add them before adding the mayonnaise.

Striped Bass & Fennel Florentine

Firm and delicately flavored, striped bass shines on a bed of vibrant spinach and fennel. Shad could also be cooked this way.

1 1/2 *pounds fresh spinach*
1 *small bulb fennel (about 1 pound)*
Four 6-ounce pieces fresh striped bass
Black pepper
Olive oil

3 *tablespoons plain yogurt*
2 *tablespoons grated Parmesan cheese*
Salt to taste
Freshly grated nutmeg to taste

1. Fill the sink with cold water. Drop the spinach leaves in one by one, tearing off and discarding tough stems and battered leaves as you go. Swish the leaves around, then let the water settle so any soil falls to the bottom of the sink. Put the spinach leaves into a colander and rinse again, then stuff them into a medium saucepan. Do not add any water other than that on the leaves. Cover and cook over low heat for 4–5 minutes, or until the leaves are tender. Stir once or twice to make sure the spinach cooks evenly. Drain in a colander and let cool. Squeeze the leaves to remove excess liquid and set aside.

2. Cut off the fennel fronds and set aside 4 of the prettiest fronds for garnish. Chop the remaining fronds and set aside. Cut off the branches and any brown or coarse outside layers and discard. Cut the fennel bulb in half lengthwise. Place each half cut-side down and cut into strips 1/3 inch wide and 3 inches long.

3. Bring a large saucepan of lightly salted water to a boil. Drop the fennel strips into the water and cook for 6–7 minutes or until crisp-tender. Drain and set aside.

4. Preheat the broiler. Season the fish with the black pepper and brush with the oil. Place in a shallow pan also brushed with the oil and broil for 7–8 minutes or until light gold on top and firm and opaque in the center of the thickest part.

5. While the fish is cooking, gently reheat the reserved spinach. Stir in the yogurt and Parmesan and season to taste with the salt and nutmeg. Keep warm on the back of the stove while you deal with the fennel.

6. Line a plate with 2 paper towels. Pour 1/4-inch oil into a medium skillet and let the oil get hot enough to lightly tremble on the surface. Drop in the reserved fennel strips, a batch at a time, so that the skillet is not overcrowded, and the strips cook quickly. Let them sizzle for 1 minute or until golden on one side. Turn and cook the other side, then transfer to the paper towels, which will absorb excess oil. Proceed in this way until all of the strips are cooked.

7. To assemble the dish, divide the spinach among 4 warmed plates. Set aside one-fourth of the fennel strips for garnish. Scatter the remaining strips on the spinach, then position 1 piece of the fish on each. Add a few strips on top of each serving and sprinkle with the reserved chopped fronds. Garnish with the reserved whole fronds and serve.

Smoked Scallop Crostini with Radish Butter

Smoked scallops are like peanuts — one is never enough. Served on crostini with radish butter, they make excellent canapés. You can serve smoked shrimp or mussels this way, too. As for radish butter, it is also good on crackers, especially if you have fresh radishes from the garden.

1 baguette
1 bunch radishes, washed and trimmed
4 tablespoons butter at room temperature
Salt to taste
Fresh lemon juice to taste
4 ounces smoked scallops
1–2 teaspoons capers
1 bunch watercress, washed

1. Cut 15 slices, each about $\frac{1}{2}$ inch thick, from the baguette. Toast one side lightly under the broiler.

2. For the radish butter, grate or finely chop 8 radishes. Mix them into the butter, adding a little salt and lemon juice to taste.

3. Spread the radish butter on the crostini. Top each with 3 or 4 smoked scallops and a few capers. Add to the top some of the tiniest leaves of watercress. Arrange the crostini on a platter with the remaining watercress and radishes in the center.

CHAPTER 3

SPRING HOLIDAYS

Eggs used to be hard to come by in the winter because, left to themselves, hens do not start serious laying until the days lengthen. Abundant eggs were therefore a spring bounty after the dearth of winter. Milk, too, was not plentiful until cows returned to outdoor grazing and gave birth to their calves. This history lives on in the foods of spring holidays. Invariably, the dishes of the national and religious holidays of springtime come freighted with butter, cream, and eggs.

Easter highlights eggs: they are decorated, hunted, or simply enjoyed in enriched breads and cakes because they promise new life and thus symbolize Christian hope. In the days when most people abstained from animal foods during Lent, the eggs and butter of Easter baked goods must have been a luxury, the first pleasure heralding the seasons of plenty.

At Passover, too, an egg, roasted and set on the traditional Seder plate, recalls Jewish Passover sacrifices at the Temple. At Shavuoth, seven weeks later, Jewish families remember God's gift of the Torah to Moses, as he was leading his people from slavery. Explanations of the symbolism vary, but one suggests that the creamy dishes recall the Promised Land, flowing with milk and honey.

New Englanders share these holidays with their co-religionists everywhere, but they also have their own special days. St. Patrick's Day, which falls on March 17, is a favorite. It venerates Ireland's patron saint, and it came to New England with the region's Irish immigrants. But with winter storms giving way to milder weather, most New Englanders don't feel they have to be Irish to celebrate the holiday, especially in Massachusetts, where nearly twelve percent of the people have Irish ancestry. Most people try to wear something green, especially if they are going to a party or watching a parade in Boston, Worcester, or Holyoke. Businesses festoon themselves with leprechauns and shamrocks. Bakeries sell cakes with emerald frosting; bars may well have green beer; green bagels are not unknown. Supper must be corned beef and cabbage, while pubs and restaurants feature Irish specialties, such as soda bread, Irish stew, Irish coffee, and desserts spiked with Irish whiskey or cream liqueurs.

As visitors from Ireland often note, it is all a lot more rambunctious than in the Emerald Isle itself.

A month later, alone of all the states, Massachusetts celebrates Patriot's Day, the April 19 anniversary of the Battles of Lexington and Concord in 1775. Public offices close, while many Boston streets also close to traffic so that runners in the annual Boston Marathon can race the twenty-six miles, 385 yards from Hopkinton to the finish line on Boylston Street.

Organized by the Boston Athletic Club and first run in 1897, the Marathon celebrates both the local heroes of the Revolutionary War and Phaedippides, the Greek runner who in 490 B.C. sped from Marathon to Athens bringing news of the Greek victory over the Persians. This mission fulfilled, he died of exhaustion. To prevent such tragedies, today's marathoners prepare for races by loading up on carbohydrate foods that boost energy and endurance. In Boston, where the Italian community is second in size only to the Irish, the carbohydrate of choice is pasta, and "carbohydrate loading" translates into a pre-Marathon pasta feast where runners stoke up on squares of lasagna and pyramids of spaghetti and macaroni. This tradition is easy to love, so as other cities around the world have followed Boston in hosting annual marathons, they have taken the prerace pasta party on board, too. It is now a part of the marathon ritual everywhere.

May brings more festivities. Rhode Islanders celebrate having been the first state to declare independence from Britain on May 4, 1776, with May breakfasts. Held all over the state in church halls, fire stations, clubs, and any facility that has room for a lot of people, these celebrations feature a variety of traditional breakfast fare: juice, bacon, ham, eggs, sausages, baked beans, apple pie, and, of course, the staple that every breakfast must include — Rhode Island johnnycakes made from white cornmeal. May baskets filled with homemade candies and the first flowers of the year are often sold at May breakfasts, with the proceeds going to good causes.

In midmonth, mothers get their day with breakfast in bed or a restaurant dinner. The last Monday of the month is Memorial Day. Instituted by the northern states in 1865, it honored Union soldiers who died in the Civil War, but in 1968, it became a nationwide commemoration of all Americans killed in combat.

Veterans' parades often occupy the morning of Memorial Day, but by afternoon, barbecues have emerged from their winter hibernation. The aroma of charcoal drifts over neighborhoods as burgers and hot dogs, steaks and vegetables sizzle on the grill. Lilacs bloom and pansies brighten flower beds. Friends and neighbors gossip over beers and munchies. Kids race from yard to yard. Swallows swoop. You might hear a distant lawn mower, or even the sharp, alarming whine of a mosquito as late spring blossoms into early summer.

JANE MCWHCRTER

Corned Beef & Cabbage

Corned beef and cabbage is an Irish-American institution on St. Patrick's Day, but it's not what the Irish back in Ireland eat. There, the meal of the day is ham served with parsley sauce and green vegetables, followed by a fancy dessert. When Irish immigrants arrived in New England in the nineteenth century, they were poor and salted beef was the nearest they could get to a ham.

3–4 pounds corned beef brisket
1 teaspoon black peppercorns
1 bay leaf
8 small beets with leaves (optional)
2–3 pounds potatoes, peeled and cut into large chunks
1 pound carrots, scraped and cut in half
1 small rutabaga, peeled and cut into large chunks
1 small cabbage, cut into large chunks

1. Put the corned beef in a large pot that has enough room for the vegetables that will go in later. Cover the meat completely with water. Add the peppercorns and bay leaf. Cover and simmer for 2–2 ¹/₂ hours.

2. If you are using beets, clean and cut off the leaves leaving 4 inches of stem still attached to the roots. One hour after starting the beef, place the beets in a large saucepan, cover with water, and bring to a boil. Cook for 20 minutes or until pierced easily by a fork. Peel or rub off the outer skin and keep warm.

3. After you have simmered the beef for 2 hours or more, remove 2 cups of the broth and set aside. Add the potatoes, carrots, and rutabaga to the beef and cook for 30–40 minutes more.

4. Twenty minutes before you plan to serve the beef, heat the reserved broth in a large saucepan and drop in the cabbage. When the cabbage and all of the vegetables are tender, about 20 minutes, remove the pans from the heat. Put the beef, either in one piece or sliced, onto a large serving platter and surround it with the drained vegetables, including the cabbage and the beets.

To make Corned Beef Hash: *Be sure to leave a large chunk of the corned beef and plenty of the potatoes; also some beets, if you are using them. The next day, chop 1 medium onion and cut the corned beef into cubes. Heat 1–2 tablespoons vegetable oil in a skillet over moderate heat and soften the onion for 4–5 minutes. Add the potatoes, increase the heat a little, and cook until the potatoes are beginning to turn golden. Add the corned beef and season; plenty of black pepper is good with corned beef hash. Add more oil if necessary to prevent sticking. Also, add the beets if you have them. Cook without stirring until everything is hot and crusty. Then fold over with a large spatula, as you would an omelette, and serve. Poached or fried eggs are excellent and traditional with hash. Hash with beets is called Red Flannel Hash, because the beet juices stain everything the color of old-fashioned red flannel.*

Muireann Glenmullen's Cranberry-Nut Soda Bread

Muireann Glenmullen of Cambridge, Massachusetts, often makes the traditional soda bread that she grew up with in Dublin. But in her recipe, she sometimes gives it the flavors of New England by adding cranberries and nuts. She explains that soda bread is best mixed with the hand so you can sense how much liquid to use.

3 $^1/_4$ cups all-purpose flour
$^1/_2$ teaspoon granulated sugar
$^1/_2$ teaspoon salt
1 teaspoon sieved baking soda
1 $^1/_2$–2 cups sour milk or buttermilk
$^3/_4$ cup dried cranberries
$^3/_4$ cup chopped walnuts

1. Preheat the oven to 450° F. Grease a baking sheet.
2. Sift the flour, sugar, salt, and baking soda into a large bowl and mix thoroughly. Make a well in the center of the mixture and pour in 1 $^1/_4$ cups of the milk all at once. Using one hand, mix the flour from the sides into the center, mixing quickly but gently, adding the cranberries and walnuts as soon as the mixture forms into a dough. Add the remaining milk, 1–2 tablespoons at a time, only if necessary to make a soft dough. The dough should not be wet or sticky.
3. Place the dough on a floured board and gently knead once or twice to shape it into a 2-inch thick disk. Score a cross on top of the disk and bake for 15 minutes. Reduce the temperature to 400° and bake for 20 25 minutes more, or until the bottom sounds hollow when rapped. Cool on a wire rack.

Leg of Lamb with Apple-Mint Sauce

Lamb is a traditional choice for Easter, especially among New Englanders of Italian, Greek, or English origin. Mint sauce from fresh mint — usually already thriving by Easter — is the perfect accompaniment as long as it is not too sweet.

ROAST LAMB
3 cloves garlic, cut into slivers
5–6 sprigs fresh summer savory
One 3 1/2-pound boned and rolled leg of lamb
1 teaspoon coarse salt
1 tablespoon vegetable oil

APPLE-MINT SAUCE
3/4 cup apple jelly
4 tablespoons cider vinegar
2/3 cup chopped fresh mint

1. Preheat the oven to 450° F. Lightly grease a roasting pan.

2. To make the lamb, put some of the garlic slivers and some of the savory leaves into the underside of the lamb where the bone was removed. Turn the lamb fat-side up and with the sharp point of a knife, make several deep cuts in the lamb. Put 1 sliver of garlic and some savory leaves into each cut. Rub the salt into the fat, then trickle on the oil. Put the lamb into the prepared pan and roast for 30 minutes.

3. Reduce the temperature to 375° and roast for 40–50 minutes more. (This amount of time gives you well done meat on the outside with medium rare, slightly pink meat on the inside. Cook for an additional 15–25 minutes for well done meat.) Remove from the oven and sprinkle any remaining savory over the meat. Let stand for 5–10 minutes.

4. To make the sauce, combine the jelly and vinegar in a small saucepan and simmer for 5 minutes. Set aside 1 tablespoon of the mint. Add the remaining mint to the jelly-vinegar mixture and simmer for 1 minute more. Keep the sauce warm until serving time. Stir in the reserved mint just before taking to the table. Serve the lamb with the sauce on the side.

Baked Ham with Cider Sauce

Ham is another traditional favorite for Easter. You can buy it off the bone and ready cut, but a ham baked on the bone always tastes better, plus you get the bone for making soup. The cider and cloves give this version an old-timey aroma and flavor.

4 cups nonalcoholic cider
1 bay leaf
½ cup raisins
2 tablespoons brown sugar
One 8-pound shank end bone-in ham
20 whole cloves
Black pepper to taste

1. Mix together the cider, bay leaf, raisins, and sugar in a medium saucepan and simmer for 10 minutes.

2. Preheat the oven to 375º F. Trim off any skin or brownish fat from the surface of the ham, exposing the white fat. Make crisscross scores over the fat so that the fat is divided into squares or diamonds. Stick 1 clove into the center of each square. Put the ham into a roasting pan, choosing a pan that leaves some space around the ham.

3. Strain the warm cider mixture over the ham and discard the bay leaf and raisins. Baste the ham thoroughly several times with the cider mixture and bake for 1 hour. Continue basting every 10–15 minutes. When the fat is golden and the cider is simmering, reduce the temperature to 350º.

4. Remove the ham from the oven and throughly baste with the cider mixture. Transfer the ham to a heated carving plate.

5. Tip the cider mixture from the roasting pan into a small saucepan. Taste for seasonings. Most likely the ham will have made it salty enough, but you may want to add a little black pepper. Bring to a boil and boil rapidly for 4–5 minutes. Remove the fat from the surface either by spooning it off or pouring the cider mixture through a low-spouted pitcher designed for the purpose. Serve the ham with the cider sauce on the side. Serves 8–12.

Hot Cross Buns

Hot cross buns are easy and fun. Children can help by working in the currants and shaping the buns, and everyone enjoys the fragrance as they cook. A minute or two after you cut the cross into the top of the uncooked buns, you see it open as the dough rises. This emblem of the Resurrection is symbolism in action. Buns with a cross of paler dough or white frosting lack this drama.

DOUGH
1 package active dry yeast
1/3 cup warm water
4 cups all-purpose flour
1/2 teaspoon salt
1/3 cup firmly packed light brown sugar
Pinch ground cloves, or 1/4 teaspoon
   ground allspice
1/4 teaspoon ground cinnamon

1 teaspoon freshly grated nutmeg
1 cup warm milk
2 eggs, lightly beaten
4 tablespoons butter
1/2 cup currants or raisins

GLAZE
2 tablespoons granulated sugar
4 tablespoons cold milk

1. To make the dough, mix together the yeast and the 1/3 cup warm water in a small bowl and set aside for 10 minutes, or until it is thick and a bit frothy.

2. In the bowl of an electric mixer or other large bowl, mix together the flour, salt, sugar, cloves, cinnamon, and nutmeg. Make a well in the center of the mixture. Pour in the reserved yeast, then the warm milk and mix thoroughly. Add the eggs, one at a time, and the butter. Knead or mix with a dough hook until the dough comes away from the sides of the bowl and does not stick to your fingers. Knead in the currants, being careful to distribute them throughout the dough. Form the dough into a ball and place it in a bowl. Cover with plastic wrap and set aside in a draft-free spot to rise. Let rise until it has doubled in bulk, about 2 hours.

3. Grease a baking sheet. Thump the dough or slap it on the counter several times, knead briefly, then divide into 12 pieces. Roll each piece into a ball and place it on the baking sheet. (As you form the buns, poke any currants on the surface into the interior to prevent them from burning during baking.) Cover with plastic wrap again and let rise until doubled again, about 30–45 minutes.

4. Preheat the oven to 400° F. With a very sharp knife or single-edge razor, slash a crisscross on top of each bun. Let sit for 10 minutes so the crosses open. Bake the buns for 15 minutes, or until the tops are golden brown and the bottoms sound hollow when rapped. Remove from the oven.

5. To make the glaze, immediately combine the sugar and milk in a small saucepan and bring to a boil. Boil until it bubbles up the sides of the saucepan. Brush the glaze onto the tops of the buns while they are still hot. This gives them a shiny top. Makes 12 buns.

Eggs in Shrimp Mayonnaise

What to do with the hard-boiled eggs of Easter? You could make deviled eggs by mashing the yolks with a little butter and hot spices or make stuffed eggs using sardines, tuna, or smoked fish worked into a yolk-based mixture. Or, you could make this simple dish of sliced eggs topped with a shrimp mayonnaise.

8 hard-boiled eggs, peeled and halved
25 medium shrimp, peeled, deveined, and cooked (about $1/2$–$3/4$ pound)
$3/4$ cup mayonnaise
$1/2$ teaspoon Worcestershire sauce
1–2 teaspoons tomato puree, ketchup, or cocktail sauce
Salt and black pepper to taste
Pinch cayenne pepper (optional)
1 tablespoon snipped fresh chives or other herbs of choice

1. Arrange the eggs cut-side down neatly on a serving platter or on individual plates if you are making the dish as a first course.

2. Reserve 8 shrimp for garnish. Coarsely chop the remaining shrimp.

3. Mix together the mayonnaise, Worcestershire sauce, and enough tomato puree to color the mayonnaise pink in a small bowl. Season to taste with the salt, black pepper, and a little cayenne if you want a slightly fiery taste.

4. Spread the mayonnaise mixture over the sliced eggs, leaving a few slices partly visible. Garnish with the reserved shrimp and sprinkle with the chives. Serves 8.

EASTER EGGS

The plentiful eggs of spring transform basic dough into the hot cross buns of England and Ireland, the tsoureki *of Greece, the dove-shaped* colomba pasquale *of Italy and dozens of other regional breads of Easter. Immigrants brought these baked goods with them to New England. While many are made only at home, bakeries in ethnic communities also produce them. Immigrants also brought other egg customs to New England. Northern Italians make Easter pies with ricotta, chard, and whole eggs, while Italians from the south use macaroni, cheese, and eggs. Poles decorate eggs, both real and wooden, with brightly colored friezes and flowers. On Easter Sunday, each Polish household cuts one hard-boiled egg into many morsels. As visitors arrive, they take a tiny piece, indicating the community of everyone in a single whole. Greek Americans dye dozens of eggs crimson, a symbol of Jesus's blood. They bake one egg right into the crust of their braided Easter loaves. Family and friends take the rest, saluting each other on Easter Sunday by tapping their eggs together to crack the shells. New England's Portuguese community, who mostly come from the Azores, also bake a hard-boiled egg on the crust of the sweet round loaves, called* folar, *that they bake for Easter.*

Rum Macaroons

During the eight days of Passover, Jewish families follow strict dietary rules, recalling their historic exodus from Egypt. They had to leave so quickly they had no time to leaven bread for their journey to the Promised Land. In memory of this, they not only eat no leavened food during Passover, but to avoid even inadvertent leavening, which can take place eighteen minutes after flour and water mix, they use only specially prepared matzo meal. Add to this the law that prohibits the consumption of meat and dairy foods in the same meal, and you have severe limits on cake and pie possibilities. Jewish cooks have therefore created a repertoire of alternative Passover desserts. Among them, macaroons made from almonds or coconut are a holiday staple. This recipe uses almond paste as a shortcut. If you have a piping bag (or a plastic bag and a piping nozzle), use the bag to make pretty shapes. If not, the macaroons taste just as good dropped from a teaspoon.

7 ounces almond paste, broken into small pieces
2 cups sweetened flaked coconut
1 egg white
4 tablespoons dark rum

1. Preheat the oven to 350º F. Place baking parchment on 2 large baking sheets.

2. Combine the almond paste, coconut, and egg white in the container of a food processor or a mixing bowl and process or stir together. Add the rum and process or beat in until you have a thick paste able to hold its shape when dropped, but not too stiff. If necessary, add a few drops more rum to get the right consistency.

3. Put the mixture into a piping bag or a plastic bag filled with a wide nozzle such as Ateco 105. (If you do not have a piping bag, make the macaroons by dropping the mixture from a well-filled teaspoon. If the edges are untidy, just push them into shape with the back of a fork.)

4. Pipe the macaroons about 1 inch or so in diameter onto the prepared baking sheets and bake for 18–22 minutes or until a warm golden brown. Makes about 2 $1/2$–3 dozen macaroons.

Spaghetti with Olives & Bay

Greek myth tells that Athena created the first olive tree as a gift to the people, who gratefully named their city after her. Another myth tells that the nymph Daphne was turned into a bay tree while running away from Phoebus, the sun god. Olives became the symbol of peace — a reminder of the Greek victory at Marathon — while bay wreaths crowned winners of classical times. The night before the Boston Marathon, runners usually load up on pasta with a basic tomato sauce highlighted with vegetables or meat. Here, olives and bay recall the origins of the race and make this a dish that vegetarians can also enjoy.

2 tablespoons olive oil
2 cups chopped onion
1–2 cloves garlic, chopped
One 28-ounce can chopped or crushed tomatoes
8 small-to-medium bay leaves
$^1/_2$ teaspoon dried thyme
Salt and black pepper to taste
24 pitted kalamata olives
8 pimiento-stuffed green olives
2 teaspoons dried oregano
1 teaspoon salt
1 pound spaghetti or other pasta of choice
$^1/_3$ cup grated Parmesan cheese
Bay leaves for garnish

1. For the sauce, heat the oil in a large skillet over medium heat. When the oil is moderately hot, add the onion and garlic and gently cook for 4 minutes, or until they are softened. Add the tomatoes, bay leaves, thyme, salt, and black pepper and simmer for 10 minutes, or until some of the juice has evaporated and the sauce has thickened. Stir in all of the olives and the oregano and cook for 5 minutes more, or until the olives are heated through.

2. Meanwhile, bring 4 quarts of water to a boil in a large pot. Add the 1 teaspoon salt and the pasta and cook for 7–8 minutes or until tender but still with substance. Drain.

3. Toss the spaghetti with half of the sauce and transfer to a warmed platter or to individual plates. Top with more sauce. Sprinkle with the Parmesan and serve more at the table. Garnish with some bay leaves and serve immediately.

Firehouse Chili-Pasta Bake

Ronzoni, the pasta company, runs a competition for recipes to feature at Boston's pre-marathon pasta party. This dish, invented by James M. Flaherty, a fireman in Quincy, Massachusetts, was one of the featured dishes for the first race of the new millennium. It is baked in a large pan, so it's a good dish to make for a crowd or to carry to a potluck.

3 cups uncooked ziti pasta
$^1\!/_2$ pound lean ground beef
1 cup diced green bell pepper
$^1\!/_2$ cup chopped onion
2 cloves garlic, finely chopped
$^1\!/_2$ teaspoon salt
$^1\!/_4$ teaspoon black pepper
1 tablespoon chili powder
One 15 $^1\!/_2$-ounce can dark red kidney beans, drained
One 14 $^1\!/_2$-ounce can chunky-style tomatoes
1 $^1\!/_3$ cups medium-hot salsa
8 ounces shredded Monterey Jack cheese

1. Cook the pasta according to package directions and drain.

2. Combine the ground beef, bell pepper, onion, and garlic in a large skillet over medium heat. Season with the salt, black pepper, and chili powder and cook, stirring occasionally, for 10 minutes, or until the vegetables are tender and the meat is thoroughly cooked. Drain off the fat and discard.

3. Stir in the beans, tomatoes, and salsa and bring to a boil. Reduce heat to simmer and cook for 10 minutes.

4. Meanwhile, preheat the oven to 375º F. Grease a 9 x 13 x 2-inch baking dish. Mix together the cooked pasta and meat mixture and pour into the prepared dish. Sprinkle with the cheese and bake until the cheese melts. Serves 6 – 8.

Rhode Island Johnnycakes

Rhode Island johnnycakes are pancakes made from white flint corn. As its name suggests, flint corn is harder than yellow corn, so johnnycakes have a texture missing from pancakes made with wheat flour or yellow cornmeal. Johnnycakes are sometimes made thin, sometimes thick. Eat them plain with maple syrup for breakfast, or serve them, as at a May breakfast, with bacon, sausage, and eggs. More johnnycake ideas come from chefs: Kerry Downey Romaniello, Executive Chef at Westport Rivers Winery, suggests serving roast turkey or ham over "tender buttered johnnycakes with a rich gravy or cranberry relish" for a cold-weather supper. Jasper White popularized thin johnnycakes served with poached eggs and caviar when he was chef at the Bostonian Hotel in Boston. Today, you'll find his dish on the menus of several fine hotels. The following recipe makes medium-thin johnnycakes.

2 cups white cornmeal
$^3/_4$ teaspoon salt
1 cup water
1 $^1/_2$–2 cups milk
1–2 tablespoons vegetable oil

1. Preheat the oven to 200° F. Mix together the cornmeal and salt in a bowl. Make a well in the center and stir in the water. The meal will thicken into a paste. Thin with $^1/_2$ cup of the milk. When it is smooth, add the remaining milk, a little at a time, until you have a thick, but pourable batter. (The amount of milk can vary, so you may need more or less than specified.)

2. Heat 1 tablespoon of the oil in a nonstick skillet over high heat. When hot, reduce the heat to moderate and pour in the batter to form pancakes 2–3 inches in diameter or as you prefer. Cook slowly until the edges look dry. Flip and cook the other side. Repeat with the remaining batter. Add the remaining oil to the pan only if necessary. (Typically, johnnycakes take a little longer than regular pancakes to cook, and they remain more moist in the center.)

3. Transfer the cooked cakes to an ovenproof platter and keep warm in the oven. Serve hot. Makes about 1 dozen.

Grilled Shiitakes

When nineteenth-century New England was the industrial powerhouse of the nation, North Adams, Massachusetts, made its living weaving textiles. Now its handsome mills have been turned to some surprising uses. One complex has become MASS MoCA (the Massachusetts Museum of Contemporary Art). Another houses the Delftree Corporation, which pioneered shiitake growing in the United States. Shiitakes are natives of Japan, where they are grown out of doors on specially treated logs. Delftree adapted this process, brought it into the old mill, and now produces premium mushrooms for restaurants in New York and throughout the region. Because they feed off wood, shiitakes are sturdy and stand up well to the grill, making them a good choice for Memorial Day barbecues and anytime you want to serve meatless burgers.

$\frac{1}{2}$ cup olive oil
$\frac{1}{4}$ cup white or red wine vinegar
$\frac{1}{3}$ cup red wine
2 teaspoons Worcestershire sauce
1 teaspoon dried marjoram or oregano
3 bay leaves
2 cloves garlic, sliced
12 large shiitake mushrooms, washed and dried

1. Whisk together the oil, vinegar, wine, and Worcestershire sauce in a shallow dish. Add the marjoram, bay leaves, and garlic.

2. Add the shiitakes, one at a time, to the oil mixture turning each one in the liquid. Marinate for a few hours or for up to 1 day in the fridge.

3. Light a charcoal fire in a barbecue grill and wait until the coals turn gray. Place the shiitakes gill-side up about 7 inches from the heat and cook for 5–6 minutes. Turn and cook for 3 minutes more. Serve on top of burgers or on burger rolls for those who prefer only mushrooms.

New England Potato Salad for a Crowd

People like potato salad so much that it is hardly worth making a little. This recipe is good for a Memorial Day cookout or for any other event where there are many mouths to feed. It can be halved.

5 pounds potatoes, washed but unpeeled
1 tablespoon prepared English mustard or other flavorful mustard
2 teaspoons granulated sugar
2 tablespoons white vinegar
1 cup mayonnaise
Salt to taste
3 stalks celery, trimmed
6 hard-boiled eggs
1 tablespoon chopped scallion or onion
12 radishes, washed, trimmed, and sliced
¹/₂ cup chopped fresh parsley

1. Put the potatoes into a large pot of cold water and bring to a boil. Cook for 20–25 minutes, or until they can be pierced by a knife blade. Drain and run cold water over the potatoes until they are cool enough to handle. Strip off the skins and cut the potatoes into bite-sized chunks. Set aside.

2. Mix together the mustard, sugar, and vinegar in a large bowl. Stir in the mayonnaise and salt.

3. Split the celery stalks lengthwise and cut into ¹/₂-inch slices. Peel the eggs. Set aside 3 eggs, and chop the remaining eggs.

4. Add the reserved potatoes, the celery, chopped eggs, scallion, and half of the radish slices to the mayonnaise mixture and toss gently until everything is coated in mayonnaise. Cover and keep in the fridge for 1 hour or so, stirring gently once or twice to allow the flavors to blend. Taste for seasonings and add more salt if needed.

5. Pile the salad into a large bowl or onto a shallow platter. Cut each reserved egg into 4 wedges. Use the wedges and the remaining radish slices to garnish the salad. Shower the parsley over the top and serve. Serves 12.

Cheese Blintzes with Cherries

Dairy foods of all kinds are traditional at Shavuoth, the Jewish holiday sometimes called the Festival of the Weeks because it occurs seven weeks after Passover, thus falling in late May or early June. In traditional agricultural societies, milk was at its most plentiful during these months, so households dealt with the excess by making butter and cheese — two ways of preserving the abundance for leaner times. The foods of Shavuoth focus on dairy products: kugels with creamy sauces, cheesecakes, and perhaps most popular of all, blintzes with cream cheese and fruit.

BLINTZES

1 cup all-purpose flour
Pinch salt
4 eggs
¼ cup milk
1–2 teaspoons vegetable oil

TOPPING

1 cup cherry jam
2 tablespoons water
¼ pound fresh cherries, washed and pitted

FILLING

8 ounces Neufchâtel cheese at room
    temperature
1 egg
1 tablespoon granulated sugar
Pinch ground cinnamon
1 tablespoon butter

1. Cut baking parchment or waxed paper into twelve 7-inch squares. You will use these to separate the blintzes as you make them.

2. To make the blintzes, mix together the flour and salt in a large bowl. Make a well in the center of the mixture. Lightly beat together the eggs and milk and pour into the well. Beat to combine the flour with the wet ingredients.

3. Lightly grease a 6-inch nonstick skillet with a little of the oil. Set over high heat and when it is hot, pour in and swirl around just enough of the batter to cover the pan. Cook until the surface looks set and is pitted with tiny holes. Remove the blintz from the pan and set it cooked-side up on a sheet of the parchment or waxed paper. Make the remaining batter into blintzes in the same way, piling them in stacks of 4 or 5, each separated from its neighbor by the paper. (Grease the pan with the remaining oil only if the blintzes stick.) You should have 12–15 blintzes.

4. To make the filling, beat the cheese, egg, sugar, and cinnamon into a smooth cream.

5. Grease a large shallow baking dish with a little of the butter. To fill the blintzes, put a dollop of the cheese mixture into the center of each blintz, keeping the cooked-side up. Fold the edge nearest to you over it, then fold in the two side edges and finally fold down the top edge. This gives you a plump pillow shape. Place the filled blintz seam-side down in the prepared dish. When all of the blintzes are made, dot each one with a tiny dab of the butter. Cover the dish with aluminum foil. (You can bake them now or prepare ahead to this point and bake them several hours later if you prefer.)

6. Preheat the oven to 375º F. Bake the blintzes for 15 minutes or until heated through.

7. To make the topping, mix together the jam and water in a small saucepan and bring to a simmer. Serve the blintzes with the cherry sauce and the cherries. Leftover blintzes reheat successfully in a microwave.

JANE MCWHORTER

Cheesecake with Irish Liqueur & Toblerone

A cheesecake makes a celebratory dessert for many occasions. This version is flavored with Bailey's Irish Cream liqueur, so it could crown a St. Patrick's Day meal. Cream cheese is in the spirit of Shavuoth, so it could appear on any of the days of this Jewish holiday. Then again, it could be something special for Mother's Day.

CRUST
7 ounces shortbread cookies
4 tablespoons butter, melted

FILLING
Three 8-ounce packages Neufchâtel cheese or other low-fat cream cheese at room temperature
1 teaspoon pure vanilla extract
$1/4$ teaspoon pure almond extract
1 cup sour cream
1 cup firmly packed light brown sugar
3 eggs
$1/3$ cup Bailey's Irish Cream or other Irish cream liqueur

FROSTING
$1/2$ cup flaked almonds
One 3.52-ounce bar of Toblerone chocolate or other milk chocolate
2 tablespoons Bailey's Irish Cream or other Irish cream liqueur

1. Preheat the oven to 325° F. Line the base of a springform pan with baking parchment or grease well. Grease the side of the pan also. The cheesecake will be baked in a water bath so you must protect the seam between the base of the pan and the side. To do this, take four sheets of heavy-duty aluminum foil, each 2 feet long, and double the sheets. Stand the pan on one doubled sheet and fold the foil around the base and side, pressing it firmly to the base. Repeat with the remaining sheets of foil, turning the pan a little each time so that eventually the sides and especially the base is thoroughly enclosed in foil.

2. To make the crust, crush the cookies into fine crumbs. Combine the crumbs and butter in a medium bowl and mix together well. Press the mixture firmly into the bottom of the springform pan and bake for 10 minutes, or until the surface looks smooth and dry. Remove from the oven and set aside. Increase the temperature to 350°.

3. To make the filling, cream the cheese in a large bowl using a slow, smooth folding motion or the paddle attachment of an electric mixer. Try to avoid beating air into the mixture because air

will make the cheesecake rise in the oven; it will then fall when you remove it, leaving a crater or crack across the top.

4. As soon as the cheese is smooth, add both extracts, the sour cream and sugar and stir with a spoon or paddle attachment until blended. Add the eggs, one at a time, blending in each one. Stir in the liqueur and pour the mixture on top of the reserved crust.

5. Place the springform pan in a large roasting pan and add water to about 2 inches up the sides of the pan. Place the outer pan on the center rack and bake for 50–60 minutes, or until a knife blade comes out clean. Check after about 25 minutes, and if the top is golden brown rather than the color of café au lait, lay a sheet of aluminum foil across the top of the pan to prevent further browning.

6. Remove the cheesecake from the large outer pan and place on a wire rack. Remove the foil wrappings from the springform pan as soon as the pan can be touched and run a thin-bladed knife between the cheesecake and the edge of the pan to loosen it. When the cheesecake has cooled to lukewarm, place in the fridge for at least 6 hours or for up to 1 day if you like.

7. To serve, cover a large flat plate with plastic wrap. Unfasten the clasp of the springform pan. Place the plastic-covered plate on top of the pan. Put your hand on the plate and invert the pan so that the cheesecake is lying upside down on the plastic wrap. Remove the metal base of the pan and the baking parchment if you used it. Now take your serving plate and place it on top of the crumb crust base of the cheesecake. Put your hand on the serving plate and invert again. Remove the plastic wrap. (This sounds strenuous and alarming, but it works.)

8. To make the frosting, preheat the oven to 300º F. Place the almonds in a shallow metal pan and toast in the oven, stirring frequently, for 5–6 minutes only, or until they are just tinged with color. Melt the Toblerone or chocolate over hot but not boiling water in a saucepan. Stir in the liqueur. Drizzle the mixture over the cheesecake. Press the toasted almonds around the edges. Serves 8–10.

CHAPTER 4

BESIDE THE SEA

Clambakes take time. Traditionally, participants began by digging their own clams. But even when you buy clams, you have to prepare a rock-lined pit, light a fire in it, wait until the rocks get hot, sweep out the embers, put in wet seaweed, pile in the clams and some corn, put more seaweed on top, cover the whole thing up, and wait again until the seaweed has cooked the corn and opened the clams. You take the clams from the shell and dunk them in butter and broth. You can eat a lot of them because each is so small. All this shelling and dunking takes time. But that's the point of a clambake — being out of doors, sharing the work, chatting while you wait, finally eating the briny, buttery darlings. It's a seaside feast, a celebration of summer on the New England coast.

It's the same with lobsters. You tackle them with nutcrackers, slipping rose-speckled meat from the claws, sucking on the skinny legs, being assiduous about getting the last little bits. You know that you are meant to work at it when you see Maine and Massachusetts' menus listing prepared lobster dishes as "Lazy Lobster."

In 1602, Bartholomew Gosnold, the first Englishman to explore the Massachusetts coast, marveled at the ease of catching fish. Compared to Newfoundland, already well known for its vast offshore shoals, he noted that off Cape Cod, fish could be caught in seven fathoms of water and within less than one league of the shore. A year later, his compatriot George Waymouth reported five-foot cod on the coast of Maine, and in 1614, John Smith, already familiar with Virginia, charted the coast of Maine south to Cape Cod, while his men hauled in fish to sell in Europe. Such tales lured the Puritans. Asked how they hoped to survive if granted land in Massachusetts, they declared that they would fish — though they had no idea how to do it.

They came to the right place. The Georges Bank, long the world's richest fishing ground, lies off the Massachusetts' coast, outstripping the state in size and providing such an abundance of fish that in 1629, Francis Higgenson of Salem called it "almost beyond believing." Eventually, the colonists became rich by fishing and especially by supplying salt cod to

Europe and the Caribbean islands. New Englanders also ate a lot of salt cod, even though their shores abounded in fresh fish. Usually they boiled it with vegetables or mixed it with potatoes to make codfish cakes and hashes. Today, salt cod is rarer, though many New Englanders, especially from Italian and Portuguese communities, still appreciate its special flavor. It remains traditional fare for the Lenten months of winter.

New Englanders still love their chowders, too. Known since at least the eighteenth century, chowder varies from region to region, but typically, contains clams or fish, salt pork, potatoes, and onions in a milky broth. There are also chowders made with scallops, lobster, and mussels, plus corn and other vegetable chowders, entirely lacking in fish. The core feature is the layering of the ingredients in the pot and the use of milk or cream, though earlier versions often called for wine, usually red.

But while many older fish dishes retain their popularity, there are also new ones. One source is immigrants, who have introduced their recipes and festivals. For example, at the end of June, the Italians of Gloucester, Massachusetts, celebrate St. Peter, patron saint of fishermen, with a ten-day *fèsta*. On the last day, the statue of the saint, followed by worshippers, is carried from church to church and to the Italian club. A cardinal or bishop comes to bless the boats and the men who venture forth to catch the fish. Crowds come to watch the display, perhaps to try their luck walking along a greasy pole and certainly to eat the hot dogs, clam rolls, and cotton candy from vendors' stalls. Meanwhile, at home, Italian families prepare feasts featuring seafood stews, breaded shrimp, stuffed calamari, and pasta with clam sauce. With a culinary heritage rich in such ocean dishes, it is no surprise that Italians run many coastal restaurants, nor that New England's tra-

ditional stock of fish dishes has been amplified by recipes from the Mediterranean.

Ironically, the decline of cod fishing has been another source of new recipes. Overfishing on the fabled Georges Bank prompted regulations forbidding cod fishing, so instead, fishing boats are bringing in previously neglected species. Monkfish, skate, and ocean catfish are delicious examples, and with their arrival on fish counters, come new recipes for using these new choices. Seafood presents a similar case. At one time, cookbooks had more recipes for oysters than any other shellfish because they were the most popular seafood in nineteenth-century New England. But by the beginning of the twentieth century, stocks were already in decline. Now they are less common than scallops and mussels, and rather than give recipes for cooking oysters, most food writers advise simply swallowing them raw.

Fortunately, aquaculture is returning oysters to tables, and regulations limiting catches off New England's marine banks are restoring fish stocks. So, although the extraordinary abundance that amazed early explorers has gone for good, summer beside the sea in New England remains idyllic; its fish and seafood, as ever, are among the best in the world.

Lobster Bisque

On the New England coast, most restaurants have lobster bisque on their menu because they have a ready supply of its main ingredient — lobster shells. Typically, the shells account for about one-fourth to one-third of the weight of the lobster, so they are as costly as the meat. It's sensible to use them for stock, especially since the stock is lovely not only for lobster bisque, but also for other lobster dishes, such as Lobster & Cucumber Risotto (see recipe on page 54) and stews, such as North Atlantic Stew (see recipe on page 57).

LOBSTER STOCK

1 tablespoon vegetable oil
1 medium onion, sliced
2 carrots, cut into large pieces
3 stalks celery, cut into large pieces
Shells from three to four 1 1/2-pound lobsters
1 bay leaf
4 cups chicken stock or water

BISQUE

1 tablespoon vegetable oil
3 ripe tomatoes, peeled, seeded, and
  chopped
1 clove garlic, chopped
1 tablespoon tomato paste
5 cups prepared lobster stock
2 sprigs fresh parsley
1/2 cup light cream
Salt and white pepper to taste
1 cooked lobster tail, sliced, or other
  lobster meat, if available

1. To make the stock, heat the oil in a large saucepan. Stir in the onion, carrots, and celery and cook for 3–4 minutes until softened. With a hammer, break the claw and any other large pieces of shell. Put all of the shells into the pan, tuck in the bay leaf, and pour in the stock. Add enough water so that it comes up to the level of the shells in the pan. Bring to a simmer, cover, and cook for 1–2 hours. (If the shells are soft, you need to cook them for only 1 hour; for the extra-hard shells of big lobsters, cook 2 hours or more.)

2. Strain the stock through a colander into another saucepan. Set aside to use in the bisque. Discard the shells.

3. To make the bisque, heat the oil in a large saucepan. Stir in the tomatoes and garlic, cover, and simmer gently in their own juices for 4–5 minutes. Stir in the tomato paste, then add the stock and parsley sprigs. Cover and bring to a boil. Let it bubble briskly for 7–8 minutes. Either cool and process in a blender or food processor or strain through a sieve into another saucepan, pressing the sieve as you go to push through the tomato.

4. Return the bisque to low heat and stir in the cream. Taste and season with the salt, if necessary, and white pepper. If you have any cooked lobster meat, put pieces into the serving bowls and pour the bisque on top. Serve hot with oyster or common crackers.

Why are some lobsters hard and some soft? *As lobsters grow, their shells become too small, so they shed them. The new shell is soft, and it will bend when you press it. Inside it will not be full of meat because the lobster has just expended its power in producing a new shell and is planning to grow into it. Some people prefer soft-shell lobster because it has more tender, sweeter meat. Hard-shell lobsters have tough shells. You will need nutcrackers and hammers to break inside and get the meat, which will be firm, chewy, and plentiful — qualities that make it the choice of many.*

What happens if you buy a lobster and it dies on the way home? *According to Harbor Fish Market of Portland, Maine, a lobster is safe to cook for 10 hours after it has died. It should be cooked separately from live lobsters, and you should check for any ammonia odor before you eat it. An ammonia smell indicates spoilage, and you should discard the lobster.*

Do you plan to carry or mail lobsters from the shore to your distant home or to friends? *If so, choose hard-shell lobsters. They survive for 24–36 hours out of water, while soft-shells live only 3–10 hours.*

HOW TO BOIL LOBSTERS

Lobsters look rather alarming. Fortunately, lobstermen fasten their claws with elastic bands as soon as they take them from their traps, so if you are boiling one for the first time, take heart. You need a large pot, and if possible, an armful of seaweed. Put the seaweed into the pot, cover with about 3 inches of water. The counsel of perfection suggests seawater, but lacking this, add 3 tablespoons of salt. Bring to the boil. Grasping the lobster in the middle of the body and ignoring the resultant display of wriggling, plunge it head first into the water. In a large pot, such as a 10-gallon canning bath or a big pasta pot, you can cook four lobsters at a time. As soon as you have them in the pot, cover and boil until they have changed from dark olive to bright red. Cooking time for 1 1/4-pound soft-shell lobsters is about 12–15 minutes; a hard-shell lobster of this size takes about 18–20 minutes. The time for 1 1/2–2-pound lobsters is 18–20 minutes for soft-shell and 22–25 minutes for hard-shell.

JANE MCWHORTER

Lobster & Cucumber Risotto

Two lobsters can serve four people when they are cooked in a dish such as this risotto, rather than being served on their own.

One English cucumber, peeled and cut into ³/₄-inch slices
4 tablespoons butter or light vegetable oil
Salt
5 cups hot lobster stock, fish stock, or lightly flavored chicken stock (see Lobster Stock on
    page 52)
1 teaspoon saffron threads
Meat from two 1 ¹/₂-pound lobsters
Lobster coral, if any, from the lobsters
¹/₂ cup chopped shallot
1 ¹/₂ cups uncooked arborio rice
³/₄ cup white wine
3 tablespoons chopped fresh parsley

1. Cut the cucumber slices into fourths, so you have wedge-shaped pieces. Heat 1 tablespoon of the butter in a small saucepan. Toss the cucumber pieces in the butter, season lightly with the salt, then cover and let sweat gently for 5 minutes over low heat, stirring once or twice. Set aside.

2. Put the stock into a large saucepan over low heat and add the saffron. Bring to a simmer, then reduce the heat. Check for seasonings and add more salt to taste. Keep the saucepan on the heat so the stock stays hot.

3. Cut the lobster meat into neat pieces. Cut any other meat from the lobsters into small bits. If you find any coral, set it aside.

4. Melt the remaining butter in a large sauté pan or skillet. Stir in the shallot and cook over moderate heat for 4 – 5 minutes or until softened. Rain in the rice and stir until all of the grains are lightly coated in butter.

5. Add the wine, then stir in ¹/₂ cup of the hot stock. When the rice has absorbed the stock, stir in another ¹/₂ cup of the hot stock. Repeat until the rice has absorbed 4 cups of the stock and is tender on the outside but still firm inside, about 20–22 minutes.

6. With a slotted spoon, scoop out the reserved cucumbers and let the butter drain from them. Fold the cucumbers into the rice along with the lobster pieces and 1 tablespoon of the parsley. Continue cooking the rice, adding more stock to keep the mixture moist. Cook until the lobster is reheated and the rice is tender but not mushy, about 6 minutes.

7. Transfer to a warm serving dish. Make sure there are some attractive bits of tail or claw showing on the surface. Scatter the remaining parsley and any lobster coral on top. Serve immediately.

Clam Chowder

New England is home to several types of clams. Quahogs have hard shells and come in three sizes: littlenecks, cherrystones, and the largest, called simply quahogs. There are also soft-shell clams, called steamers or sometimes long necks because even though they are smaller than the hard-shell clams, they have longer siphons or "necks." You can make chowder with any clams, including the large surf clams, which are often cut up and canned for making chowder or fried clams, and mahogany clams, an increasingly popular farmed clam; these are particularly easy to use because they have little or no sand inside the shell.

5 pounds quahogs, or 3 pounds mahogany or soft-shell steamer clams
2 cups water
$^1/_4$ pound salt pork
1 large white onion, chopped
4 medium potatoes, peeled and diced
1 bay leaf
$^1/_4$ teaspoon dried thyme
1 tablespoon chopped fresh parsley
4 cups milk
Salt and white pepper to taste
6 common crackers, or 1 cup oyster crackers

1. Wash the clams and put them into a large pot. Add the water and cook for 4 minutes, or until the clams have opened. Cool until they can be touched and open over the pot so you catch any juice inside the shells. Discard the shells and set aside the clams. Strain the liquid through a sieve lined with a coffee filter to remove any sand or shell bits. Set aside the liquid.

2. Cut the salt pork into $^1/_4$-inch pieces and put them into a large saucepan over moderate heat. Cover and cook until the fat is running from the pork, then uncover and continue cooking over higher heat until the pork pieces are golden. Discard all but 1 tablespoon of the melted fat. Stir in the onion, reduce the heat, and cook gently for 4–5 minutes, or until the onion has softened. Add the potatoes, bay leaf, thyme, and parsley and pour on the reserved clam liquid. If this does not cover the potatoes, add enough water to do the job. Cover and cook for 20 minutes.

3. When the potatoes are soft, add the reserved clams and the milk and season with the salt and white pepper. Bring to a simmer over medium heat, then stir in the crackers, breaking them if they are the large common crackers. Cook gently for 5 minutes. Serve hot, offering more crackers at the table.

CHOWDER TRADITIONS

Debates about the correct way to make a traditional New England chowder can get quite fierce. But ways to make it abound, and like all much-loved and long-established dishes, its ingredients have changed over time. According to Richard Hooker's The Book of Chowder, *chowders were known in both seventeenth-century England and France. They were fish stews made in a cauldron called a* chaudière, *which was anglicized into chowder. In 1751, the* Boston Evening Post *published a rhyming recipe for chowder calling for salt pork, onions, fish, and several herbs – but no potatoes or milk, and no tomatoes. These ingredients didn't appear until the early nineteenth century. By this time, New England was already famous for its chowders, and recipes began to spread westward, often losing the fish, clams, oysters, and other seafood that seem so essential to chowder and replacing them with corn and other vegetables. Even in New England, there are variants: Hooker cites a parsnip chowder from Worcester, Massachusetts, and Nantucket has some old recipes calling for chicken or veal. For an 1830 shipboard chowder, here is a recipe handed down from Captain Peleg Winslow Gifford, a captain of whaling vessels and a forebear of Professor Michael Coe of Yale University, who published it in* Petits Propos Culinaires (50) *in 1995. The pilot biscuits called for were hard ships' biscuits – a standard ingredient in old chowders; they made it into a thick stew rather than the soup we now know.*

Quarter Deck Fish Chowder

2 small Haddock or Cod, cut in chunks
1 gill stock, made from Heads, Tailes, and Bones of Fish
1 pint Port Wine
1 Pint thin Cream or Milk
³/₄ pound salt pork, diced
2 large onions, sliced
1 Tablespoon Parsley, chopped fine
4 Tablespoons Cracker Crumbs
2 Cloves
10 Pepper Corns
¹/₄ Teaspoon Salt
¹/₄ Teaspoon Paprika

Clean and bone Haddock, put Heads, Tailes, Fins, Bones, and Skin in a pot with 1 Pt. of Water; reduce by ¹/₂ and strain the Stock. Put Salt Pork in bottom of pot and try out until partly browned; then add the Onions and brown well but do not burn; add the Stock and Seasoning. Mix Port and Cream and when stew boils, add them with pieces of Haddock. Clap on the lid and cook 15 minutes. Add the Cracker Crumbs, Parsley and cook slowly for another 10 minutes. Put in Pilot biscuits, stir around the Pot and cook another 5 minutes.

North Atlantic Stew

Like all good stews, this mixture of North Atlantic fish and seafood has a long list of ingredients, but they can be varied according to what is available, and precise amounts are less important than having a flavorsome variety that includes firm fish, such as salmon or swordfish, flaky fish, such as haddock or cod, and some shellfish, such as clams, mussels, or lobster.

BROTH
2 leeks, or 1 medium onion
1 tablespoon vegetable oil or butter
1–2 cloves garlic, finely chopped
1 carrot, thinly sliced
1 large potato, peeled and diced
1/2 cup chopped fresh parsley
One 8-ounce bottle clam juice
1 cup white wine
3 cups fish, lobster, shrimp, or light chicken
  stock
1 bay leaf
1 large tomato, peeled, seeded, and coarsely
  chopped
Large pinch saffron (optional)

FISH & SEAFOOD
1 pound fresh haddock or cod
1/2 pound fresh salmon
1/2 pound fresh swordfish, or 1 cooked
  lobster tail
Salt and white pepper to taste
1 dozen fresh steamer clams, mussels, or
  some of each, cleaned

1. To make the broth, cut off the coarse tops and outer layers of the leeks. Slit them lengthwise and rinse out any soil. Cut into 1/4-inch slices. If you are using onion, simply coarsely chop.

2. Heat the oil in a large pot. Toss in the leeks or onion and stir in the garlic, carrot, potato, and 1/4 cup of the parsley. Pour in the clam juice, wine, and stock and add the bay leaf and tomato. If you are using a lobster tail, add the shell. Cover and simmer for 15 minutes. While the vegetables are cooking, soak the saffron in 1/2 cup warm water if you plan to use it.

3. To make the fish and seafood, cut the haddock, salmon, and swordfish into large bite-sized pieces. If you are using the lobster tail, cut into sections.

4. When the vegetables are tender, remove the lobster shell if you are using it. Stir in the saffron mixture. Add the salmon and swordfish and simmer for 3 minutes. Now add the haddock and lobster sections if using, stirring gently to distribute the pieces. Taste the liquid, then season with the salt and white pepper.

5. Place the clams or mussels on top. Cover and cook for 3–4 minutes more, or until the shells have opened.

6. Remove the clams and ladle the stew into a tureen or a large serving bowl. Sprinkle with the remaining parsley. Place the clams around the edge. Serve hot with garlic bread or Sesame-Herb Toasts (see recipe on page 89). Serves 8.

Baked Crackery Cod

The cracker crust on the cod keeps it moist and flavorful. Add a tomato sauce if you like or serve on a bed of ratatouille or other tender vegetables.

4 ounces Breton, Ritz, or similar crackers
1 teaspoon chili powder
2 teaspoons Worcestershire sauce
³/₄ cup mayonnaise
Four 5–6-ounce fresh cod fillets
Salt and white pepper

1. Put the crackers into a plastic bag and crush with a rolling pin or whiz in a food processor until you have fine crumbs. Put the crumbs on a plate.

2. Mix together the chili powder, Worcestershire sauce, and mayonnaise in a large shallow bowl. Stir until everything is blended.

3. Lightly grease a shallow baking dish. Season the cod with the salt and white pepper, dip each piece into the mayonnaise mixture, then place it on the crumbs. Without moving the mayonnaise-covered fish, sprinkle the crumbs plentifully over the fish until it is covered. Lift the fillets with a spatula and place in the prepared dish. Let stand for 20 minutes, while you preheat the oven to 375º F.

4. Bake the fish for 15 minutes. Serve immediately with some vegetables.

JANE MCWHORTER

Steamed Mussels

Though common on rocky shorelines, mussels were rarely eaten in New England until the early 1980s. Now raised on seafood farms, they are increasingly popular. Most mussel recipes come from Europe, where they have long been summer favorites. All recipes begin with steamed mussels, and indeed, should energy fail, you need go no further, as steamed mussels taste deliciously of the sea.

3 pounds fresh mussels
$^1/_3$ bottle white wine, or 1 cup water
4 sprigs fresh parsley
2 bay leaves

1. Wash the mussels well in cold water. Yank off any stringy bits hanging from the shells and throw out any mussels with cracked shells. Mussels gape open naturally, but they should close when you tap them on a counter edge. If they don't, they may be dead, so discard them, too.

2. Put the wine, parsley, bay leaves, and mussels into a large saucepan. Cover and cook over moderate heat for 3–4 minutes. Peek inside. If the mussels are opened, they are ready. If not, cook 1–2 minutes more. If one or two mussels fail to open, discard them.

3. To enjoy steamed mussels, scoop the mussels into a large bowl or individual bowls. Strain the broth over the mussels through a sieve lined with a coffee filter. The easiest way to eat them is to choose a mussel whose shell has an effective hinge, eat it, and use the shell as nippers with which to pluck the remaining mussels from their shells. This quantity of mussels served with bread is enough for 2–3 people.

Mussels Stuffed with Tomatoes & Olives

Stuffed mussels are popular all around the Mediterranean, often appearing as appetizers. This recipe is good to make when local tomatoes are at their best.

2 ¹/₂ dozen large mussels, steamed
Juice of 1 lemon
Salt and white pepper
2 large tomatoes, peeled, seeded, and coarsely chopped
1 large clove garlic, finely chopped
8 black olives, pitted and coarsely chopped
1 tablespoon chopped fresh parsley
1 teaspoon dried thyme
2 cups fresh bread crumbs (made from day-old bread)
¹/₂ cup grated Parmesan cheese

1. Preheat the oven to 350° F. Grease a baking pan.

2. Discard one shell from each of the mussels. Pick out 6 smaller mussels and chop them. Set aside.

3. To make the mussels easier to eat, detach the remaining mussels from their shells but sit them back in place. Place them open-side up in the prepared pan. Squeeze the lemon juice over them and season with the salt and white pepper. (It helps at serving time to put mussels from small shells into the leftover big shells.)

4. Mix together the tomatoes, garlic, olives, parsley, thyme, and the reserved chopped mussels in a large bowl. Spoon portions of the mixture over the mussels on the shells. (Don't worry if this mixture doesn't entirely cover them.) Mix together the bread crumbs and Parmesan. Scatter the mixture all over the mussels and bake for 8–10 minutes, or until the top is golden brown. They are best served hot with a pilaf or a vegetable dish. But you can also serve them at room temperature as an hors d'oeuvre. Serves 8–10 as an hors d'oeuvre and 4 as a main dish.

Seared Scallops on Leek & Carrot Stir-Fry

Surprisingly, New Englanders rarely ate scallops in the nineteenth-century. Maria Parloa, the most authoritative New England teacher and writer on cookery until Fannie Farmer got into the business, described scallops as having a "peculiarly sweet flavor." Other commentators also found the taste odd. No doubt their standard of comparison was oysters, the seafood of choice to earlier generations. No two seafoods could be more different. Oysters look and taste like congealed seawater, and they slip down the throat in an energizing instant. Scallops are white and shapely; you have to chew and savor them. Two types can be found in local waters: the large sea scallops and the smaller bay scallops, at their best when gathered in Nantucket and Cape Cod in late fall. This recipe is for chunky sea scallops. Searing them in a greased pan brings out their sweetness so they emerge golden and caramelized.

3 teaspoons butter
3 carrots, cut into 2-inch matchsticks
Salt and white pepper
$^1/_3$ cup vermouth or white wine
4 medium leeks, white and tender green parts cleaned and cut into 2-inch matchsticks
1 $^1/_4$ pounds large fresh sea scallops
2 tablespoons chopped fresh parsley
Lemon wedges

1. Grease a large nonstick skillet with 1 teaspoon of the butter.
2. Melt the remaining butter in a large saucepan over low heat. Add the carrots and season lightly with the salt and white pepper. Cover and cook for 2–3 minutes. Shake the pan once or twice to prevent sticking. When the carrots have slightly softened, pour in the vermouth, increase the heat, and let it bubble until about half of the liquid has evaporated. At this point, stir in the leeks and cover. Reduce the heat to low and cook for 4–5 minutes, or until the carrots and leeks are both tender.
3. As soon as you add the leeks to the carrots, place the prepared skillet over high heat. Pat the scallops dry with paper towels. When the skillet is hot, add the scallops, a few at a time, so you don't reduce the temperature too much. Put the biggest ones in first, as they will take a little longer to cook. Cook for 2–3 minutes per side, or until each side is a rich golden color.
4. Stir 1 tablespoon of the parsley into the carrot mixture. Cook briskly for 1 minute more, then transfer to a serving dish or divide among 4 plates. Position the scallops on top and scatter on the remaining parsley. Serve with the lemon wedges.

Monkfish in Red Peppers with Pernod Mayonnaise

In this dazzling dish, monkfish is studded with garlic slivers and baked inside whole red peppers from a jar. Buy two tall 13-ounce jars of Greek or Spanish whole peppers to be sure that you have enough peppers of suitable dimensions, then look for slim pieces of monkfish tail to fit the peppers. If your monkfish is wider than your peppers, simply trim to size. Hake or haddock can substitute for monkfish. Once when I was planning to make this dish, I picked up a jar of cut peppers by mistake, so I put the prepared fish in a baking dish and simply placed the pepper pieces on top. It was easier and still good, though not as exciting. As for Pernod, a French aperitif with an anise flavor, you could substitute gin, which tastes quite different but is nonetheless interesting.

Vegetable oil
8 large whole roasted red peppers from a jar
Eight 2–3-ounce pieces fresh monkfish
2 cloves garlic, cut into slivers
Salt and white pepper
³/₄ teaspoon dried thyme, or 2 teaspoons
   fresh dill

6 sprigs fresh parsley
2 bay leaves
¹/₃ cup white wine
³/₄ cup mayonnaise
1 teaspoon Pernod liqueur or to taste
Few drops Worcestershire sauce

1. Preheat the oven to 400° F. Lightly grease a shallow baking dish with the oil.

2. Remove the peppers from the jar and choose those that best fit the pieces of monkfish. Cut the monkfish to fit the peppers.

3. Make some cuts in the monkfish and slide the garlic slivers into them. Season the monkfish with the salt and white pepper and a tiny sprinkle of the thyme. Carefully place the monkfish into the peppers. If the peppers should tear a little, piece them together and place seam-side down when you put them into the dish.

4. Tear the parsley sprigs into 2–3 pieces and scatter evenly over the prepared dish. Break the bay leaves into 2–3 pieces and add to the dish. Place the prepared peppers so each pepper is sitting on the herbs. Pour the wine over the peppers and bake for 15 minutes. Remove the peppers to a serving dish or individual plates and keep warm in the turned-off oven.

5. While the fish is baking, mix together the mayonnaise and liqueur. Stir in the Worcestershire sauce. One tablespoon at a time, add 4–6 tablespoons of the liquid from the baking dish to the mayonnaise mixture, stirring in each spoonful before adding the next and tasting until you have the flavor that you like.

6. Spoon some of the Pernod mayonnaise around the fish. Serve with the remaining mayonnaise at the table. Plain, boiled Yukon Gold potatoes go well with both the fish-filled peppers and the mayonnaise. Also try the mayonnaise with tuna and other fish dishes.

Peppered Tuna with Sweet Potato Puree

Tuna is the meatiest of fish and works well in recipes originally designed for meat. This recipe is a tuna version of steak au poivre. It is excellent when cooked medium or medium rare, rather than well done, which dries out the tuna. The soft sweet potato puree contrasts nicely.

SWEET POTATO PUREE
1 large sweet potato (about ³/₄ pound)
Salt to taste
¹/₄ teaspoon dried thyme
¹/₃ cup sherry
¹/₄–¹/₂ cup milk
Few drops fresh lemon juice

PEPPERED TUNA
3 teaspoons black peppercorns
1 teaspoon dried green peppercorns
¹/₂ teaspoon allspice berries, or ¹/₄ teaspoon ground allspice
Four 6-ounce pieces fresh tuna (each 1 inch thick)
Salt
Vegetable oil
Lemon wedges and sprigs fresh thyme for garnish

1. To make the puree, peel the potato and cut into small chunks. Boil in salted water for 20 minutes or until tender. Drain. Return the potato to the pan and mash until smooth. Add the salt. Mash in the thyme and stir in the sherry. Add ¹/₄ cup of the milk and form into a thick puree. Set aside.

2. To make the tuna, put all of the peppercorns and the allspice berries into a mortar or spice mill and grind or whiz them to a very coarse powder, then pour onto a plate.

3. Season the tuna pieces lightly with the salt and brush with the oil. Press one side firmly on the plate of ground pepper. (You may find that the first couple of pieces take up more than their share of the pepper. In this case, press the remaining pieces on top of them to take off the excess.)

4. Pour a film of oil into a skillet and heat until just beginning to tremble. Place the tuna pieces, peppered-side down into the skillet and cook for 2 minutes. Turn over and cook for 4–6 minutes more, depending on the thickness of the tuna and how well done you like it. (Tuna should remain deep pink inside; if it changes to pale beige, it will be too dry.)

5. While the tuna is cooking, reheat the reserved potato puree, adding more milk if necessary. It should have a consistency halfway between a thick sauce and mashed potato. At the last moment, add the drops of lemon juice.

6. Pour a portion of the puree on each of 4 plates. Position 1 piece of tuna on each plate and garnish with the lemon wedges and thyme sprigs.

Baked Bluefish with Sautéed Confetti Tomatoes

This recipe tastes of summer in New England. Tomatoes are a favorite crop for amateur and commercial growers alike, while bluefish is a summer visitor to the coast and is unobtainable the rest of the year. It is a flavorful, oily fish at its best when set off by contrasting flavors and textures. Here the oats add crispness, the three types of tomatoes add a sweet-sour touch, and the basil and oregano bring depth of flavor. If you or your friends don't have green tomatoes in your gardens, substitute tomatillos, a distant Mexican relative of the tomato. A tomatillo looks like a shiny green ball in a papery sheath and can often be found among the tropical vegetables in the produce departments of larger supermarkets.

BLUEFISH
Four 6–8-ounce bluefish pieces, or one
*   *1 ¹/₂–2-pound bluefish fillet*
Salt and black pepper
2 tablespoons Dijon mustard
¹/₂ cup rolled oats

CONFETTI TOMATOES
2 large firm red tomatoes
1 large green tomato, or 3 tomatillos
15 orange cherry tomatoes
1 tablespoon olive oil
¹/₄ cup chopped shallot or onion
1 clove garlic, chopped
Salt and black pepper
3 fresh basil leaves, torn
³/₄ teaspoon dried oregano
Sprigs fresh basil for garnish

1. Preheat the oven to 375° F. Grease a shallow baking dish.

2. To make the bluefish, season the fish pieces with the salt and black pepper and brush the mustard on the flesh side. Sprinkle the flesh side thoroughly with the oats and press in the oats with your hands. Place the pieces in the prepared dish and bake for 10–12 minutes.

3. To make the tomatoes, cut the red and green tomatoes into 8 thick slices, then cut across three times so you have wedge-shaped pieces. Halve the cherry tomatoes.

4. Heat the oil in a shallow saucepan. Add the shallot and garlic and soften for 3–4 minutes. Add the green tomatoes and cook for 3 minutes over moderately high heat, turning occasionally. Add the red and orange tomatoes, season with the salt and black pepper, and stir in the basil. Cook briskly for 2–3 minutes more, or until the tomatoes are heated through. (Do not let the tomatoes get soft — the pieces should remain chunky and separate.)

5. During the last minute of cooking, stir in the oregano. If you are using fish pieces, serve on heated plates, add a spoonful of tomatoes on each serving, and garnish with the basil sprigs. If you are using one fillet, transfer the fish to a serving platter, surround with the tomatoes, and garnish with the basil sprigs.

CHAPTER 5

BERRY SEASON

You have to stoop to pick strawberries, and you generally get mud on your shoes or even between your toes if you are wearing sandals. But discomfort is a small price to pay for the pleasure of peeping under the trefoiled leaves, reaching for the fattest berries, lured on by the idea of getting just a few more. For sure, no strawberry ever tastes better than the one you've just picked, rubbed clean, and popped, all juicy, right into your mouth. It makes picking strawberries one of the big thrills of June in New England.

Raspberries come soon after, and then there are blueberries. You must cradle raspberries gently into your basket, but you can rain blueberries into a bucket slung round your shoulders — a most satisfying sound. Fruit from the wild is even more thrilling. Spying a gang of shining blackberries hiding beneath a parasol of leaves is a pure joy if you have the hunter-gatherer instinct. Scratches scored by brambly branches are honorable wounds in the battle for this hoard. What if cultivated blackberries are bigger? Those you discover yourself are more lovable.

All these berries grow in both Europe and America, and people have always valued them. Native Americans dried blueberries (cranberries, too) and used them in their preserved meat, pemmican. They also picked gooseberries, shadberries, dewberries, wild currants, and wild grapes — fruits that still grow by the roadside or in the woods, but are now rarely gathered except by foragers.

As the first fruit of the year, strawberries were a special favorite with Native Americans, and some nations celebrated their arrival with a festival giving thanks for the strawberry harvest and praying for the success of crops still to come. In Europe, too, the strawberry used to have religious significance. It has blooms and berries at the same time, so it symbolizes the Virgin who gave birth, while its three-in-one leaf represents the Trinity. The sheer beauty of the plant — heart-shaped berries coexisting with tiny wild rose flowers, all framed by elegant sawtoothed leaves — has made it a favorite motif in carvings and embroidery, and especially on china.

When English settlers sailed up New

Hampshire's Piscataqua River in 1630, they were so thrilled to see its banks covered in wild strawberries that they named their settlement Strawberry Banke. (Today, it's called Portsmouth.) Back in Europe, gardeners had been bringing the tiny strawberries in from the wild since the Middle Ages to secure a private supply. They also hoped to develop bigger berries, but it took several centuries and the strawberries of two continents to reach this goal. The first step came when seventeenth-century botanists took scarlet berries from the east coast of North America to England and France. They could not be crossed with European berries, but they were cultivated alongside them. The big breakthrough was achieved when an eighteenth-century French naval officer took a yellow, pineapple-flavored, Chilean strawberry back to France. The French botanist Dechesne crossed it with berries from North America and produced berries with the larger size and flavor of the Chilean berry and the bright color of the northern strawberries.

By the early nineteenth century, growers in France and England had produced many named varieties of the new strawberries, of which Keens' Seedling became the most popular. In 1829, horticulturalist Charles Mason Hovey of Boston procured some of these, but they failed to thrive in New England's tough winters and torrid summers. Hovey decided that he would have to produce a big, bright strawberry of his own. Starting with seeds from his imported plants, he created Hovey's Seedling and exhibited it at the Massachusetts Horticultural Society in 1838. Such was its success that in the 1840s both plants and berries sold for double the price of other strawberries.

Today, growers in California and Florida develop larger berries with tough skins and firm flesh so they can weather the journey to supermarkets all over the country. Virtually all of them lack the fragrance and flavor of smaller wild varieties; often they appear simply as a garnish — a testament to their looks rather than to their taste. However, their bigness and firmness make them adaptable to new uses. You can slice them in salads, dip them in chocolate, or even stuff them.

Raspberries and blackberries belong to the same genus as strawberries, and they also hybridize, often managing very nicely without human help — hence their rainbow colors: shades of pink and red, as well as yellow, orange, purple, and black. They can also range in size from the large, cultivated loganberries and boysenberries to the small, ground-clinging dewberries. There are black raspberries and red underripe blackberries that look so similar, it's hard to tell them apart. The difference is that raspberries come away from their central core so they are hollow, while blackberries and their kin cling to their centers.

The blueberry family also has relatives growing on both sides of the Atlantic. Wild blueberries carpet many coastal and northern areas of Maine and New Hampshire. Tiny — no bigger than a bird's eye — they are more flavorful than cultivated berries, good even when canned. Hybrids of these wild berries have been commercially raised only since the early twentieth century. These plump, bloomy berries, growing on high bushes from whence they are easily picked, are less flavorful than their wild relatives, but obligingly collapse into lovely, juicy sploshes in muffins and pancakes. The wild low-bush blueberries make perfect pies and jam.

New England's berry harvests chase each other through the summer with July's raspberries and blueberries coming close on June's strawberries, and blackberries flourishing through August until mid-September. Each harvest prompts festive meals. Strawberry teas and suppers have been popular church money-raisers since the nineteenth century. A family trip to a pick-your-own farm prompts strawberry shortcake for dessert, blueberry muffins for breakfast, or — simply deliciously — bowls of berries with ice cream.

A hoard of berries also leads to the pleasure of preserving. Few kitchen tasks satisfy more deeply than stashing bags of berries in the freezer and squirreling away the jars of jam in a closet. This pleasure can be rationalized as putting by foods when they are cheap or getting a head start on holiday gifts. But it is surely more atavistic, rooted in the most ancient and serious satisfaction of Having Provided.

A. BLAKE GARDNER

Strawberry Shortcake

Picking fruit at pick-your-own farms is such a luxury. You reap where you have not sown — not necessarily a bad thing according to the Biblical parable of the talents. Gardeners would disagree. Theirs is the joy of planting and cultivating and watching the baby things peek through, develop and bear fruit. Theirs is the work of all this, too. U-pickers can just sally forth, cash in hand, and with a minimal effort, go merrily home with the harvest stashed in the back of the car. A strawberry shortcake is the thing to make with just-picked local strawberries. This version has raisins in it. They are not traditional, but I like them because they add moments of chewiness. Omit them if you prefer.

SHORTCAKE
2 cups all-purpose flour
1 tablespoon baking powder
6 tablespoons cold butter
$^1/_2$ cup granulated sugar
$^3/_4$ cup golden or dark raisins
1 egg
$^1/_2$–1 cup milk

FILLING
1 quart fresh strawberries, washed,
  hulled, and sliced
$^1/_2$ cup granulated sugar
1 cup heavy cream
2 tablespoons confectioners' sugar

1. Preheat the oven to 425° F. Grease a small baking sheet or a pie pan.
2. To make the shortcake, mix together the flour and baking powder in a large bowl. Cut the butter into several bits and rub them into the flour mixture until it looks like coarse crumbs. Stir in the sugar and raisins. Make a well in the center of the mixture. In a small bowl, beat together the egg and $^1/_2$ cup of the milk, then pour the mixture into the well. Working quickly, stir to form a soft but not sloppy dough. Add the remaining milk, a little at a time, until you have achieved this soft dough.

3. Form the dough into a 1-inch-thick disk. Place on the prepared baking sheet and bake for 20 minutes, or until a toothpick inserted in the center comes out clean. (Alternately, you can form the dough into 8 individual shortcakes, each 2 $^1/_2$ inches across. These take only 15 minutes to bake.) Cool on a wire rack.

4. To make the filling, toss the sliced strawberries and sugar in a bowl and let stand at room temperature for 1 hour, or until they soften and juice appears.

To make Blueberry Shortcake: *Follow the shortcake directions above. For the filling, toss together 1 pint blueberries and 2 tablespoons honey in a large saucepan. Cook over gentle heat until juicy. To thicken the mixture, make a thin paste with 1 tablespoon cornstarch and 1 tablespoon water. Stir some of the blueberry juice into the cornstarch mixture, then pour the mixture into the saucepan of berries and stir over moderate heat until the mixture looks glossy and thick. Cool to room temperature and stir in $^1/_2$ pint fresh blueberries. Have another $^1/_2$ pint blueberries on hand as a final garnish.*

5. Whip the cream into soft clouds. Sift in 1 tablespoon of the confectioners' sugar and whip again.

6. Halve the shortcake horizontally and carefully lay the top piece on one side. Put the bottom piece on the serving dish and strain the juice from the berries onto it, reddening all the surface. Spread about half of the sliced berries over the top, then spread on the whipped cream. Lightly replace the top and sift the remaining confectioners' sugar over it.

7. Slice the shortcake and add extra sliced berries to each serving. (If using individual shortcakes, simply slice, spoon on berries and juice, then some whipped cream and replace the top. Add more whipped cream or confectioners' sugar, plus a berry slice or two on the top.) Serve.

Stuffed Strawberries

The ultimate in red desserts, stuffed strawberries are easy, elegant, and dramatic. If you have a big black plate, use it to serve the berries, not crowded together but each berry sitting in splendid isolation.

12–15 large well-shaped fresh strawberries
$^1/_4$ cup mascarpone or cream cheese at room temperature
3–4 teaspoons confectioners' sugar
Grated zest of half a lemon
2–3 drops Boyajan lemon oil or grated zest of half a lemon and lemon juice to taste

1. Choose the biggest, reddest, and most handsome strawberries you can find. Hull the strawberries by cutting off the leaf tuft and hollowing the berries with the point of a knife. Sit the berries open-side down. If they wobble, trim the base to make them stable.

2. Mix together the mascarpone, 2 teaspoons of the confectioners' sugar, the lemon zest, and lemon oil or juice to taste. Using a small spoon, such as a coffee spoon or a $^1/_4$-teaspoon measuring spoon, fill the hollowed berries with this mixture. Stand them open-side down on either a large serving plate or individual serving plates. They look best when you set them far apart.

3. Sift a light snow of the remaining confectioners' sugar on top. You can make the strawberries up to 4 hours ahead of serving time, but don't sift on the sugar until just before serving.

To make Chocolate-Stuffed Strawberries: *If you like chocolate-dipped strawberries, you'll probably like strawberries with a chocolate stuffing. For 12–15 large berries, you will need 1 tablespoon mascarpone or cream cheese and 2 tablespoons chocolate chips or grated bittersweet chocolate. Melt the chocolate chips or grated chocolate in a small bowl over hot water or in a cup in a microwave. Stir in the mascarpone. Hull and hollow the berries and fill with the chocolate mixture while it is still runny. Place the stuffed berries open-side up, propping them up with a wad of aluminum foil or sitting them in eggcups until the filling has set. Then carefully place the berries open-side down on the serving plate. If you don't plan to serve them immediately, put them in the fridge and lightly cover with plastic wrap. They'll be safe for at least 4 hours. Dust with $^1/_2$ tablespoon confectioners' sugar mixed with $^1/_2$ tablespoon cocoa powder just before serving.*

Fresh Berry Jelly

Making jellies took time and trouble in the nineteenth century. The gelling agent had to be prepared, either from the bones of calf's feet or from isinglass made from the swim bladders of cod, hake, or other fish. Juice also had to be squeezed by hand. Not surprisingly, cooks only ventured on this task for special occasions. Life became dramatically easier in the 1890s when Charles B. Knox created unflavored powdered gelatin, and Pearl Bixby Wait invented a flavored gelatin called Jell-O. This is now such a popular substitute for fresh fruit gelatins that few people now make them from scratch. But armed with a package of unflavored gelatin and berry juice, you can make a shimmery summer dessert without the chemicals contained in commercial products.

2 quarts fresh strawberries, washed, hulled, and sliced, or 1 $^1/_2$ quarts fresh raspberries, washed
2 tablespoons granulated sugar
$^1/_2$ cup water
1 package unflavored gelatin
$^1/_2$ cup light corn syrup
$^1/_4$ teaspoon rosewater or pure vanilla extract (optional)

1. Set aside 1 cup of the smallest and most nicely shaped berries for serving with the jelly.

2. If using strawberries, put them into a large saucepan and add the sugar and $^1/_4$ cup of the water. Set the pan over very low heat and cook for 30 minutes, stirring occasionally, and never letting the berries do more than just simmer. If using raspberries, simply put them into a large saucepan and proceed as for strawberries.

3. Place a sieve over a deep bowl and drain the berries. Let stand in the colander for at least 15 minutes so the juice drips through, but don't press them because the juice will become cloudy.

4. While the berries are draining, mix together the gelatin and the remaining water in either a very small saucepan or a small jug sitting inside a pan of hot water. Let stand for a few minutes, then heat it over low heat, stirring until the gelatin loses its granular look.

5. Measure 1 $^1/_2$ cups of the strained strawberry juice into a bowl and stir in the gelatin mixture, corn syrup, and rosewater or vanilla extract if you are using it. If you don't have enough juice, add water to make up the amount, but if you have more, set aside for using with another recipe. Don't add it to the gelatin, or you will have too much liquid to set.

6. Rinse either a fancy mold with cold water or choose a nonstick cake or pie pan. Pour the mixture into the container and place in the fridge until set, about 4 hours, though you can leave it longer if you like. (Rinsing a mold makes it easier to get the jelly out at serving time, but easiest of all is using a nonstick pan.)

7. Fill the sink with hot water and immerse the bottom of the mold in the water for 5 seconds only, taking care that no water sloshes onto the jelly. Place the serving dish on top of the mold, then with one hand under the mold and one hand on top of the serving dish, invert the mold with a sharp shaking movement. Place the serving dish on a level surface and remove the mold. Scatter the reserved berries around the jelly and serve.

Trifle with Jelley & Flowers

A trifle sounds like it should be a tiny morsel, just right for people watching their weight. Far from it. Trifles are big, and their layers of cream, custard, and cake will not help anyone get any slimmer. Still, people always love a trifle. Make it as a special treat for Father's Day or when you have guests. Don't let the lengthy instructions fool you into thinking that a trifle is troublesome. Each layer is simple, and all can be made ahead of time. This recipe is inspired by the recipe that Amelia Simmons gave in *American Cookery*, published in 1796 and the first cookbook written specifically for Americans. "Garnish with jelley and flowers," is her final instruction. A hundred years later, the Deerfield, Massachusetts, parishioners who gathered recipes for *The Pocumtuc Housewife* repeated her recipe with the same garnishing advice.

CAKE & JELLY LAYERS
3 cups crumbled pound cake or plain sponge cake
½ cup sherry or white wine
1 pint fresh strawberries, washed and hulled, or raspberries, washed
1 recipe strawberry or raspberry jelly (see recipe on page 71)

CUSTARD
5 eggs, separated
3 tablespoons cornstarch
3 ¼ cups milk
½ cup granulated sugar
1 teaspoon pure vanilla extract

TOPPING
½ pint heavy cream
¼ teaspoon freshly grated nutmeg or
*   rosewater*
Edible flowers: pansies, rose petals, violets,
*   or nasturtiums, rinsed*

1. To make the layers, take a large attractive glass or ceramic bowl and crumble the cake into the bowl. Pour on the sherry and stir to make sure all the cake is moistened. Slice the strawberries. (If you are using raspberries, you can leave them whole.) If your trifle dish is glass, set some of the berries near the edge where they will be visible. Set aside.

2. Prepare the jelly following the recipe on page 71. While the jelly is still liquid, pour half of it over the berries and cake. Pour the remaining jelly in a shallow dish. Put both the jelly and the trifle into the fridge for 4 hours or until set.

3. Make the custard while the jelly is setting. Beat together all of the egg yolks and 2 of the egg whites in a large bowl until light and foamy. Discard or save the remaining egg whites for use in other dishes. Mix together the cornstarch, ½ cup of the milk, the sugar, and vanilla into a smooth paste, then whisk the cornstarch mixture into the eggs. Heat the remaining milk until it is hot but not boiling.

4. Pour the hot milk into the egg mixture, stir well, then transfer it to the top of a double boiler or to a saucepan set inside a larger pan of simmering water. Stir over moderate heat until the

custard thickens. Cool, then pour the custard onto the trifle and return the trifle to the fridge for 1 hour or longer if more convenient.

5. To make the topping, cut the remaining set jelly into little squares or random shapes and set aside. Whip together the cream and nutmeg and spread or pipe on top of the trifle. Decorate with the reserved jelly squares and the flowers. (Do not use any flowers except those you know are edible and have been grown without the use of pesticides and other chemicals.) Serves 8–10.

TRIFLES, FOOLS & SYLLABUBS

Trifles and syllabubs became popular in late sixteenth-century England, a time when the spiced and elaborate foods of the Middle Ages were giving way to simpler dishes. Trifles and fools were made of thickened and flavored cream, while syllabubs were wine or cider mixed with creamy milk to give a frothy head. By the eighteenth century, fools were a simple mixture of cream or custard with fruit. Gradually trifles became more complex. They included almond-flavored ratafia biscuits or ladyfingers, fruit jelly or jam, custard topped with a foamy syllabub, and decorations of comfits or crystallized fruits. They have never lost their popularity in England, and they were favorite party dishes in eighteenth- and nineteenth-century New England. Amelia Simmons's recipe is typical: "Fill a dish with biscuit finely broken, rusk and spiced cake, wet with wine, then pour a good boil'd custard (not too thick) over the rusk, and put a syllabub over that; garnish with jelley and flowers." As for the syllabub, one of her two recipes tells the cook to "Sweeten a quart of cyder with double refined sugar, grate nutmeg into it, then milk your cow into your liquor, when you have thus added what quantity of milk you think proper, pour half a pint or more, in proportion to the quantity of syllabub you make, of the sweetest cream you can get all over it." Simmons based this syllabub on Hannah Glasse's recipe in The Art of Cookery *(1747). She omits, however, Glasse's tip for those who don't happen to have a cow on hand. "You may make this Syllabub at Home, only if you have new Milk: make it as hot as Milk from the Cow, and out of a Tea Pot or any such Thing, pour it in, holding your Hand very high." Whether you use a cow or a teapot, the technique was to pour a thin stream of warm milk into the cider in order to develop a creamy head.*

Raspberry Meringue Pie

The pink meringue topping makes this one of the prettiest meringue pies. It is also very easy. Pasteurized egg whites are a convenient product to use in recipes calling for egg whites but not yolks. They are also good for dishes cooked at temperatures too low to kill the dangerous organisms that occasionally occur in fresh eggs.

PASTRY

1 1/4 cups cake flour
Pinch salt
2 teaspoons granulated sugar
6 tablespoons cold butter
2 tablespoons ice-cold water

FILLING

3 cups fresh raspberries, washed
3/4 cup plus 1 tablespoon superfine or
  granulated sugar, divided
2 tablespoons pasteurized dried egg white
  (Just Whites), or 2 fresh egg whites
6 tablespoons warm water
1 drop red food coloring (optional)

1. Preheat the oven to 400° F. Grease a 7- or 8-inch pie pan with sloping sides.

2. To make the pastry, mix together the flour, salt, and sugar in a bowl. Cut the butter into several bits and rub them into the flour mixture until it looks like coarse crumbs. Make a well in the center of the mixture. Pour in the ice-cold water and mix until the pastry coheres. If it is too dry, add more water. You may need up to 4 tablespoons in all.

3. Form the pastry into a ball and place it in the center of the prepared pie pan. With your knuckles, push it outwards to cover the base and sides of the pan. Make sure it is as even as you can make it. Prick the bottom several times with a fork. Place a sheet of aluminum foil on the bottom and fill with dried beans or rice. Bake for 18 minutes or until pale gold. Discard the foil and beans. Place the baked pie shell in the oven and let the surface dry for 1–2 minutes. Remove from the oven and reduce the temperature to 300°.

4. To make the filling, place the berries in the pie shell and sprinkle with 6 tablespoons of the sugar.

5. Put the dried egg whites into a large bowl. Add the warm water and let stand for 2–3 minutes. Stir for 1–2 minutes until the whites have dissolved. With a whisk or an electric mixer, whisk the whites until they are bulky and foamy and the whisk leaves deep trails in them as it moves. Add 2 tablespoons of the sugar and whisk until the mixture looks glossy. Whisk in 2 more tablespoons of the sugar. Finally, add 2 more tablespoons of the sugar and whisk until the whites look like ruffled satin. Stir in the food coloring if you are using it and whisk until the mixture is pale pink.

6. Pile the egg mixture on top of the raspberries in the pie shell, taking care that no raspberries peek through and that there are no gaps between the shell and the meringue. Sprinkle with the remaining sugar and bake in the bottom third of the oven for 20 minutes, or until the top is a swirly pink and gold and slightly crisp. Let stand for 20 minutes or longer before serving.

Fudge Brownie Tart with Raspberries

This tart looks elegant and dramatic, but it is easy to make — a good choice for a large party. The recipe comes from Kristine Elison of Portabella Catering of Amherst, Massachusetts.

One 12-ounce bag semisweet chocolate chips
1 teaspoon pure vanilla extract
³/₄ cup sifted all-purpose flour
¹/₄ teaspoon baking soda
¹/₄ teaspoon salt
6 tablespoons unsalted butter
²/₃ cup granulated sugar
2 tablespoons water
2 eggs, beaten
¹/₂ cup seedless raspberry preserves
16 large perfect raspberries, washed
16 fresh mint leaves, rinsed and dried

1. Preheat the oven to 350º. Grease an 11- or 12-inch tart or springform pan. It also helps to line the base with baking parchment.

2. Mix together the chocolate chips and vanilla in a large bowl. In another bowl, mix together the flour, baking soda, and salt.

3. Heat the butter, sugar, and water in a small saucepan, stirring occasionally to dissolve the sugar. When the mixture boils, pour it over the chocolate mixture. Add the eggs and mix well, then thoroughly blend in the flour mixture. Spread into the prepared pan and bake for 25 minutes, or until the center is set. Cool completely.

4. Warm the raspberry preserves over low heat in a small saucepan. Pour over the cooled tart and smooth. Let stand. Cut into 16 wedges with a serrated knife and garnish each wedge with a fresh berry and a mint leaf. Serves 16.

To make a Fudge Brownie Tart with Cherries: *Unlike just-picked raspberries, jars of maraschino cherries are available year-round. For a fall and winter variation of this dish, replace the raspberries with 16 maraschino cherries with stems. Replace the ¹/₂ cup of raspberry preserves with ¹/₃ cup of red currant or apple jelly thinned with 1–2 tablespoons of the juice from the jar of cherries.*

Gooseberry Cream

Gooseberries used to be so common in New England that an islet in Maine's Casco Bay is called Gooseberry Island, and every nineteenth-century cookbook had recipes for gooseberry pies, puddings, and preserves. In the twentieth century, gooseberries more or less disappeared when planting was discouraged because gooseberry plants harbor a pest that does them no harm but injures white pines. Today, gooseberries are reappearing as farmers plant crops to appeal to innovative cooks, and supermarkets import berries and other fruits grown in the Pacific Northwest. Most gooseberries have the tints and translucency of jade, but some may be pink or deep purple. They may be as small as a cranberry or as big as a large grape. Typically, they are tart (hence their use in France in sauces for mackerel and other oily fish), but a few varieties are sweet; they can replace more common fruits in cobblers, crisps, and other baked goods. In England, this recipe, adapted from *The Cook's Own Book,* an anonymous dictionary of recipes published in Boston in 1832, would be called gooseberry fool, and it is one of the easiest and best-loved of summer desserts.

2 cups washed fresh gooseberries
$^1/_2$ cup granulated sugar
1 tablespoon water
1 egg yolk
$^1/_2$ teaspoon pure vanilla extract
1 cup heavy cream

1. Put the gooseberries, sugar, and water into a large saucepan. Cover and cook over low heat, stirring occasionally, until the gooseberries are tender and juicy, about 20 minutes.

2. Mix together the egg yolk and vanilla in a small bowl. Pour in $^1/_3$ cup of the very hot berry juice and quickly whisk to blend. Return the mixture to the pan and cook over moderate heat, stirring constantly, until the mixture has thickened. Pour the mixture into a bowl and chill it in the coldest part of the fridge until it is very cold and thick. (To speed things, you can put it in the freezer and chill until it is just above the freezing point.)

3. Whip the cream. Fold in the chilled gooseberry mixture. Pour into small bowls or sherbet cups and serve immediately accompanied by crisp cookies. (Cookies with a dark chocolate filling or frosting are especially good.)

Cobbler Quartet

Cobbler topping is less fuss to make than pie pastry. Here are four variations on the cobbler theme using summer berries. Dictionaries are unclear about why biscuit-topped dishes are called cobblers. Maybe it is because they are so forgiving that they can be just cobbled together with fresh fruit and kitchen staples.

Blackberry-Apple Cobbler

COBBLER FILLING
2 large apples, peeled
1 quart fresh blackberries, washed
¹/₂ cup granulated sugar
1 tablepoon water
1 tablespoon cornstarch
2 tablespoons cold water

COBBLER TOPPING
1 ¹/₂ cups all-purpose flour
¹/₄ teaspoon freshly grated nutmeg
1 tablespoon baking powder
1 stick (4 ounces) butter
¹/₂ cup plus 1 tablespoon granulated sugar
1 egg
³/₄ cup buttermilk, or ³/₄ cup milk with
    1 teaspoon fresh lemon juice
1 teaspoon pure vanilla extract

1. Preheat the oven to 400° F. Grease a 9-inch square ovenproof baking dish or any shallow 2-quart baking dish.

2. To make the filling, core and quarter the apples, then cut across each quarter to make small slices. Put the sliced apples, blackberries, sugar, and the 1 tablespoon water into a large saucepan. Cover and cook over low heat for 15 minutes, or until the berries are juicy and the apple slices are tender. Mix together the cornstarch and the 2 tablespoons cold water in a small bowl. Stir in ¹/₄ cup of the juice from the pan, then return the mixture to the pan. Stir until thickened, then pour into the prepared dish.

3. To make the topping, mix together the flour, nutmeg, and baking powder in a large bowl. Cut the butter into several bits and rub them into the flour mixture until it looks like fine crumbs. Stir in ¹/₂ cup of the sugar. In a separate bowl, beat together the egg, buttermilk, and vanilla. Pour the egg mixture into the flour mixture and stir to form a soft dough of dropping consistency.

4. Using a tablespoon, drop the dough in dollops more or less evenly over the filling. Spread lightly to make the dollops join up, but don't worry if some of the fruit remains uncovered. Sprinkle the surface with the remaining 1 tablespoon of sugar. Place in the center of the oven and bake for 20–30 minutes, or until a toothpick inserted in the center comes out clean. Serve warm. Serves 6.

Strawberry-Rhubarb Cobbler

6 long stalks fresh rhubarb
³/₄ cup granulated sugar
1 tablespoon butter
1 tablespoon cold water
1 quart fresh strawberries, washed and hulled
One recipe Cobbler Topping (see recipe on page 77)

1. Preheat the oven to 400° F. Grease a 9-inch square ovenproof baking dish or any shallow 2-quart baking dish.

2. For the filling, wash the rhubarb, cut off both ends of each stalk, and strip off any stringy skin. Cut the rhubarb on the diagonal into 1-inch pieces. Put the pieces into a large saucepan and add the sugar. Toss the rhubarb pieces in the sugar, then add the butter and cold water. Cover and gently cook over very low heat letting the rhubarb soften, without stirring, until tender.

3. Slice the large berries in half but keep the smaller ones whole. When the rhubarb is tender, add the berries and cook for 1 minute more, then pour the mixture into the prepared dish.

4. Make the topping as directed in the recipe and dollop on top of the fruit. It probably won't quite cover the fruit, and some juice may seep up, but that's fine. Sprinkle on the remaining 1 tablespoon sugar and bake for 20–30 minutes, or until the top is golden and a toothpick inserted in the center comes out clean. Serve warm.

Blueberry-Maple Cobbler

1 quart fresh blueberries
¹/₂ cup Grade B or other dark maple syrup
¹/₂ cup plus 1 tablespoon maple sugar or firmly packed light brown sugar
One recipe Cobbler Topping (see recipe on page 77)

1. Preheat the oven to 400° F. Put the blueberries into a 9-inch deep-dish pie plate and pour the maple syrup over the berries.

2. Make the topping as directed in the recipe, but substitute ¹/₂ cup maple sugar or light brown sugar for the ¹/₂ cup granulated sugar. Dollop the topping onto the berries. The topping may not cover the fruit, and some juice may seep up, but that's fine. Sprinkle on the remaining 1 tablespoon maple sugar and bake for 20–25 minutes, or until the top is golden and a toothpick inserted in the center comes out clean. Serve warm with cream or ice cream.

Raspberry-Peach Cobbler

3 large ripe peaches
Boiling water
²/₃ cup granulated sugar
1 pint fresh raspberries, washed
One recipe Cobbler Topping (see recipe on page 77)

1. Preheat the oven to 400° F. Grease a 9-inch square ovenproof baking dish or any shallow 2-quart baking dish.

2. Score the skin of the peaches crisscross across the stem end. Put the peaches into a large bowl and pour the boiling water over them. Let stand for 1–2 minutes, then remove them from the water. Starting with your crisscross scores, peel them as you would peel a tomato.

3. Slice the peaches and put them into a medium saucepan. Stir in the sugar. Cover and cook gently for 15 minutes, or until the peaches have released their juice.

4. Put the peach slices and 1 cup of the juice into the prepared dish. Set aside any remaining juice for serving with the cobbler. Scatter on the raspberries.

5. Make the topping as directed in the recipe and dollop the topping onto the fruit. The topping may not cover all the fruit, and some juice may seep up, but that's fine. Sprinkle on the remaining 1 tablespoon sugar and bake for 20–25 minutes, or until the top is golden and a toothpick inserted in the center comes out clean. Serve warm, with the reserved juice if you have any.

Blackberry Jelly

Most jelly recipes are daunting because they assume that you are using masses of fruit and that you have a candy thermometer to test it, a jelly bag to strain it, and a boiling water bath to can it. Neither the vast amount of berries nor the special equipment is necessary. Working with smaller quantities is easier, and the results are better. Any strainer lined with a coffee filter works as well as a jelly bag. There are lots of ways to test for a set without a thermometer. And canning homemade jelly (or jam) in a boiling water bath ruins its color and mars its flavor. Canning also wastes time and energy when you are making just a few jars that will be eaten within a few weeks.

2 quarts fresh blackberries, washed
1 tablespoon water
Granulated sugar
Juice of 1 large lemon

1. Put the blackberries into a large saucepan and add the water. Cover and cook over low heat for 1 hour, or until you have a lot of juice and the berries are pale and very soft. Stir once or twice in the first 15 minutes of cooking time to move the berries from the top of the pan to the bottom, but don't stir repeatedly because this will mush up the berries, which may later cloud the jelly.

2. Line a steamer basket, a large sieve, or a colander with a large, round coffee filter. Two or three coffee filters may be necessary to make sure that all of the apertures are covered. Balance your steamer basket over a pan or bowl on which it sits steadily. Pour in the berries and all of their liquid. Cover lightly with a lid or cloth and let stand overnight so that the juice can drip through into the pan below. Do not press the berries in order to extract more juice as it may cloud the jelly.

3. Put a couple of small plates in the freezer. Wash some small lidded jars for the jelly, then fill the jars with boiling water and let stand.

4. Choose a large pan, preferably shallow. It should hold about five times more liquid than you actually have, so when the jelly bubbles up, it won't spill. Measure the juice. Measure an equal amount of sugar: 1 cup of sugar for 1 cup of juice. Bring to a boil and boil rapidly, stirring frequently with a long-handled wooden spoon or a long plastic-handled metal spoon so you don't burn your hand.

5. At first, the bubbles will be tiny. Gradually they will get larger as the jelly gets hotter and its consistency changes. You can tell that it is getting thicker when it runs from the spoon in drops rather than a stream. Watch for these stages. They will occur in 3–6 minutes depending on how rapidly the liquid in the mixture is evaporating. As soon as you think that the jelly is thickening, even slightly, pour a little onto one of the small, chilled plates; the cold plate will cool it quickly. If the surface of the cooled jelly wrinkles when you tip the plate, the jelly is set. Keep testing every 30 seconds until the surface wrinkles.

6. During the final minutes of cooking, empty the water from the jars and dry them with paper towels. As soon as the jelly sets, pour it into the jars. Place a paper towel over the top to absorb the steam and to protect the jelly as it cools, then cover with screw tops. Keep unopened jars in the

fridge. As for opened jars, they are better kept in a closet; jelly (or jam) tastes much better at room temperature. The yield varies depending on the juiciness of the berries, but you should get 2–3 half-pint jars. Use within 6 weeks.

JELLY: WHAT'S IN A NAME?

If it's fruity, in a jar, and you spread it on toast, it's most often called jelly — but some people call it jam or preserves. Technically, there is a difference. According to the U.S. Food and Drug Administration, jelly is the overall term for any food set by gelatin or pectin, a natural setting agent found in many fruits. More specifically, jellies are made from fruit juices or other liquids, such as stock or wine; jam is made from whole fruit and is therefore thicker, while preserves have chunks of fruit embedded in them. To add to the complexity, if you see a nineteenth-century recipe for a jelly, it may well be for the sort of dessert that we now call a gelatin — Fresh Berry Jelly on page 71, for example.

Sugar-Top Blueberry Muffins

Blueberry muffins set the standard that all other muffins must meet. This version has a sweet and crunchy top.

15 sugar cubes
2 eggs
$^2/_3$ cup milk
1 teaspoon pure vanilla extract
$^1/_4$ teaspoon ground nutmeg or mace
Pinch salt
6 tablespoons butter, melted but not hot
2 cups all-purpose flour
1 tablespoon baking powder
$^1/_3$ cup granulated sugar
1 $^1/_2$ cups washed fresh blueberries

1. Preheat the oven to 400° F. Prepare a 12-cup muffin pan either by fitting muffin papers in the cups or by greasing the cups. Crush the sugar cubes by putting them in a bag and bashing them into little chunks with a rolling pin. Set aside the crushed sugar.

2. Whisk together the eggs, milk, vanilla, nutmeg, and salt in a large bowl. Stir in the melted butter.

3. Mix together the flour, baking powder, and sugar in a bowl. Put the flour mixture on top of the egg mixture and stir it in, working quickly. As soon as the dry ingredients are moistened, fold in the berries. The batter will be lumpy. Nevertheless, spoon it into the prepared muffin pan, filling the cups about $^3/_4$ full.

4. Scatter the reserved crushed sugar on top and bake in the top third of the oven for 20 minutes, or until a toothpick inserted in the center comes out clean. (The toothpick may show blueberry juice, but as long as it shows no moist batter, the muffins are ready.) Cool on a wire rack and serve warm. Makes 12 muffins.

> **For Apple-Crunch Muffins:** *Add $^1/_2$ teaspoon of cinnamon; substitute 2 medium apples, peeled, cored, and diced, for the blueberries.*

Blueberry-Almond Tart

The almond top makes this more flavorful than the usual double-crust blueberry pie, and since the blueberries are not cooked before they go in the shell, they stay whole and fresh tasting.

SHELL
1 ¹/₂ cups cake flour
1 tablespoon cornstarch
2 teaspoons granulated sugar
1 stick (4 ounces) cold butter
1 egg yolk
2 tablespoons cold water

FILLING
3 cups fresh blueberries, washed
1 ¹/₂ cups confectioners' sugar
1 cup ground almonds
2 eggs
¹/₄–¹/₂ teaspoon pure almond extract to taste
1 tablespoon water
¹/₃ cup sliced almonds (optional)

1. Preheat the oven to 400° F. Grease an 8-inch pie pan with sloping sides.

2. To make the shell, mix together the flour, cornstarch, and sugar in a large bowl. Cut the butter into several bits and rub them into the flour mixture until it looks like coarse crumbs. Mix together the egg yolk and cold water and pour it into the flour mixture. With your hands, pull it together to form a pastry ball. If it is too dry, add more water, 1 teaspoon at a time, until the pastry coheres.

3. Roll out the pastry on a floured surface, then line the pie pan with the pastry. Cover with aluminum foil and ¹/₂ cup dried beans or rice and bake 18–20 minutes. Remove from the oven and discard the foil and beans. Reduce the temperature to 325°.

4. To make the filling, put the berries into the baked tart shell. Mix together the confectioners' sugar and ground almonds in a bowl. Lightly beat together the eggs, almond extract, and water in another bowl. Stir the sugar mixture into the egg mixture and pour the mixture over the berries. If you are using the sliced almonds, sprinkle them on top. Bake for 35–40 minutes, or until the top is golden with perhaps a few juicy blueberries peeking through. Serve warm.

Duck Breasts with Blueberry-Lavender Sauce

This is the type of recipe that sounds complicated, but in fact it is straightforward and quite quick to make as both the blueberry-lavender sauce and the duck breasts cook rapidly. Traditionally, New Englanders have always used lavender for perfumes or medications rather than as a flavoring. But lavender works well in creamy desserts and in sauces for rich meats and poultry. In this recipe, the flavor stays in the background but adds a haunting note to the sauce. If you enjoy it, try adding a little more the second time you make the dish.

SAUCE

1/3 cup duck or chicken stock or water
1 cup washed fresh blueberries
1/4 teaspoon dried lavender
Pinch salt or to taste
1/4 cup port or other full-flavored red wine

DUCK BREASTS

4 large boneless duck breasts
Salt and black pepper
3 tablespoons olive oil
2 tablespoons fresh blueberries (optional)
Fresh sprigs lavender (optional)

1. To make the sauce, put the stock and blueberries into a small shallow saucepan and simmer until the berries soften. Sprinkle on the lavender and salt, then increase the heat and boil until about half of the liquid has evaporated. Set aside.

2. To make the duck, season the meat side of the breasts with the salt and black pepper. Turn over and stab the skin side several times with the tip of a sharp knife. This will let the fat run out during cooking thus crisping the skin. Sprinkle with more salt and rub it into the skin.

3. About 15 minutes before serving time, heat the oil in a skillet. When it is slightly shivery, put the breasts skin-side down into the skillet and cook over high heat for 7–8 minutes, or until they are a rich appetizing brown. Turn them over and cook for 4–6 minutes more, depending on the size of the breasts and whether you want the interior pink or well done.

4. As the breasts are getting close to ready, return the reserved blueberry sauce to the heat, bring to a boil, then stir in the port. Let it bubble for 1 minute. Taste for seasonings and add more salt if necessary.

5. Spoon some of the sauce on each of 4 plates and settle a duck breast on the sauce. Garnish with the blueberries and lavender sprigs if you have them. If you like, slice each breast into several thin slices and fan these on the pool of sauce. Serve extra sauce at the table.

Turkey & Zucchini Salad with Raspberry Vinaigrette

Raspberry vinegar used to be made with lots of sugar to make a sweet-sour base for drinks. Today, it is generally made by packing raspberries in a jar, filling the jar with vinegar, and leaving the jar in the sun for 3–4 weeks. When it is strained, the vinegar is a pink and flavorful condiment. If you don't have a bottle of raspberry vinegar, and you want a little for a recipe, you can pour 3 tablespoons vinegar over $^1/_4$ cup ripe raspberries, mash them, let stand for a few minutes, then strain the liquid through a sieve. It's not the same, but it's better than nothing and works fine in this recipe.

5 medium zucchini
1 teaspoon salt
12 ounces cold roast turkey
$^1/_4$ cup light olive oil
2 tablespoons raspberry vinegar or white wine vinegar
1 teaspoon Dijon mustard
$^1/_2$ teaspoon dried thyme or oregano
Freshly ground black pepper to taste
$^1/_2$ cup fresh raspberries, washed

1. Wash the zucchini and trim off the ends. Slice the zucchini lengthwise into 4–5-inch long pieces. Cut the pieces into strips 2–2 $^1/_2$ inches long by $^1/_4$ inch wide.

2. Bring a large saucepan of water to a boil and add the salt. Have another pan filled with cold water and ice cubes. Drop the zucchini strips into the pan of boiling water. Let cook only until the water returns to a boil, then drain and dump the strips into the pan of water and ice cubes. Swish them gently to cool them off, then drain thoroughly and pat dry with paper towels.

3. Cut the roast turkey into strips about the same size as the zucchini strips. Set aside.

4. Whisk together the oil, vinegar, and mustard in a bowl. Divide into 2 portions and add the thyme to 1 portion only. Pour the thyme portion over the reserved turkey, grind on the black pepper, and toss gently. Let the turkey mixture stand for 20 minutes, or up to 2 hours if you want to prepare ahead of time.

5. Just before serving, toss the zucchini strips in the remaining portion of dressing, then mound the strips in a hill on a serving platter or on individual plates.

6. Fold $^1/_4$ cup of the raspberries into the turkey mixture and gently toss the mixture, then pile it on top of the zucchini. Garnish with the remaining raspberries and serve.

To make a Turkey & Zucchini Salad with Cranberry Vinaigrette: *For a Thanksgiving and winter variation on this dish, use 1 tablespoon of white vinegar and 1 tablespoon of cranberry juice instead of the 2 tablespoons of raspberry vinegar, and substitute $^1/_3$ cup of dried cranberries for the raspberries.*

CHAPTER 6

SHAKERS & GARDENERS

There are summer days when creamy clouds, lofty trees, and flowery gardens give rural New England a Utopian air, and never more so than in the Shaker villages of Hancock, Massachusetts, Canterbury, New Hampshire, and Sabbathday Lake, Maine. And little wonder — the Shakers built these communities so they could pursue earthly perfection.

A small and welcoming Shaker community remains at Sabbathday Lake, still following the principles of Mother Ann Lee, a charismatic religious visionary, who in 1774 led eight disciples from the north of England to America. Traveling through western New York and New England and withstanding some violent attacks, she converted disciples to her vision of a stainless life. They were called Shakers because they quivered and danced in their religious celebrations.

By the mid-nineteenth century, Shakers had built nineteen villages, most of them in New England. They lived communally but in celibacy. Mother Ann's injunction "Put your hearts to God and your hands to Work" served her followers well. They grew vegetables, fruits, and grain, raised sheep, cows, and poultry, and made furniture, baskets, brooms, boxes, cloaks, washing machines, cheeses, preserves, candies, and herbal medicines — all models of their kind. Their villages were immaculate. They had big dwellings, where men lived on one side and women on the other, a meetinghouse, and a school, where the Shakers educated the many orphans who they adopted. Dairies, barns, forges, and workshops surrounded by pastures, orchards, and gardens completed the scene.

With large numbers of people to take care of, including children and the elderly, the Shakers valued laborsaving devices. At Hancock, one of their largest villages and now a museum preserving the Shaker heritage, there is a spectacular, round stone barn with three levels so that the herdsmen could drive cattle in at one level, load hay on another, and remove manure from the third. The brothers at Hancock also built "sliding shelves" — a dumbwaiter to haul food from the kitchen to the dining room. A Shaker sister in Harvard, Massachusetts, is credited with inventing the circular saw. At Canterbury, they devised an oven with revolving shelves that made it easier to check on the hoard of pies baking inside. As early as 1926, the Canterbury sisters were lauding their newly acquired Kitchen Aid mixer in a little poem:

> When we cooks now play the Kitchen Aid
> All the grinders, sieves and fancy beaters
> Have now been relegated to the shelf,
> For we simply touch a little lever,
> And the ice cream makes itself.

Today, at Sabbathday Lake, Sister Frances A. Carr is just as proud of the new dishwasher and microwave as she is of the huge nineteenth-century oven equipped to bake dozens of loaves or pies. "Technology gives one more time to give to God," she notes.

Sister Frances arrived at Sabbathday Lake as a child of ten in the 1930s. Shaker children learned many skills because villagers rotated from one job to another. At Sabbathday Lake, groups of four worked in the kitchen: a head cook and a baker, assisted by a vegetable cook and a sink girl, who did cleanup jobs. Sister Frances enjoyed cooking, so at nineteen, she became a head cook, creating meals for sixty people. She recalls times when the kitchen was filled with steam from the nineteenth-century arch kettle, "It was great for anything needing a lot of water: corn, bundles of asparagus, boiled eggs." The nineteenth-century, wood-fired oven in the bake room is as big as a modern side-by-side refrigerator. Now it stores baking pans, but Sister Frances remembers when pies were baked twelve at a time. She explains, "The brothers would often start work before eating. When they came in, they needed a hearty breakfast, and pie was a traditional part of it."

Since they were well equipped for large-scale cooking, many Shaker villages served meals to the public. A writer for the *Brooklyn Eagle* in 1885 described a lunch that he had eaten at Hancock: "Cold beef, white bread, brown bread, butter, boiled rice, baked beans, potato cake, apple pie, milk, pickles, cream cheese, cottage cheese, blackberry jam, blackberry pie, cake, doughnuts. And the bill was twenty-five cents!" Local people willingly walked a mile from the trolley stop to sample the chicken fricassee made in Hancock. In the 1930s and 1940s, residents of Concord, New Hampshire, bought their weekend baked beans from the Canterbury sisters, who made the beans in the village and drove them down to the city.

Shaker villages were also famous for their herbs. The 1864 *Catalogue of Herbs, Roots, Barks and Powdered Articles, Etc.,* prepared by the Sabbathday Lake Shakers, lists over 150 items, many sold in various forms, with details of the ills that they might relieve. In contrast, the catalogue had only four "sweet herbs" for the kitchen: marjoram, sage, summer savory, and thyme. This narrow range sufficed for mid-nineteenth century cooks, but having so many herbs on hand, the Shakers led the way in introducing herbs to the kitchen. Today, the Sabbathday Lake Shakers still grow and market culinary herbs packed in cans that are as close as possible to the cans of yesteryear.

Similarly, they maintain the tradition of preserving. The catalogue of 1864 offered "Horse Radish in jars, Apple Sauce by the gallon or barrel; Peach Water and Rose Water, by the gallon or bottle." Current favorites in the village are bread-and-butter cucumber pickles, zucchini relish, and a favorite mustard pickle relish, which takes a blue ribbon every year at the Common Ground Fair in Unity, Maine.

This commitment to excellence — not special techniques or recipes — marks all Shaker cooking. As the interpreters who greet visitors in the pleasant kitchen of the large Dwelling House at Hancock Shaker Village point out, Shaker cooking differed little from that of their neighbors because converts simply brought their recipes into their new communal home.

Sister Frances Carr agrees, "Shakers have always cooked simple country food, and always in abundance." Jeffrey Paige, Chef at the Creamery Restaurant in Canterbury, now also a museum village, finds inspiration in the Shakers' philosophy of using what they had at hand: tossing dandelion and beet greens into salads because they abhorred waste, for example, and preferring maple sugar to white sugar and dried blueberries to raisins because they could make them themselves.

Beyond this focus on local ingredients, Sister Frances notes, "If there is one thing that I think we have done differently it is our use of herbs." Her cookbook, *Shaker Your Plate: Of Shaker Cooks and Cooking* (United Society of Shakers: Sabbathday Lake, ME, 1985), has recipes for broccoli topped with rosemary butter and asparagus dressed with a sweet cicely, for example. Among the breads are sesame toasts with basil, rosemary, marjoram, and chives. Rosewater perfumes her Floating Island dessert and tarragon her grilled fish.

This thoughtfulness about flavor celebrates the importance of cooking. Early on, Mother Ann instructed kitchen sisters to produce pleasant meals," so that when the Brethren return from their labors in the fields, they can bless you and eat their food with thankfulness, without murmuring."

Later, Shakers enjoyed food festivities of many kinds. In the 1980s, Eldress Bertha Lindsay of Canterbury recalls her childhood excitement when the sisters made candy and popcorn balls as after-supper treats for the children, and also the fun of catching fish in their Ice Mill Pond and eating it al fresco with biscuits made on an old open-air woodstove. Early twentieth-century photographs of Canterbury show the sisters laughing over giant wedges of watermelon served at a summer picnic. Another photograph shows two brethren preparing a clambake, while a sister in the background seems to look on with anticipation. The brothers had to travel to Rhode Island to buy the fish and seafood, so it was special occasion fare. When they celebrated July 4, 1924, in their Cow Barn, they served clam chowder, vegetable soup, steamed clams, clam cakes, lobsters, quahogs, two kinds of pie, and watermelon.

This festive philosophy of eating — at once joyful and practical — lives on. No sign speaks more directly to the New England soul than the July placard announcing "Native Corn." Homeward-bound commuters screech up to flatbeds of freshly picked ears and to farm stands displaying the latest crops: bushel baskets of summer squash and green beans, trays of shining tomatoes, cucumbers, and bell peppers. The cabbages that you find on these stands are giants — twelve- and fifteen-pounders are common in the Connecticut Valley. The rough-skinned muskmelons are sweet and juicy. Potatoes and carrots may come in fifty-pound bargain sacks from farms that grow acres and acres of them or in quart boxes holding tiny new potatoes or unusual varieties, such as Peruvian blue potatoes or banana-shaped Russian fingerlings. Saturday morning farmers' markets may yield heirloom tomatoes, Asian greens, baskets of berries, or plums fresh from someone's backyard tree.

Each crop in its turn prompts its own celebration. Must buy corn while it is so tender that it scarcely needs to see the pot! Must make fresh pasta sauce while the tomatoes are so juicy! Must tackle the piles of zucchini by making zucchini bread and zucchini pickles! Green and yellow beans go into multibean salads; cabbages become coleslaw; cucumbers and beets fill pickle jars; basil highlights salads or turns into pesto. And on it goes. Summer fleets by in New England; you must enjoy it while you can.

Tomato Soup with Shaker Sesame-Herb Toasts

Few soups taste better than a homemade tomato soup made with height-of-the-summer local tomatoes. One Shaker recipe calls for topping the soup with lightly salted whipped cream — a stroke of culinary genius. To make this topping, simply season 1 cup whipped cream with ¼ teaspoon salt or more to your taste. At Sabbathday Lake, Sister Frances Carr often serves soups with Sesame-Herb Toasts. The following recipe is adapted from her *Shaker Your Plate: Of Shaker Cooks and Cooking.* The crustless triangles in this version look ladylike; for chunkier toasts to go with a stew, use 1-inch thick slices of French bread.

TOMATO SOUP

6 large ripe tomatoes (about 2 ½ pounds)
Boiling water
1 tablespoon vegetable oil
2 stalks celery, chopped
1 medium onion, chopped
2 cloves garlic, minced
4 leaves fresh basil
1 sprig fresh parsley
1 teaspoon salt or to taste
1 teaspoon granulated sugar or to taste
½–1 cup light cream or milk
Fresh basil leaves for garnish

SESAME-HERB TOASTS

½ cup butter at room temperature
1 tablespoon all-purpose flour
1 egg, well beaten
2 tablespoons sesame seeds
¼ teaspoon dried marjoram
¼ teaspoon dried basil
¼ teaspoon dried rosemary
1 tablespoon dried chives, or 2 teaspoons
   chopped fresh chives
12–14 slices toasted bread

1. To make the soup, score the tomatoes, place in a large bowl, and cover with the boiling water. Let stand for 1–2 minutes, then remove them one by one, and peel, starting with the scored spot. Cut out and discard the stalk end and the tough piece of tomato underneath.

2. Cut the tomatoes in half and scoop out the seeds with a teaspoon. Do this over a sieve set on a bowl to catch the juice. Chop the tomatoes and set aside.

3. Heat the oil in a large saucepan. Stir in the celery, onion, and garlic. Reduce the heat to low, cover, and cook for 3–4 minutes to soften. Add the reserved chopped tomatoes, their juice, the basil, and parsley. Season with the salt and sugar. Cover and simmer over low heat for 30 minutes. Extract and discard the basil leaves and parsley and let the soup cool to lukewarm. Then process the soup in a food processor or blender or pass it through a sieve, returning it to a clean saucepan.

4. Just before serving, stir in the cream and taste for seasonings. Add more salt and sugar as you deem fit. Reheat the soup over moderate heat without letting it boil. Pour into soup bowls and garnish with the basil leaves.

5. To make the toasts, preheat the oven to 350° F. Grease a baking sheet.

6. Mix together the butter and flour in a bowl. Stir in the egg, then the sesame seeds, marjoram, basil, rosemary, and chives. Cut off the crusts from the bread and spread the slices with the egg

mixture. Slice diagonally to make triangles. Place them herb-side up on the prepared baking sheet and bake for 12–15 minutes, or until they are lightly browned. Serve warm with the soup.

7. Store leftovers in an airtight container. Rewarm them in a warm oven before serving. If you have leftover sesame-herb mixture, cut the crusts of the bread into cubes, toss them in the mixture, and bake on a nonstick baking sheet for 10 minutes. Use as croutons for soups and salads.

Baked Eggplant, Tomato & Summer Herb Salad

The combination of cooked eggplant, uncooked tomatoes, and fresh herbs makes lots of flavor and texture contrasts in this salad.

VEGETABLES
¼ cup olive oil
One 1 ¼–1 ½-pound eggplant
3 tablespoons salt
3 large ripe tomatoes, halved
12 orange or yellow cherry tomatoes, halved
1 small zucchini or yellow summer squash
8 fresh basil leaves, torn
1 tablespoon fresh summer savory, thyme, marjoram, or a mixture
2 tablespoons chopped tender celery leaves or fresh parsley
Salt and black pepper to taste
1 large sprig fresh basil for garnish

DRESSING
⅓ cup pine nuts
2 tablespoons olive oil
½ teaspoon Dijon mustard
Few drops fresh lemon juice

1. Preheat the oven to 475° F. Grease a large baking tray with some of the oil.

2. To make the vegetables, wash the eggplant, trim off the ends, and cut into slices about ⅓ inch thick. Put the slices into a colander, sprinkling them with the salt as you go. Let stand for 1–2 hours, then rinse off the juice that will have accumulated on the surface and pat dry with paper towels.

3. Arrange the eggplant slices on the prepared tray in a single layer and brush them with the remaining oil. Bake near the top of the oven for 15 minutes, or until the surface is golden and the peel is slightly wrinkled. Loosen the slices from the tray and cut the large rounds into quarters and the small rounds into halves. Place the eggplant pieces in a salad bowl.

4. Position a sieve over a bowl and squeeze each tomato half into it so that the juice runs through and the seeds are left in the sieve. Discard the seeds and set aside the juice for the dressing. Coarsely cut the tomatoes into small pieces and add to the eggplant, then add the cherry tomatoes.

5. Halve the zucchini lengthwise, then slice. Add the zucchini, basil, summer savory, and celery leaves to the eggplant mixture. With your hands, gently mix everything together.

6. To make the dressing, preheat the oven to 325° F. Put the pine nuts into a single layer in a shallow pan and toast in the oven for 5–7 minutes, or until they turn golden brown. (You can also toast them in a microwave oven. They take 1–2 minutes only, but you need to stir them once during the cooking time.)

7. Whisk together 2 tablespoons of the reserved tomato juice, the oil and mustard. Add the drops of lemon juice to sharpen the flavor. At serving time, season the vegetables with the salt and black pepper. Pour on the dressing and toss gently to mix. Garnish with the toasted pine nuts and the basil sprig. Serves 6–8.

Broccoli & Rosemary Quiche

Shakers combined vibrant greens, such as spinach and broccoli, with rosemary — an idea that underpins this recipe. It's excellent for brunch or as a vegetarian main dish.

PASTRY
1 ¹/₂ cups all-purpose flour
Pinch salt
1 teaspoon granulated sugar
1 stick (4 ounces) cold butter
3 tablespoons cold water

FILLING
1 broccoli crown (about 2–3 ounces)
¹/₄ teaspoon dried rosemary
3 – 4 fresh mushrooms, sliced, or 8 strips
   cooked red bell pepper
1 tablespoon vegetable oil
1 ¹/₂ cups grated Vermont Cheddar cheese
Salt and black pepper
4 eggs
1 ³/₄ cups milk

1. Preheat the oven to 400° F. Grease a 9-inch deep-dish pie plate.

2. To make the pastry, mix together the flour, salt, and sugar in a large bowl. Cut the butter into several bits and rub them into the flour mixture until it looks like coarse crumbs. (Alternately, you can make the pastry in a food processor, pulsing until the mixture reaches a crumblike stage. Transfer to a bowl at this point.) Make a well in the center of the mixture. Pour in the cold water and mix together with your hands. Add more cold water, 1 tablespoon at a time, if necessary to make the mixture cohere into pastry.

3. On a floured board, roll out the dough into a large circle and fit it into the prepared pie plate. Cover with aluminum foil, fill with a layer of dried beans or rice, and bake for 20 minutes. Remove the foil and discard the beans or rice (or save for the next time you bake a blind pie shell). If the surface looks moist, return it to the oven for 2 minutes to dry out. This helps keep the crust firm when it is filled.

4. Preheat the oven to 425° F. To make the filling, break the broccoli crown into small florets, trimming the stems of each neatly. Steam the florets for 2–3 minutes or until just lightly cooked but still bright green. Sprinkle on the rosemary and set aside.

5. Meanwhile, toss the mushroom slices with the oil in a small skillet and sauté for 1–2 minutes, or until they are just wilting slightly.

6. Sprinkle the cheese over the prepared pie crust. Arrange the reserved broccoli florets on top. Add the mushroom slices or strips of red pepper and season with the salt and black pepper.

7. Whisk the eggs in a bowl, add the milk, then mix thoroughly. Pour the egg mixture over the vegetables and bake in the center of the oven for 10 minutes. Reduce the temperature to 350° and bake for 15 minutes more, or until a knife inserted in the center comes out clean. Serve hot.

Salad of Baby Beets & Greens

For this salad you need beets that are no bigger than ping-pong balls complete with their stems and red-veined leaves. Don't choose bunches whose leaves look coarse or battered. Whenever you boil beets, always leave a few inches of stem on the root; it lessens the amount of juice that bleeds out.

12 small beets with their leaves
Salt
Boiling water
¹/₂ teaspoon grated lemon zest
2 tablespoons fresh lemon juice
2 tablespoons olive oil
¹/₄ teaspoon ground coriander or allspice
2 teaspoons finely chopped fresh parsley

1. Cut off the beet leaves, leaving 4–5 inches of stem on the beets. Wash the beets and the leaves separately.

2. Put the beets into a large saucepan and cover with cold water. Simmer for 20–25 minutes, or until the beets are tender when pierced with a knife blade. Drain and rinse the beets under cold running water. Peel them by rubbing off the skins with your fingers. Discard the stems or leave them if you prefer.

3. While the beets are cooking, wash the leaves, discarding any battered or coarse-looking leaves or stems. Put the leaves into a saucepan with the salt and pour on just enough of the boiling water to cover them. Cover and simmer until the greens are tender but still green, about 6 minutes. Drain and cool under cold running water.

4. For the dressing, whisk together the lemon zest, lemon juice, oil, and coriander.

5. Season the beets and their leaves lightly with salt. Pour about half of the dressing over the beets and place the beets on one side of a shallow serving dish. Sprinkle them with the parsley. Toss the leaves lightly in the remaining dressing, arrange them on the other side of the plate, and serve.

Sugar Snap Peas & Potatoes

A recipe for Peas and New Potatoes in Cream in *The Best of Shaker Cooking* by Amy Bess Miller and Persis Fuller inspired this dish. Here, lean bacon replaces the salt pork of the original, sugar snap peas replace shelled peas, and the cream and butter of the original disappear altogether. This recipe is excellent with chicken dishes, and you can even turn it into a quick meal for two or three people by cooking extra bacon and maybe some tomatoes to serve as a side dish. For a no-meat version, omit the bacon and cook the peas in 2 tablespoons vegetable oil. If sugar snaps are not available, use shelled peas.

3 pieces Irish or center-cut bacon
15 baby red potatoes (about 1 pound)
Salt to taste

$^1/_2$ pound fresh sugar snap peas
Boiling water
Freshly ground black pepper

1. Broil the bacon until golden brown in a shallow pan. Remove it from the pan and cut into $^1/_2$-inch pieces. Set aside the pieces and bacon fat.

2. Wash the potatoes and remove any damaged parts but do not peel. Cut the potatoes into $^1/_2$-inch slices. Drop the slices in a saucepan of cold water, add the salt, and boil for 12 minutes or until tender.

3. Meanwhile, wash the peas, trim away both tips, and strip any string from the side of the pod.

4. Put 2 tablespoons of the reserved bacon fat into a shallow saucepan over high heat. When it sizzles, add the peas and sauté over high heat, stirring constantly, for 1 minute. Add $^1/_3$ cup of the boiling water and simmer for 3–4 minutes, or until the pea pods are just tender.

5. Drain the potatoes. Add the potatoes and the reserved bacon pieces to the peas and stir over moderate heat. Season with the black pepper. (Salt will probably not be necessary because the bacon is salty). Serve immediately.

Heavenly Squash

This sunny-colored mixture of yellow squash and eggs flavored with herbs and cheese looks like summer in a dish. Serve it for brunch or as a nonmeat entrée. This recipe, originally from Hancock Village, is adapted from *The Best of Shaker Cooking* by Amy Bess Miller and Persis Fuller.

6–8 small yellow summer squash (about 1 $1/2$ pounds)
2 teaspoons salt
2 ears fresh corn, shucked
1 clove garlic, chopped
1 teaspoon dried marjoram, oregano, or thyme
Salt
3 eggs
$3/4$ cup milk
2 cups grated sharp Vermont Cheddar cheese

1. Preheat the oven to 375º F. Grease a 1 $1/2$-quart baking dish.
2. Wash the squash, cut it into quarters lengthwise, then chop into $1/2$-inch pieces. Put it into a colander and sprinkle with the 2 teaspoons salt as you go. Let stand for 45 minutes, then rinse off the liquid that will have accumulated on the surface and pat dry with paper towels.
3. Cut the corn from the cob. Put the squash, corn, garlic, and marjoram into the prepared dish. Season lightly with the salt and toss to combine everything.
4. Whisk together the eggs and milk in a bowl and stir in 1 $1/2$ cups of the cheese. Pour the cheese mixture over the squash mixture and sprinkle the remaining cheese on top.
5. Cover and bake for 40 minutes, or until the squash is fork-tender. Avoid cooking for so long that the squash collapses into a mush. For a browned top, uncover about 5 minutes before you take the dish from the oven. Serves 2–3 as a main dish and 4–6 as a side dish.

Chicken with Corn

Shaker villages had herds of cows so they had plenty of dairy products, both for themselves and for sale. Many of their recipes called for generous amounts of butter, cream, and cheese. In *Shaker Your Plate: Of Shaker Cooks and Cooking,* Sister Frances A. Carr writes, "I often think back to those days, especially when making a recipe that seemed to be especially delicious due to the cream and butter no longer so readily available." Yet she admits that even if the good dairy foods were still to be had, they would now be eaten "with a guilty conscience knowing of the cholesterol involved." This recipe for Chicken with Corn is adapted from a recipe of the Hancock Shakers. The original recipe called for 1 cup sour cream and ¹/₄ cup butter. I find that the cider provides such good flavor that 1–2 tablespoons cream are much nicer than a cupful, and a little oil can replace a lot of butter.

1 tablespoon vegetable oil
One 3-pound frying chicken, cut into 8–10 serving pieces, or 8–10 chicken thighs
2 cups coarsely chopped onion
1 tablespoon all-purpose flour
1 cup cider (preferably hard cider)
2 tablespoons coarsely chopped fresh tarragon
Salt and white pepper
4 ears fresh corn, shucked
3 tablespoons sour cream

1. Preheat the oven to 325° F. Grease a baking dish.

2. Heat the oil in a large skillet over high heat. Place the chicken pieces in the skillet, skin-side down, and cook briskly for 7–8 minutes, or until the chicken is golden brown. Turn over, reduce the heat to medium, and cook for 8 minutes on the other side. Transfer the chicken to the prepared dish and bake for 15 minutes.

3. Discard all but 2 tablespoons of the fat in the skillet. Add the onion and cook over medium heat for 5–6 minutes or until softened. If they turn golden, that's fine, but don't let them get dark brown.

4. Remove the skillet from the heat and stir in the flour. When it is blended, stir in the cider and tarragon and season with the salt and white pepper. Return the skillet to fairly high heat and bring to a boil, stirring constantly until the mixture has thickened. Cook for 2–3 minutes.

5. Cut the corn from the cobs. Add the corn kernels to the mixture in the skillet. Reduce the heat and cook gently for 2 minutes. Remove from the heat and stir in the sour cream. Taste and adjust the seasonings as you see fit. Return the chicken to the skillet and place over the heat. Cook gently, letting it do no more than just simmer, for 5 minutes. Serve with potatoes, rice, or tortellini and summer vegetables.

Multibean Salad

Once you start mixing beans in a salad, it's difficult to know when to stop. Three kinds, one of which should be fresh, seem to be the minimum. Beyond that, the only limit is the number of bean varieties you can find. This recipe makes enough for a large summer gathering.

1 teaspoon ground mustard or ready-made hot mustard
$^1/_3$ cup white vinegar
1 tablespoon granulated sugar
$^1/_3$ cup vegetable oil
1 tablespoon dried oregano
1 teaspoon cumin seeds
1 pound fresh green beans, washed
$^1/_2$ pound fresh wax beans, washed
1 teaspoon salt
Boiling water
One 15-ounce can chickpeas
One 15-ounce can kidney beans
One 15-ounce can black beans
One 15-ounce can navy beans or cannellini beans
$^1/_2$ cup chopped fresh parsley
Salt and black pepper to taste

1. Mix together the mustard and vinegar in a large bowl. Stir in the sugar, then the oil, oregano, and cumin seeds. Set aside.

2. Top and tail the green and wax beans and cut into 1-inch pieces. Put them into a large saucepan with the 1 teaspoon salt and pour boiling water over them to cover. Cook briskly for 3–4 minutes, then drain. Set aside $^1/_2$ cup of the cooking liquid. Tip the warm beans into the reserved dressing and stir them around.

3. Drain and rinse the chickpeas well and set aside. Put the kidney beans, black beans, and navy beans, one can at a time, into a colander or sieve and rinse well under cold running water to remove any thick liquid clinging to them. (The spray attachment is the easiest way to do this.) Add the reserved chickpeas to the rinsed beans.

4. Add about one-third of these canned beans and one-third of the parsley to the beans in the dressing. Season with the salt and black pepper and toss gently to mix. Add another one-third of the beans and parsley and season and toss again. Add the remaining beans and parsley. Taste for seasonings and add more salt and black pepper if you think necessary. Serves 8–12. Leftovers keep well for up to 1 week if stored in a plastic container in the fridge.

Mustard Relish

Visitors to Hancock Shaker Village can see the handsome kitchen devoted exclusively to preserving and the shelves where the sisters kept their good things for the winter. They were not alone in their efforts; all rural households used to make preserves for winter, and many still do. Mustard relish combines a variety of vegetables in one relish. Exact amounts of each vegetable are not important. Onions and cucumbers there must be, but if you don't have one of the items suggested below, it can be omitted; alternately, if you have an abundance, you can use more than specified. This recipe makes a small amount, which is easier than dealing with vast quantities, but if you want a stash of relish, double or triple the quantities below.

VEGETABLES
1 large onion, coarsely chopped
2 medium green tomatoes, cut into $^1/_2$-inch pieces
1 medium red bell pepper, deveined, seeded, and coarsely chopped
3–4 stalks celery, cut into $^1/_4$-inch pieces
1 cup tiny cauliflower florets
$^1/_2$ pound fresh green beans, wax beans, or a mixture, trimmed and cut into $^1/_4$-inch pieces
Two 6-inch cucumbers, peeled
$^3/_4$ cup pickling or kosher salt

PICKLING MIXTURE
2 cups white vinegar
2 bay leaves
$^1/_2$ teaspoon allspice berries
6 whole cloves
4 tablespoons ground mustard
$^1/_2$ teaspoon ground turmeric
3 tablespoons all-purpose flour
3–5 tablespoons granulated sugar to taste

1. Prepare the vegetables the day before you plan to make the relish. Make sure that all of the vegetables are clean and that none is bruised or damaged. Cut the cucumbers in half, remove the seeds with a teaspoon, then cut each half into 3 strips. Cut the strips into $^1/_4$-inch pieces. Choose a large glass or ceramic dish and put the prepared vegetables into the dish. Sprinkle with the pickling salt. Cover and let stand until the next day, stirring once or twice.

2. To make the pickling mixture, put 1 $^1/_2$ cups of the vinegar, the bay leaves, allspice berries, and cloves in a large saucepan. Cover and simmer for 10 minutes. Strain to remove the bay leaves and spices and return the flavored vinegar to the pan. Set aside.

3. Mix together the mustard, turmeric, flour, and sugar in a bowl. Add the remaining vinegar and stir the mixture into a paste. Set aside.

4. Drain the vegetables, then rinse thoroughly by swishing them around in a large bowl of cold water. Drain and swish a second time to reduce excess salt. Put them into a large saucepan, cover with cold water, then simmer for 4 minutes. Drain and rinse under cold running water.

5. Meanwhile, reheat the reserved flavored vinegar. Add the cooked vegetables and return to a simmer. Pour off a little of the cooking liquid into the reserved mustard mixture and stir, then add this mixture to the vegetables, stirring until it thickens. Simmer for 2–3 minutes, stirring to make sure that no lumps develop. Let cool.

6. Pour into sterilized jars and cover with the lids. After the relish has cooled, remove the lids, wipe the insides to dry off any condensation, then replace the lids and tighten them. Store in a cool place. (To sterilize jars, boil them in water for 10 minutes. Do not remove from the water until you are about to use them and dry each one with a paper towel.)

Apple-Raisin Hand Pies

In her book, *Seasoned with Grace,* Eldress Bertha Lindsay of Canterbury Shaker Village writes, "Sometimes the Shakers would make picnic lunches that included little hand pies, sandwiches, a piece of cake, and a beverage. Hand pies make a delicious picnic dessert." They are also good for school lunch boxes and for an easy cooking project to share with children. Today, the bakery housed in the former Power House at Canterbury Shaker Village makes hand pies with a variety of fillings. The recipe Eldress Bertha gives in her book specifies apples and raisins, and this recipe is adapted from hers.

FILLING	CRUST
1 pound apples, peeled, cored, and diced	*6 cups all-purpose flour*
¹/₂ cup granulated sugar	*2 tablespoons granulated sugar*
Pinch ground cloves or cinnamon	*¹/₂ cup vegetable shortening or lard*
1 tablespoon water	*¹/₂ cup butter*
¹/₃ cup raisins	*Cold water*
	1 egg
	3 tablespoons milk

1. To make the filling, put the apples, sugar, cloves, and water into a large saucepan. Cover and cook over low heat until the apples are soft. If they are very juicy, cook, uncovered, for a few minutes to evaporate some of the liquid. Stir in the raisins. Remove from the heat and let cool. (You can make the filling a day ahead of time, if you prefer.)

2. To make the crust, mix together the flour and 1 tablespoon of the sugar in a large bowl. Add the shortening and the butter, which has been cut into several bits. Rub the shortening and butter into the flour mixture until it looks like coarse crumbs. Make a well in the center of the mixture and pour in ¹/₄ cup cold water. Mix the water into the dry mixture. Add more cold water, 1 tablespoon at a time, until the pastry coheres.

3. Preheat the oven to 400° F. Grease 2 large baking sheets or line them with baking parchment.

4. Whisk together the egg and milk to make an egg wash. Take half the pastry and roll it out. Using a 3 ¹/₂- or 4-inch cutter, cut out circles. Brush each circle lightly with the egg wash and transfer to the prepared baking sheets. Pile 1 heaping teaspoon of the apple-raisin filling in the center, leaving a ¹/₂-inch border.

5. Roll out more pastry and cut out more circles. Cut a 1-inch long vent in the center of each, then place on top of the filled circles, pressing the edges together. Brush once more with the egg wash, then sprinkle lightly with the remaining sugar. Continue this way, rerolling pastry scraps as necessary. Bake for 15 minutes or until golden brown. Makes about 1 dozen hand pies.

To make Peach Hand Pies: *Follow the recipe for Apple-Raisin Hand Pies (page 100), but make the filling from 2 large ripe peaches, peeled and cut into ¹/₂-inch pieces. Cook the pieces with ¹/₃ cup granulated sugar and a tiny pinch ground cinnamon in a small, covered saucepan for 15–20 minutes. Make a paste with 1 tablespoon cornstarch and 1 tablespoon water. Add a little juice to the paste, then mix this mixture into the fruit in the pan and stir until the juice has thickened. Chill before using to make hand pies.*

CANTERBURY SHAKER ARCHIVES, CANTERBURY, NH

SHAKER DRINKS

Before the days of bottled soda, rural New Englanders made their own cooling beverages for summer days. "Switchel" was important for people spending hours working in the hot sun; it had molasses and brown sugar for quick energy and vinegar and ginger for a refreshing tang. Home-brewed hop beer was another standby for haymakers. With their many varieties of herbs, Shakers made mint cups and herbades with borage, lemon balm, mint, citrus juices, and even goldenrod. They also made drinks and wine from Concord grapes, rhubarb, raspberries, and blackberries. Eldress Bertha Lindsay, one of the last Shakers to live in Canterbury, recalls cold spring days when sisters were cleaning chilly cellars and an Eldress would come around with "tiny glasses of blackberry wine for us to have." In the summer, the sisters picked dandelions and combined them with oranges to make "a very fine golden wine." They also made raspberry and elderberry wines and a variety of herbal teas. In the winter, she writes, "A cup of catnip tea seemed to cure a cold in hardly any time."

Shaker Lemon Pie

This unusual lemon pie seems to have originated in a Shaker community in Ohio, but it appears also in collections of Shaker recipes from New England, no doubt because it is so delicious that New England Shaker communities added it to their repertoire of pies. Thin-skinned lemons are the best to use because they have less bitter white pith. If your lemons have thick skins, discard some of the pithy parts from the pointed ends. Before doing so, grate or strip off the flavorful yellow zest.

FILLING
2 large lemons
2 cups granulated sugar
6 eggs

PASTRY
2 ¹/₄ cups all-purpose flour
1 tablespoon granulated sugar
¹/₂ cup vegetable shortening
¹/₄ cup butter
Cold water
1 tablespoon half-and-half or milk

1. To make the filling, wash the lemons very well and cut off any rough bits of peel. Grate the zest from the pointed ends of the lemon or scrape it off with a lemon zester. Cut off the ends and discard all except the flesh. Using a sharp knife, slice the lemons very thinly ("paper thin" says the original recipe).

2. Put the lemon slices, grated lemon zest, and sugar into a bowl and let stand for several hours or overnight, stirring occasionally. The lemon juice eventually dissolves the sugar. When it is time to make the pie, beat the eggs and stir them into the lemon mixture.

3. Preheat the oven to 450° F. Grease a deep-dish pie plate.

4. To make the pastry, mix together the flour and 1 ¹/₂ teaspoons of the sugar in a large bowl. Rub the shortening and the butter, which has been cut into several bits, into the flour mixture until it looks like coarse crumbs. Make a well in the center of the mixture. Add 3 tablespoons cold water and blend it into the flour. Add more cold water, 1 tablespoon at a time, until the pastry coheres. Divide the pastry into 2 portions, one slightly larger than the other.

5. Roll out the larger portion of the pastry on a floured board and line the prepared plate with the pastry. Pour in the lemon filling. Roll out the second portion of pastry. Place it over the top of the pie and crimp the edges together. Brush the top crust with the half-and-half and sprinkle on the remaining sugar. Cut 3 vents in the center and bake for 15 minutes. Reduce the temperature to 375° and bake for 15–20 minutes more, or until a knife point inserted into one of the vents comes out clean. Serves 6–8.

Floating Island

Floating Island has a long history. The earliest English version appears in Hannah Glasse's *The Art of Cookery* in 1747. Her version has "islands" of French roll topped with jelly floating on a sea of cream and wine. She advises making it in a large glass bowl, noting, "It looks very pretty in the middle of a Table with Candles round it." The origin is the French *île flottante*. Later cooks used an island of meringue, so it resembled *oeufs à la neige*, "snow eggs," a confection of several egg-sized meringues surrounded by custard. Both dishes were favorite company desserts in nineteenth-century New England. The Shaker version is distinguished by the rosewater flavoring. The Hancock Village made large amounts of rosewater, and it is still made at Sabbathday Lake. In a note to her recipe for Floating Island, Sister Frances A. Carr recalls that "As children, this was a great favorite of ours." Interestingly, her recipe has a note adding "a tiny bit of stiff jelly to the egg white." Hannah Glasse also advised a touch of color using "what Jellies, Giams [jams] and Sweet-meats you have." A dish of berries or sliced peaches is a nice accompaniment; crisp cookies are good when peaches are not in season.

5 eggs, separated
1 tablespoon cornstarch
3 1/4 cups milk
8 tablespoons granulated sugar
1/4 teaspoon pure vanilla extract
1/2 teaspoon rosewater

1. For the custard lake on which the islands float, whisk together the egg yolks until they are bulky and pale, using an electric mixer.

2. Mix together the cornstarch and 1/4 cup of the milk into a paste. Stir this paste into the egg yolks and mix thoroughly.

3. Heat the remaining milk until hot but not boiling in a small saucepan. Stir in 4 tablespoons of the sugar and the vanilla, then add to the egg mixture. Mix well, then pour the mixture into the top of a double boiler and cook, stirring constantly, over low heat until the mixture has thickened. (If you don't have a double boiler, you can produce the same effect — cooking over water so the custard doesn't scorch — by placing the pan inside a larger pan of simmering water.) When the mixture has thickened to saucelike consistency, pour into a shallow serving dish. Cover the surface with plastic wrap to prevent a skin from forming. Let cool.

4. For the islands, whisk 3 egg whites until they are stiff. Discard or save the remaining egg whites. Add 2 tablespoons of the remaining sugar and whisk until the egg whites look glossy. Add the remaining 2 tablespoons sugar and the rosewater and whisk again.

5. Bring a large skillet half-filled with water to a boil. Using a rounded soup spoon or something similar, drop dollops of the egg white mixture onto the water. Let them poach for 2 minutes, then turn them over and poach for 1 minute more. Remove from the skillet with a slotted spoon, letting excess water drain off. Place the islands on the custard lake and serve within 1–2 hours.

HERITAGE DAYS

Throughout the summer and fall, the peoples of New England celebrate their heritage with picnics, powwows, and festivals.

The two that everyone shares are Halloween — a dark night frolic that heralds winter — and the summery Fourth of July. In earlier days, when wild salmon ran up the rivers, New Englanders often served salmon on the Fourth. Green peas, in season at the same time, became its natural accompaniment. Henry Wadsworth Longfellow captured the correctness of the combination in 1868, when he described John Endicott as "A solid man of Boston, A comfortable man, with dividends, And the first salmon, and the first green peas." Salmon and green peas taste just as good today, when the salmon comes from Maine's fish farms. But so, too, do contemporary choices for the holiday: grilled hamburgers and hot dogs, now two archetypal American foods.

Similarly, at community get-togethers, people choose dishes that link them to their homelands. When Puerto Rican families gather at the July Puerto Rican Parade and Hispanic Family Festival in Holyoke, Massachusetts, the specialties include arroz con gandules (rice with

pigeon peas), pastelitos (little meat pies), and flan — the caramel custard that is one of the favorite desserts of Spanish-speaking countries.

In Manchester, New Hampshire, Franco-Americans celebrate their patron saint, John the Baptist, with a midsummer supper honoring the Franco-American of the year. Other Franco-American festivals include the July Festival de Joie in Lewiston, Maine, and La Kermesse in Biddeford, Maine. Here French-Canadians and their descendants can explore their history in New England in the genealogical tent. They can also tour exhibitions illustrating life in the shoe factories and logging camps, where earlier generations came to work. More light-heartedly, there are dancing and clogging to Quebecois music and feasting on favorite dishes, such as pea soup or boudin fried with onions and served with piles of French fries.

For Greek-Americans, September brings Glendi, a celebration organized by St. George's Greek Orthodox Cathedral in Springfield, Massachusetts. Glendi means "festival" in Greek, and the event occurs over a three-day September weekend: time enough for joining hands in traditional dances, for touring the exhibits of Greek art, and for shopping in the Greek marketplace. Friends can chat over little cups of strong coffee and Greek pastries at the Greek *kafenion* set up for the festival. For something more substantial, a tent in the Cathedral parking lot offers moussaka or pastitsio, souvlaki, or stuffed peppers and eggplant. Horiatiki — the Greek salad of cucumbers, lettuce, and tomatoes topped with feta cheese and dotted with olives — accompanies everything.

Italians also celebrate traditional holidays. Fishing families of the New England coast honor St. Peter in June, while Boston's North End, once home of Paul Revere and now an Italian community packed with Italian restaurants and groceries, celebrates the Assumption on August 15.

On October 12, the anniversary of Columbus's arrival in the New World, the Italian flag flutters its green, white, and orange stripes to honor the country's most famous explorer. The weather is invariably perfect; the trees splash their colors over the hillside, and villages throb with Oktoberfests, craft fairs, and apple festivals.

For Jews, these gorgeous days of fall bring the High Holy Days with Rosh Hashanah, the start of a new year in the Jewish calendar, celebrating the bounty of life. Jewish families gather for festive meals that begin with apple slices dipped in honey. Beef brisket is a popular choice for the main course, usually cooked with sweet vegetables such as carrots flavored with dried fruit. Sweet foods symbolize the hope for a sweet year and usher in days of reflection leading to Yom Kippur, a solemn time of fasting and repentance.

In 1763, the first Jewish synagogue in the United States was built by Sephardic Jews from Spain and Portugal in Newport, Rhode Island. By the nineteenth century, Ashkenazic Jews

from Eastern Europe were settling in Portsmouth, Boston, and other cities, which were already home to immigrants from Ireland and Italy. Seamen from the Azores and the Italian coast manned the whaling and fishing boats of New Bedford, Nantucket, Gloucester, and Cape Cod. Inland, Polish farmers were settling on the fertile land of the Connecticut River valley, while Greeks and French Canadians worked in the metal, paper, and textile mills of Massachusetts and New Hampshire. In the post-Viet Nam era, refugees from Viet Nam and Cambodia found homes all over New England; many opened restaurants to introduce the foods of their homeland. More recent immigrants include Russians and Yugoslavs. As for Hispanic peoples, most large cities have Puerto Rican and Latin American communities, helping to make New England one of the most culturally varied regions of the country. Ethnic groceries and restaurants thrive, and even modest supermarkets can be depended on for Polish kielbasa and pierogis, Puerto Rican pigeon peas and sofrito, Italian oils and canned vegetables, Greek olives and feta cheese, Southeast-Asian sauces, Portuguese sausages, and Irish tea.

Foods from afar are nothing new in the cooking of New England. As early as 1833, Lydia Maria Child's book, *American Frugal Housewife*, gave instructions on how "To Curry Fowl" and recipes for sago and tapioca puddings. By the mid-nineteenth century, cookbooks had recipes for ketchups and chutney, all dishes that call for ingredients from Asia and South America. New England's sailors brought these foods back from their voyages to the East along with exotics such as coconuts and pineapples. The idea that New England fare is plain fare has thus never been wholly true, and certainly not today, when foods from the many communities of the region bring big flavor and vast variety to the culinary repertoire.

Passamaquoddy Hulled Corn Soup

Yellow-eyed beans are a Maine specialty. They look like black-eyed peas, with a yellow patch instead of a black eye. At the Sipayik Reservation in Pleasant Point, Maine, Passamaquoddy cooks team these beans with hulled corn, also called hominy, in a soup that could be served any time, but especially at celebrations. Donald Francis outlined the following recipe. He does not include salt, though you may want to add it.

$1/_2$ pound dried yellow-eyed beans
2 ounces salt pork, cut into $1/_2$-inch cubes
1 large onion, chopped
6 cups water
1 can golden hominy (hulled corn), drained
1 medium potato, peeled and cut into 1-inch dice
Salt to taste (optional)

1. Pick over the beans in case they have any little stones or other debris among them. Rinse in cold water, then soak overnight or for at least 3 hours in enough water to cover them by at least 2 inches. Drain and set aside.

2. Put the salt pork in a large saucepan over low heat and cook for 5–10 minutes, or until the fat has melted and the bits are golden brown. Remove the bits from the pan and pour off all except 1 tablespoon of the fat. Return the salt pork bits to the pan and add the reserved drained beans, the onion, and water. Bring to a simmer and cook until the beans are tender. (Cooking time can vary from 1 hour or more, depending on the age of the beans and how long they have soaked.)

3. Add the hominy, potato, and salt if you are using it and simmer for 25 minutes more, or until the potato is cooked through. Serve immediately.

Ten-Thousand Dollar Burgers

After Rob Chirico of Greenfield, Massachusetts, had spent some time in Argentina, he found American beef lacking in flavor compared to the meat he had been eating there. Trying to recapture the taste he loved, he began tinkering with his hamburger recipe. Eventually he came up with the following mixture of ground beef and ground lamb confected with a little feta cheese for moistness. It pleased him so well that he entered it in a 1991 Build A Better Burger contest run by Sutter Home, the California winery. It won him the $10,000 top prize. It's the perfect choice for a Labor Day backyard barbecue.

CILANTRO-MINT CHUTNEY

¹/₃ cup plain yogurt
2 tablespoons chopped yellow onion
1 ¹/₂ tablespoons peeled and chopped
  fresh gingerroot
³/₄ cup fresh cilantro leaves
¹/₃ cup fresh mint leaves
1 large clove garlic, chopped
¹/₂ teaspoon salt
Pinch granulated sugar

BURGERS

1 pound lean ground sirloin
1 pound lean ground lamb
1 clove garlic, minced
¹/₂ cup crumbled feta cheese
¹/₃ cup pitted minced kalamata olives
1 teaspoon salt
6 medium-sized thick pita bread pockets
¹/₄ cup fruity extra-virgin olive oil
1 teaspoon ground cumin mixed with 1
  teaspoon ground coriander
Vegetable oil

1. To make the chutney, combine all of the ingredients in a blender or food processor and blend thoroughly. Cover and chill for several hours or as long as 24 hours.

2. In a grill with a cover, prepare a medium-hot fire, preferably with natural hardwood charcoal, for direct-heat grilling.

3. To make the burgers, combine the sirloin, lamb, garlic, cheese, olives, and salt in a large mixing bowl. Handling the meat as little as possible to avoid compacting it, mix well. Divide the mixture into 6 equal portions and form into round patties to fit the pita bread. Brush the patties with the olive oil and sprinkle with the cumin mixture.

4. When the fire is ready, brush the grill rack with the vegetable oil. Place the patties on the grill, cover, and cook until browned on the bottom, about 4 minutes. With a wide spatula, turn the patties and cook until done to preference, about 4 minutes more for medium-rare.

5. During the last few minutes of cooking, place the pitas on the outer edges of the grill and turn to toast lightly on both sides. Place the patties inside the pita pockets and add the chutney. Serves 6.

Flan de Coco

In Spanish-speaking countries the favorite dessert is flan, a caramel custard that differs from the French crème caramel only in being richer in egg yolks. Flan is often simply flavored with vanilla or cinnamon. Flan de coco, a version popular in Puerto Rico and the Dominican Republic, is made with coconut milk. Stores that have a section of Puerto Rican foods usually sell packaged mixes for flan de coco, but homemade is easy and tastes a lot better, especially if you use freshly grated coconut. Flan is always better made a day ahead of serving, giving the caramel time to bond to the custard rather than the cup. It keeps well in the fridge for 2–3 days, making it one of the best do-ahead desserts. Almost everybody likes it.

1 ¹/₂ cups granulated sugar
4 whole eggs plus one egg yolk
1 ¹/₂ cups milk
1 ¹/₂ cups coconut milk
¹/₄ cup shredded coconut
Shredded coconut for garnish

1. Preheat the oven to 325° F. Warm an ovenproof ceramic or glass soufflé dish or another dish that can act as a mold. Set it beside the stove.

2. Pour 1 cup of the sugar into a heavy skillet and place over low heat. If the sugar has lumps, press them out with a wooden spoon or discard them. Let the sugar cook until it liquefies at the edges. (This takes 4–5 minutes and you should watch it carefully.) As the sugar liquefies into caramel, use a wooden spoon to stir the uncooked sugar into it. The caramel darkens within seconds. When it reaches a rich golden brown, pour it into the prepared dish. Wearing oven mitts or using pot holders, quickly tilt the dish while the caramel is still liquid to swirl it about 1 inch up the side.

3. Whisk together the eggs, egg yolk, and the remaining sugar in a large bowl. Heat the milk and coconut milk in a small saucepan, but don't let them boil. Pour the milk mixture into the egg mixture and whisk to blend. Stir in the coconut. Pour the custard on top of the caramel.

4. Place the dish in a roasting pan and add hot water to come about half way up the side. Bake in the center of the oven for 45–55 minutes, or until a knife blade inserted in the center comes out clean. Let cool, then chill in the fridge for at least 12 hours or preferably 1 day.

5. To unmold, run a knife blade between the custard and the dish. Place a shallow serving platter on top of the dish, then invert with a shaking motion. Add a little mound of shredded coconut to garnish the center. Serves 4–6.

Puerto Rican Corn Sticks

These little corn sticks, called *surullitos* in Spanish, often come with a drink and a savory dip — salsa is a good choice. Puerto Ricans also sometimes serve them plain with a cup of coffee or a glass of milk. They are best freshly made and eaten warm; if possible, within 2–3 hours.

2 cups water
1 ¹/₂ teaspoons salt
1 ¹/₂ cups yellow cornmeal
1 cup grated Cheddar or Colby cheese
Vegetable oil or shortening

1. Bring the water to a boil in a medium saucepan. Add the salt, then pour in the cornmeal in a stream. Stir briskly until smooth, about 1–2 minutes. Remove from the heat and immediately stir in the cheese. Set aside until lukewarm.

2. Take small portions of the cornmeal mixture and roll them in your hands until you have cylinders about the size of your index finger. When all of the mixture is formed into sticks, heat the oil to the depth of about ¹/₂ inch in a skillet.

3. When a tiny bit of bread sizzles and rises to the top as soon as it is dropped in, begin cooking the corn sticks a few at a time. They need to be turned over so don't crowd the skillet. Cook for 4 minutes or until golden all over, then remove with tongs to a plate lined with paper towels.

4. Serve either warm or cold with a dip such as salsa if you like. Makes about 3 dozen.

Boudin with Onions & Apples

Boudin is a French-styled blood sausage sold in supermarkets in Maine, New Hampshire, and other areas with large Franco-American populations. Morcela is a similar, though spicier, Portuguese sausage, available in Massachusetts, especially in the southeastern part of the state, which has many people of Portuguese ancestry. Black puddings are the British version, and they, too, can sometimes be found in supermarkets. This recipe, French in conception, works with all of these sausages. Since the sausage, onions, and apples take only a few minutes to cook, they make a quick and flavorful meal.

1 1/2 pounds boudin sausage
2 tablespoons vegetable oil
2 medium onions, coarsely chopped
1/2 teaspoon dried thyme or savory
Salt and black pepper
2 tablespoons butter
2 medium apples, peeled, cored, and thickly sliced

1. Preheat the broiler. Grease a shallow pan.

2. Cut the sausage into 5–6-inch lengths, then cut in half lengthwise. Place cut-side up in the prepared pan and set aside.

3. Heat the oil in a skillet and toss in the onions. Sprinkle with the thyme and season with the salt and black pepper. Stir well, then reduce the heat. Cover and cook, stirring frequently, until tender, about 6–8 minutes.

4. Melt the butter in another skillet and toss in the apple slices. Cover and cook over gentle heat, stirring occasionally, for 5–6 minutes or until tender.

5. As soon as you have the onions and apples started, put the reserved sausage under the broiler and cook for 5 minutes, or until the surface is black and slightly dry.

6. Arrange the onions on a serving platter with the sausage on top and the apple slices to the side. Serve immediately.

Souvlaki

Souvlaki, grilled skewers of pork (or sometimes chicken), are Greek soul food. Rigani, an especially fragrant form of oregano, is the signature herb used in the marinade. It can be found in Greek and Middle-Eastern specialty stores. If unavailable, its close relatives oregano or marjoram do very well. Serve souvlaki with a rice dish, such as Bell Peppers Stuffed with Pilaf on page 112, or with pita bread and a salad.

4 thick-cut boneless pork chops (about 1–1 ¹/₂ pounds)
¹/₄ cup olive oil
1 tablespoon fresh lemon juice
2 cloves garlic, chopped
2 teaspoons dried rigani, oregano, or marjoram
6 bay leaves
Salt and black pepper
2 lemons, each cut into 4 wedges

1. Cut the pork into bite-sized cubes. Leave any fat on the meat as it is useful in cooking.

2. Mix together the oil, lemon juice, garlic, and rigani in a shallow dish. Break each bay leaf into 2 pieces and stir into the mixture. Put the pork cubes into the dish and stir them around. Place in the fridge for 2–3 hours, stirring occasionally.

3. Preheat a charcoal or gas grill or the broiler of the stove. Grease 6 skewers with a piece of paper towel soaked in a little vegetable oil. Season the pork cubes well with the salt and black pepper, then string the cubes onto the skewers, adding 2 pieces of bay leaf to each one.

4. Grill or broil the meat until it is browning on the edges. Use leftover marinade to brush the pork as it cooks. To check for doneness, insert a knife point and press firmly. If the juice is clear, the meat is cooked. If it is pink, cook for a little longer. Cooking generally varies from 6–9 minutes depending on the size of the meat and the temperature of the grill. Avoid overcooking because it dries out the cubes of meat.

5. As you remove the souvlaki from the heat, squeeze 2–4 lemon wedges over the meat. You can remove the meat from the skewers before serving if you wish. Discard the bay leaves. Add a lemon wedge to each plate and serve.

Bell Peppers Stuffed with Pilaf

This favorite Greek dish is perfect in late summer, when bell peppers abound. You can serve the peppers cold or lukewarm before the main course, as Greeks often do, or straight from the oven. They are good alongside pork, lamb, or chicken dishes, but equally good on their own served as a first course or as a vegetarian main dish.

1 cup uncooked long grain rice
3 tablespoons olive oil
¹/₂ cup chopped onion
1 teaspoon salt
¹/₂ teaspoon ground allspice
1 teaspoon dried rigani or oregano
2 cups water
1 bay leaf
²/₃ cup currants or golden raisins
4 large bell peppers of various colors
Salt
¹/₂ cup peeled, seeded, and diced fresh tomato
¹/₃ cup pine nuts or slivered almonds

1. Cover the rice with cold water, swish it around, and leave for a few minutes, then drain.

2. Heat 1 tablespoon of the oil in a medium saucepan. Add the onion and gently soften for 3–4 minutes. Add 1 more tablespoon of the oil, then stir in the drained rice. When it is glistening, season it with the salt and allspice and stir in the rigani. Add the water and bay leaf and bring to a boil. Reduce the heat to simmer and cook steadily, uncovered, for 10 minutes, or until the liquid has evaporated. (The rice will be partly cooked.) Stir in the currants, cover, and cook on the lowest possible heat for 5–6 minutes more.

3. Preheat the oven to 400° F. Grease a shallow baking dish just big enough to hold the pepper halves in a single layer. Cut the peppers in half and discard the seeds and any pale-looking internal ribs. Place the pepper halves in the prepared dish cut-side up and lightly season the interior with the salt.

4. When the rice is tender but not soft, gently stir in the tomato. Taste and season with more salt or allspice if necessary. Fill each pepper half with some of the rice. Drizzle the remaining oil over the tops and sprinkle on the pine nuts or slivered almonds. Cover with aluminium foil and bake for 30–40 minutes, or until the peppers are tender. Uncover during the last few minutes of cooking time to brown the nuts if necessary.

Gingerbread Pancakes with Lemon Sauce with maple syrup on the side, and (bottom right) Latkes with Applesauce.

Farmers make maple syrup in late winter and early spring, but they sell it at roadside stands throughout the year.

A springtime Spinach & Radish Salad served with Maple-Mustard Dressing.

New Englanders relish fish and shellfish soups, such as (left) Salmon, Leek & Corn Chowder, (Center) North Atlantic Stew, and (right) Lobster Bisque.

Runners in the Boston Marathon always eat pasta the evening before the race. For marathoners and other pasta lovers, Spaghetti with Olives & Bay (left), and Firehouse Chili-Pasta Bake.

Corned Beef & Cabbage is a New England tradition for St. Patrick's Day (March 17), shown here with Muireann Glenmullen's Cranberry-Nut Soda Bread.

Ham is a traditional Easter choice in New England. Here Baked Ham with Cider Sauce is shown with asparagus and radishes — two of the earliest spring crops.

A special dessert fit for any special occasion: Cheesecake with Irish Liqueur & Toblerone.

A classic New England clam chowder made from clams, potatoes, onions, milk and a little salt pork.

Today, Steamed Mussels are favorite choices from seafood menus.

The Maine Lobster Festival is the highlight of August in Rockland, Maine.

Lobsters are served at all kinds of food fairs. Here, diners enjoy themselves at the Machias Blueberry Festival, Machias, Maine

Steaming lobsters at the Maine Lobster Fair, Rockland, Maine.

Lobster still-life at the Maine Lobster Fair, Rockland, Maine

Seafood, always traditional in New England cuisine, lends itself to modern treatments, as shown here: Peppered Tuna with Sweet Potato Puree (left), Monkfish in Red Peppers with Pernod Mayonnaise (center front), and Baked Bluefish with Sautéed Confetti Tomatoes (right rear).

Wild blueberries are a pride of Maine.

Duck Breast with Blueberry-Lavender Sauce is an easy dish to make, but its evocative flavors give it a sophisticated special-occasion taste.

New Englanders love pies. Here (bottom left) Blueberry-Almond Tart, (top left) Apple Streusel Pie, and (right) Raspberry Meringue Pie.

A pastry shell, some raspberries and sugar, and a bowl of meringue: ingredients for Raspberry Meringue Pie.

Rosewater flavors the Shaker version of Floating Island, while pansies prettify the eighteenth-century Trifle with Jelley & Flowers.

This Fudge Brownie Tart with Raspberries is an easy dessert for a crowd.

Summer and fall bring berry harvests: (left to right) blueberries, cranberries, and blackberries.

Pumpkins, squash, and gourds spell fall in New England. Here a hollow pumpkin makes a tureen for Pumpkin-Peanut Soup.

An herb-flavored mixture of eggplant and tomatoes fills this Early Autumn Roulade, equally delicious as an appetizer or a meat-free main dish.

Cows, goats, and sheep graze New England's pastures, producing the milk that inspires the regions's cheese makers.

Roast Turkey with Two Stuffings & Giblet Gravy, Cranberry-Lime Sauce, Parker House Rolls, and an array of vegetables star on the Thanksgiving table.

Corn and peppers — two new-world vegetables — team up in this dazzling Sautéed Red Bell Peppers & Baby Corn.

New England breads include (clockwise from bottom left), Ginger-Pumpkin Bread, Nantucket Portuguese Bread with Vermont Shepherd cheese (left) and Berkshire Blue cheese (center), Anadama Bread, Mint, Cucumber & Cheese Bread, and Vermont-made butter (center).

Pasta with Sardines

At festivals, pasta with sardines is one of the more unusual Italian treats that might appear on the menus of Italian restuarants in Boston's North End. It is a Sicilian dish whose Arabic origins are witnessed by such ingredients as saffron, currants, and pine nuts. In Sicily, the sardines may be fresh, salted, or canned. This version calls for canned sardines from Maine, whose five sardine canneries make it America's major producer.

1 medium-large bulb Florentine fennel
¹/₄ cup pine nuts
2–3 tablespoons tomato paste to taste
1 large pinch saffron
¹/₃ cup warm water
¹/₄ cup currants or raisins
3 quarts water
1 tablespoon salt

2 tablespoons olive oil
2–4 anchovies to taste
1 large onion, chopped
Two 3 ¹/₄-ounce cans sardines packed in oil
2 tablespoons chopped fresh parsley
Salt and black pepper to taste
12 ounces spaghetti or other pasta

1. Put the fennel into a large saucepan, cover with water, place a lid on the pan, and bring to a boil. Cook the fennel for 8–10 minutes or until tender. Drain the water into a large pot in which you will cook the pasta, pressing the fennel with a spoon to squeeze out as much liquid as possible. Chop the cooked fennel and set aside.

2. While the fennel is cooking, lightly toast the pine nuts either by microwaving for 1–2 minutes, or until they are golden, or by baking in a 300º oven for 6–7 minutes. Set aside.

3. Mix together the tomato paste with 2 cups of the liquid from the fennel and set aside. In a small bowl, soak the saffron in the ¹/₃ cup warm water and set aside. In another small bowl, cover the currants with cold water and set aside.

4. Add the 3 quarts water and the 1 tablespoon salt to the fennel liquid in the large pot. Cover and bring to a boil for the pasta.

5. Meanwhile, heat the oil in a skillet. Rinse the anchovies and stir them into the oil, pressing a bit so they break up. Add the onion and cook gently for 4–5 minutes, or until it has softened. Add the reserved chopped fennel, stir for 2 minutes, then pour in the reserved tomato mixture and the reserved saffron mixture.

6. Drain 1 can of the sardines and stir them in, breaking them up as you go. Drain the currants. Add the currants and 1 tablespoon of the parsley. Season with the salt and black pepper. Cover and simmer the mixture gently for 10 minutes. Check it several times and add a little water if it seems to be dry. Drain the remaining can of sardines, add them to the pan, breaking them as little as possible. Spoon on some of the sauce and continue cooking gently.

7. Add the pasta to the boiling water and cook until al dente according to package directions. Drain through a colander and place the pasta on a serving platter and top with the sardine sauce. Sprinkle on the remaining parsley and the reserved pine nuts. Serve immediately.

SARDINES

Sardines were one of the first foods to be canned, and in Europe at least, one of the very few canned foods appreciated by connoisseurs, who discriminate among French, Spanish, and Portuguese producers, and also by vintage years: In general, the best canned sardines are made in the years that favor olives — sardines in olive oil being the only ones worth attention at this rarefied level. No sardines swim off New England's coast, but when canned sardines became fashionable in the late nineteenth century, canning companies in Massachusetts and Maine entered the business using small Atlantic herring. At that time, sardines were fancy food, and hostesses on both sides of the Atlantic had china or glass dishes sized to take a sardine can. Sardine enthusiasts could thus see the brand label, much as wine lovers like to check the label on a wine bottle.

Today, Maine's five sardine canneries still use Atlantic herring, which swim plentifully off the coast and are one of over twenty species of fish that qualify as sardines according to international regulations. Within a day of being caught, the fish are tucked into their cans. Sometimes you'll find four chunky fish sharing a can; sometimes eight slim fish nestle up to each other. What you get depends on what the fishermen caught, and that depends partly on their nets and other technology. If you really adore the minifish, look for cans that specify small sardines. If you enjoy the texture of the chunkier fish, try canned herring steaks: They are simply bigger "sardines."

With the omega–3 oils that protect against heart disease and significant amounts of calcium for bone health, sardines are nutritious. Nevertheless, they lack their former prestige, possibly because they cost very little. Prestigious or not, they taste as good ever — and are more varied. Today, sardines come packed in the traditional oil — soy or olive oil — and also in water or in various sauces, including Cajun, tomato, and mustard.

Beef Tzimmes

Many Jewish families have favorite tzimmes that they make for holiday dinners. Tzimmes vary tremendously, but all tzimmes are stews of sweet vegetables and fruits, usually with beef brisket or ribs. Since a long list of ingredients and the cook's pride can be involved in tzimmes, the word has come to mean "a big fuss" in Yiddish slang. But as long as you start well ahead of time, tzimmes are easy to make, and many people say they taste even better the next day — good news for cooks who like to get the work done ahead of time.

3 – 4 pounds flat-cut beef brisket
Salt and black pepper
1 tablespoon vegetable oil
1 large onion, coarsely chopped
2 cloves garlic, chopped
1 stalk celery, halved
2 bay leaves
8 carrots
2 cups beef stock or water
1 cup red wine
2 tablespoons cornstarch
20 prunes
1 large sweet potato, peeled and thinly sliced

1. Preheat the oven to 350º F. Wash the beef and season with the salt and black pepper.

2. Heat the oil in a large ovenproof pan and put the fattiest side of the beef in the oil. Let the beef sear for 3 – 4 minutes, then turn it over. Sprinkle on the onion and garlic. Tuck the celery halves, bay leaves, and 2 of the carrots, each cut in half, around the beef. Pour on the stock and wine. Bring to a simmer and cook on top of the stove for 5 minutes, then transfer to the oven. Let simmer, checking and basting two to three times for 2 hours.

3. Remove the pan from the oven. With a slotted spoon, remove and discard the carrot and celery pieces. Also remove 1 cup of the broth and set aside. In a small bowl, mix the cornstarch with enough cold water to make a smooth paste. Stir in the reserved 1 cup of broth, then add the cornstarch mixture to the pan, stirring it into the liquid. Add the remaining carrots, cut into 1-inch pieces, and the prunes. Taste for seasonings and add salt and black pepper if necessary.

4. Add the sweet potato slices, keeping them on top. Cover and bring to a simmer on top of the stove. Return to the oven and let simmer for 20 minutes. Remove the lid and cook for 15 minutes more, or until the sweet potatoes are lightly browned.

5. Remove the beef and slice. Put the slices on a platter and partly cover them with the vegetables and the gravy from the pan. Serve the remaining vegetables and the gravy separately on the side. This recipe can be expanded as needed for larger gatherings. Serves 6.

Portuguese Kale Soup

Kale soup is a staple in Nantucket, Cape Cod, and southeastern Massachusetts. Debates about the proper way of making it rage as fiercely as debates about chowder. Does the sausage go in with the soup, or is it cooked separately? Does it have vegetables other than potatoes and kale? Kale soup, also called by its Portuguese name *caldo verde* ("green soup") came to New England with Portuguese fisherman from the Azores, a windswept archipelago off mainland Portugal. This version stays close to the original Portuguese form — simple, but surprisingly good. Serve it as a main course with bread — either chunks of Nantucket Portuguese Bread (see recipe on page 117) or a corn bread, a common accompaniment in Portugal.

5 medium-large potatoes, peeled and sliced (about 2–2 $^1/_2$ pounds)
2 quarts water
1 teaspoon salt
1 large onion, chopped
2 cloves garlic, chopped
4–6 tablespoons olive oil
6–8 cups fresh kale, washed
1 pound linguica or kielbasa
$^1/_2$ pound chourico or chorizo

1. Put the potato slices, water, salt, onion, garlic, and 1 tablespoon of the oil in a large pot. Bring to a boil and cook for 20 minutes. Mash the potatoes still in their liquid, leaving some small solid pieces.

2. Cut the kale leaves into $^1/_4$-inch wide strips, discarding any tough stems. Drop the strips into the pot and add 2 more tablespoons of the oil and more salt if you think it is needed. Cover and cook for 7–8 minutes, or until the kale is tender.

3. Meanwhile, cook the linguica and chourico in a large ovenproof pan by baking them in a 400° F oven for 15 minutes or by frying them on top of the stove. In either case, prick the sausages first. Slice them after they are cooked. Set aside.

4. Put some pieces of the sausages in each soup bowl and ladle the soup on top. Add some of the remaining oil to each serving or serve the oil at the table so people can add their own. (The sausage is also sometimes served at the table along with the bread.)

Nantucket Portuguese Bread

Nantucket Portuguese bread is a white bread that gets its characteristic flavor and crust from dried milk and high-gluten flour of the sort recommended for bread machines. It makes terrific toast. The Portuguese bread of Fall River and southeastern Massachusetts is enriched with eggs and lightly sweetened and spiced — a bread for eating with tea or coffee rather than with soup or as sandwiches.

1 package active dry yeast
1 teaspoon granulated sugar
$^1/_3$ cup lukewarm water
3–4 cups flour for bread machines
$^1/_2$ cup dried milk powder
1 tablespoon salt
$^1/_2$ cup lukewarm water

1. Put the yeast and sugar in a small bowl and stir in the $^1/_3$ cup lukewarm water. Set aside for 10 minutes, or until it is slightly frothy on the surface.

2. Preheat the oven to 250º F. Mix together 3 cups of the flour, the milk powder, and salt in a large ovenproof bowl and put it into the oven to warm slightly.

3. Remove the bowl from the oven. Make a well in the center of the flour mixture and pour in the reserved yeast. Add the $^1/_2$ cup lukewarm water and mix to form a dough. Add more lukewarm water as needed to form the dough; you may need as much as another $^1/_2$ cup. Knead the dough until it is smooth and no longer sticks to your hands or the sides of the bowl. (If needed, you may add a little more flour.) Kneading takes about 15 minutes by hand or 6–7 minutes in the bowl of an electric mixer. When the dough is ready, grease a bowl, form the dough into a ball, and roll it in the greased bowl. Cover the bowl with plastic wrap and let stand in a draft-free spot until the dough has doubled in bulk, about 2 hours.

4. Punch down the dough. Knead it again for 2–3 minutes, then form it into a ball and let rise until doubled again, about 1 $^1/_2$ hours.

5. Grease a baking sheet or shallow pan. Punch down the dough again and form into a ball. Place it on the prepared baking sheet and cover loosely with plastic wrap. Let it rise again. When it has almost doubled in bulk, dust 1 tablespoon of the flour over the surface by shaking it through a sieve, then slash the surface with a single-edged razor blade or a very sharp knife. Some bakers slash the bread only once, in the middle; others make three or four slashes across the top.

6. While the slashes are opening out, preheat the oven to 425º F. When the slashes have opened, about 15 minutes, bake the bread for 10 minutes. Reduce the temperature to 375º and bake for 15–20 minutes more, or until the bread sounds hollow when rapped on the bottom. Cool on a wire rack. Makes 1 loaf.

Kielbasa with Horseradish

Kielbasa is a Polish smoked sausage, traditionally made with pork or a mixture of pork and beef, but now also obtainable in reduced-fat turkey versions. In Polish homes, kielbasa invariably comes with horseradish, and many Polish farmers and gardeners in the Connecticut valley grow their own horseradish solely to ensure a pungent supply of this favorite condiment. Some Polish families also make *kapusta,* a form of sauerkraut, for serving with kielbasa. Potatoes and fresh cabbage are other typical side dishes. As for kielbasa sandwiches, in Polish families the bread must be dark rye with caraway seeds.

1 pound kielbasa
1 tablespoon butter or oil
1 tablespoon all-purpose flour
$^1/_3$ cup cold water
2–4 tablespoons prepared or freshly grated horseradish or to taste
$^1/_2$ cup sour cream
Salt to taste
1–2 teaspoons white vinegar (optional)

1. Prick the kielbasa in 3–4 spots, then place it in a skillet. Cover with cold water and bring to a simmer over low heat. Cook gently, never letting it do more than simmer, for 10 minutes. (Gentle cooking prevents the kielbasa from bursting.)

2. Heat the butter in a small saucepan. Off the heat, stir in the flour so that you have a paste. Stir in the $^1/_3$ cup cold water, return to low heat, and cook gently for 1 minute. Stir in 2 tablespoons of the horseradish and the sour cream. Season lightly with the salt. Taste and add more horseradish or salt if you would like it and add vinegar if you want a tarter sauce. (Typically, fresh horseradish is best and is very hot, so you may not need extra. Grated horseradish from a jar is milder, so you may want an additional tablespoon or two. Generally it is packed in vinegar, so you probably won't need vinegar if you use this form.)

3. Slice the kielbasa for serving. Offer the horseradish sauce on the side.

CHAPTER 8

HARVEST FESTIVAL

In September, many New Englanders take the day off work and go to the Big E, the annual fair and exhibition that celebrates the region and its products.

By 9:30 a.m., people already throng the grounds in West Springfield, Massachusetts. Though the bright sky promises warmth, morning chill still spritzes the air, and in the Rhode Island building, eager hands reach for bags of clam fritters hot from the oil or maple-gilded johnnycakes just lifted from the griddle. A line of early birders wends its way into the Maine building, where baked potatoes go as fast as servers can dollop them with sour cream and sprinkle on the bacon bits. Outside, a Vermont emu farmer offers tastes of emu sausage, while a Massachusetts sausage maker displays Portuguese-style chourico and linguica.

On the other side of the vast grounds, there are prize cows and baby chicks, displays of horsemanship, concerts, demonstrations, and every whirling fairground ride that you can imagine. But to get to them, you have to walk the gauntlet of food kiosks selling cotton candy, deep-fried mushrooms, turkey drumsticks, steak sandwiches, pierogis, tempura, gyros, and souvlaki. Some folks bite into hot, sugar-dusted fried dough as they walk. Others share bags of French fries or onions cunningly cut and battered so they open into savory petals. No, it's not what the nutritionist ordered, but fair food is part of the fun of the Big E and the abundance that is fall.

The message of plenty also murmurs from the mushrooms on the forest floor. Brassy pumpkins belt it out from farm stands, where the corn, eggplant, and bell peppers of late summer keep company with the onions, cabbage, squash, and carrots of autumn. Tucked among them, you may spot Jerusalem artichokes. They look like the gingerroot of the tropics and taste (a bit) like the globe artichokes of the Mediterranean. Nonetheless, their botanical home is New England. Samuel Champlain, the French explorer, sampled them on Cape Cod in 1605, where the Wampanoags cultivated them.

Champlain reported their artichokelike taste in letters back home, and soon Jerusalem artichokes were the latest American novelty in Europe. In return, European settlers brought apples to New England, where they quickly became staples. Some went into pies; others were dried or stored in barrels for winter. Yet others went to the cider press. Growers developed varieties for all these uses, giving them enticing names like Sops of Wine and Westfield Seek-No-Further. Today, McIntoshes, Macouns, and Cortlands have replaced them as favorites, but old orchards sometimes still have dainty red-cheeked lady apples, or Baldwins, Pound Sweets, and best of all, Northern Spies — big apples that make the tastiest desserts and pies.

Throughout fall, there are apple festivals, perhaps none bigger than that at Dummerston, Vermont, where a church fund-raiser held on the Sunday before Columbus Day draws crowds, including out-for-the-day motorcyclists, to sample the 1,500 pies baked by the townspeople. Homemade ice cream, doughnuts, cider, and Vermont Cheddar cheese complete the offerings.

Vermont Cheddar gets its characteristics from a cheese-making practice, invented in Cheddar, England, where the curd is chopped and piled into slabs to drain off the whey. Other New England cheeses also follow European methods. Calabro Cheese of East Haven, Connecticut, founded by Sicilian Joseph Calabro, makes Italian cheeses such as ricotta and mozzarella. New Hampshire's Fanny Mason is a Swiss cheese. Vermont Shepherd derives from the sheep cheese of the Pyrenees, while the Vermont Butter and Cheese Company makes cow's and goat's milk cheeses modeled on the cheeses of France, Greece, and Germany.

Yet while tradition (and sometimes regulation) commits New England's cheese makers to using European names for their products, they quickly point out that their cheese inevitably differs from its antecedents because it captures the essence of the fine pastures grazed by the animals who produce the milk. Thus, quite simply, it tastes of New England — another harvest, preserving the lush milk of summer in a form to savor months later, when chill has settled on the earth and animals and people keep indoors.

Early Autumn Roulade

This roulade looks pretty but therefore daunting, and the longish list of ingredients does nothing to inspire confidence. But, truly, it is easy. The vegetable filling can be altered at whim as long as you have a mixture that forms a cohesive mass. Ratatouille, for example, is good, as are mushroom mixtures.

FILLING

One 12–16-ounce eggplant, washed
2 tablespoons salt
2 tablespoons vegetable oil
1 medium onion, chopped
2 cloves garlic, chopped
2 cups chopped fresh tomatoes
1 teaspoon cumin seeds
1 teaspoon ground allspice
1 teaspoon herbes de Provence or other
  herb mixture
Salt to taste

ROLL

$^1/_2$ stick (4 tablespoons) butter
3 tablespoons all-purpose flour
$^1/_2$ cup milk
1 cup grated extra-sharp Vermont
  Cheddar cheese
Pinch cayenne pepper
4 eggs, separated
1–2 tablespoons grated Parmesan cheese
Cherry tomatoes or sliced tomatoes for
  garnishing

1. To make the filling, cut the eggplant into 1-inch cubes. Place them in a colander, sprinkling them with the 2 tablespoons salt as you go. Let stand for 1 hour, by which time the surface will be moist with the juices drawn out by the salt. Rinse with cold water, then pat dry with paper towels.

2. Heat the oil in a skillet. Add the onion and garlic and cook for 3–4 minutes. Stir in the eggplant, then add the tomatoes and sprinkle with the cumin seeds, allspice, and herbes de Provence. Season lightly with the salt, then cover and cook over low heat until the mixture is soft, about 40 minutes. Check from time to time and add extra water as necessary to get a moist consistency. Finally, mash the mixture so that you have a lumpy puree. (You can make this filling up to 1 day ahead if you like.)

3. To make the roll, preheat the oven to 400° F. Grease a jelly-roll pan and line it with baking parchment or waxed paper.

4. Melt the butter in a saucepan over low heat. Remove from the heat and stir in the flour until you have a smooth paste. Add the milk and return to low heat. Cook, stirring constantly, until the mixture thickens. Add the cheese and cayenne pepper. When the cheese has melted, add the egg yolks, one at a time, stirring to blend each into the mixture before adding the next. Set aside to cool to lukewarm.

5. Whisk the egg whites by hand or with an electric mixer until they are billowy. Gently fold together the whites and the reserved cheese sauce. When thoroughly blended, pour into the prepared jelly-roll pan and bake in the center of the oven for 15–20 minutes. The roll may puff up or

crack across the surface. Don't worry about this. To test for doneness, insert a knife blade into the center and if it comes out clean, the roll is ready.

6. Place a clean kitchen towel on your counter. Run a knife around the edge to loosen the roll from the pan, then invert onto the towel. Let stand for 1 minute to cool, then strip off the baking parchment. Keeping the towel in your hand, roll up quite tightly from the long side of the roll. The towel will be rolled into the roll as if it were the filling. (This makes it easier to roll the filled roll later on.) Let cool for 10–15 minutes, then unroll to free the towel. The roll will probably not lie flat.

7. Spread the eggplant mixture over the roll leaving a 1-inch border at the short sides and along the long side farthest from you. Roll up the roll starting with the long side closest to you. Be firm though not rough as you roll it. Cut off the edges to expose the spiral effect of the filled roulade. Place it on a narrow platter. Sprinkle the surface with the Parmesan cheese garnish with the tomatoes, and serve. This roulade keeps amazingly well. Wrap any leftovers in plastic wrap and store in the fridge for up to 2–3 days.

JANE MCWHORTER

Chicken & Leek Pie

Chicken pies used to be a staple of family cooking in New England, but many people no longer make them because of time constraints and pastry-making anxieties. The packaged frozen puff pastry used here makes life easier.

One 4-pound roasting chicken, with
  giblets removed
1 stalk celery, halved
2 medium carrots
1 bay leaf
8 sprigs fresh parsley
1 teaspoon salt

3 large leeks, coarse tops and outer leaves
  removed
3 tablespoons all-purpose flour
1 cup plus 2 tablespoons milk
Salt and black pepper to taste
One 17-ounce package frozen puff pastry
1 egg, beaten

1. Rinse the chicken and pat dry with paper towels. Put it into a large pot and cover with water. Add the celery, the 2 whole carrots, bay leaf, 4 sprigs of the parsley, and the 1 teaspoon salt. Bring to a simmer, skim off the scum that rises to the surface, cover, and simmer for 1 hour.

2. Remove the chicken from the pot and let it cool enough to handle, then remove and discard the skin. Cut the meat from the carcass, leaving the meat in fairly large chunks. Remove the carrots and set aside. Discard the celery, bay leaf, and parsley.

3. Cut the leeks lengthwise without cutting them in half and run cold water through the layers to remove any gritty bits. Cut the leeks into rounds and put them into a large saucepan. Skim the fat from 1 cup of the chicken broth and pour the broth over the leeks. Cover and simmer for 5 minutes.

4. Mix together the flour with ¼ cup of the milk in a small bowl. Gradually mix in ¾ cup of the remaining milk. Stir in a little of the hot liquid from the leeks, then add the flour mixture to the leeks, stirring gently until thick. Add the chicken pieces. Chop the remaining parsley and slice the reserved cooked carrots and add them to the leek mixture. Season to taste with the salt and black pepper. Set aside.

5. Preheat the oven to 400° F. Lightly grease a 2-inch deep pie plate. Have your pastry in 2 portions. Roll out 1 portion and cut three or four 2-inch strips. Arrange the strips so they cover the edge and overlap the rim of your pie plate.

6. Join the remaining pastry from the first portion to the second portion, then roll it out so you have a circle somewhat larger than the diameter of the plate. Fill the pie plate with the chicken and leek mixture. Mix together the remaining 2 tablespoons of the milk and the egg to make a wash and brush it on the pastry around the rim. Place the pastry circle on top. Press it to the rim to seal the pie.

7. Trim off any excess pastry. (If you like, you can cut the pastry scraps into leaves or other decorations — brush one side of the decoration with the egg wash and stick it on the pie, then brush the top of the pie with the egg wash.) Cut 4–5 vents in the pastry with a sharp knife. Place the pie on a baking tray in the center of the oven and bake for 10 minutes. Reduce the temperature to 350° and bake for 15 minutes more. Let the pie stand for 5–10 minutes before serving.

Vermont Cheddar & Potato Soup

Cheese soup made with the local Cheddar is a tradition in Vermont. This version starts with vegetables, so it is not as rich as recipes that call for lots of cheese and cream. For lunch, serve it with Anadama or another hearty bread; for serving before an entrée, offer it with oyster crackers. For a vegetarian meal, serve this soup with whole-wheat bread and a salad.

1 cup peeled and $1/2$-inch cubed potatoes
$1/2$ cup sliced carrots
$1/4$ cup chopped onion
1 stalk celery, thinly sliced
2 cups water
1 teaspoon salt
4 ounce (about 1 $1/2$ cups) grated extra sharp Vermont Cheddar
$1/4$ cup grated Parmesan cheese
1 teaspoon ground mustard, or tiny pinch cayenne pepper
1 $1/2$–2 cups milk
Salt and white pepper to taste
2 tablespoons finely chopped fresh parsley or snipped fresh chives

1. Put the potatoes, carrots, onion, celery, water, and the 1 teaspoon salt into a large saucepan. Cover and simmer for 15–20 minutes, or until the vegetables are tender.

2. In a food processor, process the vegetables and their liquid in batches or pass them through a sieve or a food mill. Return the mixture to the pan and add the Cheddar and Parmesan. If using the mustard, mix it to a thin paste with $1/4$ cup water and add it to the mixture; if using the cayenne pepper, simply stir it into the mixture. Stir 1 $1/2$ cups of the milk into the mixture.

3. Reheat, stirring frequently, to melt the cheese and mix everything together. Do not allow to boil. Add the remaining milk if you want a thinner soup and season to taste with the salt and black pepper. (You will probably not need much more salt as the cheese and cooking liquid already have some.) Pour the soup into serving bowls and garnish with the parsley or chives. Serve immediately.

For Vermont Cheddar & Potato Soup with Beer: *Use only 1 cup of water and 1 cup of milk. You will need a 12-ounce bottle of New England bitter ale or India Pale Ale (also called IPA). Cook the potato, carrot, celery, and onion in a saucepan with 1 cup of water and 1 cup of beer. Proceed as in the basic recipe until you have added the cheeses and mustard or cayenne. Now add the remaining beer and cook until the cheeses have melted. Thin the soup to the consistency you want with the milk and season to taste.*

The Cheeses of New England

In 1882, Winfield Crowley of Healdville, Vermont, built a cheese factory. His family had been making cheese in their kitchen since 1824, so the 30 x 30-foot factory, now a National Historic Place, was a major expansion. Today, Crowley is America's oldest continuously operated cheese producer, making 600 pounds of cheese a day from local hormone-free milk. Cheese makers thrive throughout New England, creating an array of artisanal cheeses. Here are some to look for:

Berkshire Blue (Great Barrington, Massachusetts) Michael Miller, who studied cheese making in England, works alone and by hand to make this delectable blue cheese that balances the tang of two blue molds and one white mold with the creamy flavors of unpasteurized Jersey milk.

Cabot (Cabot, Vermont) Compared to the giant cheese companies of Wisconsin, Cabot is the David that regularly takes the prize for the best Cheddar in America, and in 1998, won acclaim as the best Cheddar in the world. Compared to other New England cheese companies, however, Cabot is the Goliath, founded as a cooperative in 1919 and now employing 300 people making cheeses that can be found in every New England supermarket. Their extra-sharp Cheddar is superb, as are their other aged Cheddars. Among flavored cheeses, their Five Peppercorn is a prize-winner.

Calabro Cheese (East Haven, Connecticut) Founded by Joseph Calabro, a Sicilian immigrant who came to America in 1948, Calabro Cheese specializes in Italian-style cheeses. The main products are whole-milk ricotta, whey ricotta, and mozzarella. The company also makes smaller amounts of specialty Italian cheeses, including *fior di latte* mozzarella, which comes in balls ranging from cherry to grapefruit size.

Crowley (Healdville, Vermont) Long ago, U.S. government classifiers typified Crowley as a Colby cheese, but Colby is in Wisconsin, and the makers of Crowley insist that their creamy, fast-maturing cheese is from Vermont and properly called Crowley. Like many cheese makers, Crowley makes a smoked cheese. Their version is mild and especially delicious.

Fanny Mason Farmstead Cheese (Walpole, New Hampshire) Made from raw milk from Boggy Meadow Farm's holstein herd and vegetable rennet, Fanny Mason is a Swiss cheese with a creamy taste rarely achieved in supermarket Swiss. Good on its own, it grates easily and does not separate when used in cooked dishes.

Grafton Cheddar Cheese (Grafton, Vermont) Grafton Cheddar is a raw-milk cheese. Long aging creates a mellow balance of creaminess and sharpness.

Great Hill Blue (Marion, Massachusetts) Made by dairy farmer Tim Stone, Great Hill Blue is a well-veined, raw-milk blue cheese with sharp tang reminiscent of Danish Blue.

Smith's Country Cheese (Winchendon, Massachusetts) This Gouda-style cheese is made from milk produced by the cows of the Smith farm. It comes plain or flavored with caraway, sun-dried tomatoes, or cumin — a favorite in Holland, the homeland of Gouda.

Vermont Butter and Cheese Company (Websterville, Vermont) Working with chefs to produce the dairy foods needed in fine cooking, cheese maker and co-owner Allison Hooper, who trained in France, makes European-style cultured butter and an acclaimed range of goat's and cow's milk cheeses, including crème fraîche, mascarpone, quark, feta, chèvre, impastata, Fontina, chevrier, and Bonne Bouche, an ash-ripened goat cheese. Her Torta Fresca, made from mascarpone layered with either smoked salmon and leeks or with roasted pine nuts and basil, far exceeds any other flavored cheese.

Vermont Shepherd (Putney, Vermont) Trained in the French Pyrenees, cheese maker Cynthia Major developed Vermont Shepherd and Shepherd's Tomme with milk from ewes grazing summer pastures. Hints of clover and thyme infuse her prizewinning cheese. Several nearby farms now also make the cheese using her techniques, aging it in a cave on the Major farm and participating in a rigorous grading process. Cynthia Major also makes Timson, a soft cow's milk cheese named after a favorite hillside road.

Westfield Farms (Hubbardston, Massachusetts) Since the late 1970s, this farm has been making Capri, a fresh goat cheese. More recently, they have added Bluebonnet, a log-shaped blue goat cheese, and Hubbardston Blue Goat and Hubbardston Blue Cow, two blue Camembert-style cheeses. All have won awards in cheese shows.

Mushroom Lasagne

Some cultures are mushroom-gathering cultures, and others are just not. Russians, Poles, and Italians belong to the first, while all but a few New Englanders belong to the second — even though the woods of the region abound in edible species. Unfortunately, they also abound in poisonous types, so though this mushroom lasagne calls for porcini — *boletus edulis* — the mushroom most prized by mushroom hunters, don't risk disaster by picking your own. Specialty stores sell imported dried porcini from Italy or Poland. They look unprepossessing, but they add intense flavor when reconstituted in water. Even one or two porcini can highlight the most humdrum cultivated mushrooms. Try to choose dried porcini in large pieces from the cap rather than the scruffier bits of stem. Many people describe the flavor of porcini as "meaty." They certainly have a hearty taste that makes this lasagne a delight for both meat-eaters and vegetarians alike.

FILLING

¹/₃ cup dried porcini mushrooms
3 cups water
3–4 ounces shiitake mushrooms, washed and stems trimmed
10 ounces baby portabella or crimini mushrooms, washed and stems trimmed
1 medium onion, chopped
1 medium carrot, grated
Salt and black pepper
1 tablespoon cornstarch
2 tablespoons water

CHEESE SAUCE

1 tablespoon butter
2 tablespoons all-purpose flour
1 ³/₄ cups milk
4 ounces Fontina or Cheddar cheese, sliced or grated
¹/₃ cup finely grated Parmesan cheese
Salt and black pepper to taste
8 ounces uncooked no-boil lasagne

1. To make the filling, put the porcini and the 3 cups water in a bowl and let soak for 4 hours. Remove them from the liquid and chop. Put the chopped porcini in a large saucepan and strain the soaking liquid over them. Cover, bring to a simmer, and cook for 15–20 minutes or until tender.

2. Cut the shiitake and portabella mushrooms into thick slices or halve them if they are small. Add these mushrooms, the onion, and carrot to the pan of porcini and lightly season with the salt

and black pepper. Cover and cook for 5 minutes. Check the liquid. If it is scanty, add up to 1 cup water and continue cooking.

3. Mix together the cornstarch and the 2 tablespoons water in a small bowl. Stir in some hot liquid from the mushrooms, then stir the cornstarch mixture into the mushroom mixture. Taste and add more seasoning if necessary.

4. Preheat the oven to 400º F. Lightly grease a 9 x 13-inch lasagne pan.

5. To make the sauce, melt the butter in a medium saucepan. Off the heat, stir in the flour until the mixture is smooth, then stir in $1/2$ cup of the milk and return to the heat. Stir until the mixture thickens, then add the remaining milk and bring to a simmer. Stir in three-fourths of the Fontina and 2 tablespoons of the Parmesan. When the cheeses have blended, season to taste with the salt and black pepper. Remove from the heat.

6. To complete the dish, pour 1 cup of the mushroom mixture into the lasagne pan. Cover it with sheets of lasagne. Add the remaining mushroom mixture, spreading to cover the pasta. Scatter on the remaining Fontina. Place another layer of lasagne on top. Reheat the cheese sauce and pour it over the last layer of lasagne. Sprinkle with the remaining Parmesan.

7. Cover the pan with aluminum foil and bake near the top of the oven for 15 minutes. Reduce the temperature to 350º and bake for 30 minutes more, or until the lasagne feels tender when pierced with a knife blade. Remove the foil and bake for 5 minutes more, or until the top is lightly golden. Remove from the oven and let stand for 5 minutes before cutting into rectangles for serving. Serve hot. Serves 4–6.

JANE MCWHORTER

Sautéed Butternut Squash
with Peppers & Deviled Chestnuts

When the Native American word *askootasquash* was anglicized into "squash," it perhaps encouraged settlers to think that the vegetable should appear in a squashed sort of condition. In any case, New Englanders generally do just that, mashing squash into mounds or pureeing it for soups. Here butternut squash is cut into slices and sautéed, emerging from the pan firm and tender, a fine foil for the deviled chestnuts served on top. This chestnut recipe is adapted from Fannie Farmer's 1896 *The Boston Cooking-School Cookbook*. In her day, chestnut trees abounded in America, but they were all stricken by a blight that arrived with trees imported from the Far East. The chestnuts that appear in stores in late fall now come from Italy or Spain. But disease-resistant forms of native chestnuts are on the way back. Look for them in farmers' markets. Serve this as a main dish, omitting the bacon for vegetarians. Alternately, use it as a dramatic accompaniment to steak or pork chops.

1 butternut squash	*10–12 chestnuts, roasted, boiled, or*
1 tablespoon salt	*canned*
4 strips lean bacon (optional)	*1 tablespoon butter*
¼ cup all-purpose flour	*½ cup ¼-inch cut roasted red bell pepper*
2 teaspoons dried thyme	*Salt*
¼ cup vegetable oil	*Few drops Tabasco or hot sauce*

1. Cut off the bulbous end of the squash and discard or use for another recipe. Peel the straight neck of the squash and cut it into ½-inch slices. Sprinkle with the salt and let the slices stand for 20–30 minutes. Beads of moisture will appear on the surface. Dab them off with paper towels.

2. Broil the bacon and set aside. Mix together the flour and thyme in a bowl. Place the squash slices in the bowl, one at a time, to lightly dust.

3. Heat the oil in a large skillet over moderately high heat. Put the squash slices in a single layer and cook for 4 minutes. Check the underside. If it is golden with one or two brown patches, turn it over; if not, cook for 1–2 minutes more before turning. Cook for 7–10 minutes more, reducing the heat if necessary to prevent burning. The slices are ready when you can pierce them with a fork and the edges are perhaps a little brown.

4. While the squash is cooking, slice the chestnuts into 2–3 pieces if they are whole. Heat the butter over low heat in a small skillet. Toss in the chestnuts and bell pepper pieces and sauté for 1–2 minutes. Season lightly with the salt and stir in the Tabasco. Cut the reserved bacon into 1-inch pieces and add to the mixture.

5. For serving as a main dish, arrange 3 slices of the squash on each of 2 dinner plates and sprinkle with the chestnut mixture. For a side dish, arrange the squash in a single layer on a serving platter, scattering the chestnut mixture on top. Serves 2 as a main dish, 4–6 as a side dish.

Pumpkin-Peanut Soup

Many pumpkins live out their lives as decorations, but all of them, the large field pumpkins as well as the smaller sugar pumpkins, are edible. To prepare them, cut them into chunks, remove the seeds and stringy bits from the center, then bake in a 400° F oven for about 45 minutes, or until they are tender. At this point, they are easy to peel, then mash or puree in a food processor. Sugar pumpkins cooked this way excel in this unusual soup, but canned pumpkin (or squash) is fine, too. Using canned pumpkin, the soup can be made in less than 30 minutes, so it is worth keeping a couple of cans on hand.

1 tablespoon vegetable oil
1 clove garlic, chopped
1 large onion, chopped
2 teaspoons curry powder or to taste
1 teaspoon ground ginger or coriander
2 cups cooked or canned pumpkin
$^1/_4$ cup creamy peanut butter
3 cups water
Salt and black pepper to taste
1 cup milk
2 tablespoons chopped peanuts or chopped fresh cilantro

1. Heat the oil over low heat in a large pot. Add the garlic and onion and cook gently, stirring occasionally, for 3–4 minutes. Stir in the curry powder and ginger, then add the pumpkin and peanut butter. Add the water, salt, and black pepper. Stir well to mix in the peanut butter. Cover and simmer for 10 minutes, stirring occasionally.

2. Remove from the heat and stir in the milk. Let the soup cool a little, then process, in batches, in a food processor or blender.

3. Return the soup to the pot. Test for seasonings and thickness. Add more salt and black pepper if necessary. For a thinner soup, add more milk or water. (Generally, leftovers thicken considerably, so extra liquid is needed at reheating.) Serve topped with the chopped peanuts or chopped cilantro.

Ginger-Pumpkin Bread

Pumpkin quick bread is a fall favorite in New England. This version includes chunks of crystallized ginger.

4 ounces crystallized ginger
6 tablespoons butter at room temperature
$^1/_2$ cup firmly packed light brown sugar
2 eggs
1 cup cooked or canned pumpkin
1 tablespoon ground ginger
1 teaspoon ground cinnamon
$^1/_2$ cup all-purpose flour
1 tablespoon baking powder
$^1/_4$ teaspoon salt
$^1/_4$–$^1/_2$ cup milk

1. Preheat the oven to 375° F. Grease a 9 x 5-inch loaf pan. Cut the crystallized ginger into bits about the size of a pea. Set aside.

2. Cream the butter with the sugar in a large bowl. Beat in the eggs, one at a time, and when thoroughly blended, mix in the pumpkin, ground ginger, reserved crystallized ginger, and the cinnamon.

3. Mix together the flour, baking powder, and salt in a bowl, then add to the pumpkin mixture. Add enough milk to make a dough that is spreadable but not runny. (Generally, you will need less milk if using pumpkin you cooked yourself, more if using canned pumpkin.)

4. Put the mixture into the prepared pan and bake for 35–45 minutes, or until a tester inserted in the center comes out clean. Cool in the pan on a wire rack for 15–20 minutes, then remove from the pan and finish cooling before cutting.

Jerusalem Artichoke & Seafood Salad

Jerusalem artichokes have nothing to do with Jerusalem, and their only link to artichokes is a flavor resemblance. They are the underground tubers of *Helianthus tuberosus,* a sunflower that often grows 8 feet or more. The epithet Jerusalem comes from *girasole,* literally "turning to the sun" or sunflower. "Girasole" quickly became "Jerusalem" when the tubers arrived in England in the seventeenth century. Jerusalem artichoke soup is called also Palestine soup because the nineteenth-century English cooks who invented it assumed that the vegetable must be linked to the Holy Land. The Russians took a different tack, calling the tubers "earth pears" — possibly a reference to their texture. They are a perennial that tends both to take care of itself and to spread — worth planting if you like their taste and you are a gardener. Harvest them in October and November, after the late-blooming flowers have died and frost has struck the ground and brought out their sweetness. In *Jane Grigson's Vegetable Book,* the author suggests teaming them with prawns in a salad. This hint led to the recipe below, a useful dish for the first course of a dinner party and good also served on crostini or crackers.

1 pound Jerusalem artichokes
2 tablespoons fresh lemon juice
1/2 teaspoon lemon zest
1/2 pound fresh bay scallops
1/2 pound medium (51–60 per pound)
  fresh shrimp, cooked

1 medium carrot
Salt and white pepper to taste
1 tablespoon coarsely chopped fresh parsley
1 tablespoon snipped fresh chives
1/2 teaspoon dried thyme
1/2 cup mayonnaise

1. Wash the artichokes and scrape off the peel. Cut off and discard any tiny knobs, which are a nuisance, but peel larger ones. Cut into $1/2$-inch slices. Drop the slices into a saucepan of boiling salted water and cook for 7–8 minutes or until just tender. (Do not let them get mushy, which they readily do if you don't keep an eye on them.) Drain in a colander, put them into a bowl, and toss with the lemon juice and zest. If any pieces are larger than bite-sized, cut them up.

2. Spray a nonstick skillet with cooking spray, heat, then add the scallops in a single layer. Cook, turning once, until they are opaque, about 4 minutes. Add the scallops to the artichokes.

3. Select 8–10 nice looking shrimp and set aside for garnish. Remove the tails from the remaining shrimp and cut the shrimp into pea-sized bits. Add the bits to the artichoke mixture.

4. Using a swivel-blade peeler, cut the carrot into ribbons. Then cut across these so you have flat bits about $3/4$ inch long. (Alternately grate the carrot on a coarse grater.) Add to the artichoke mixture.

5. Season the mixture with the salt and white pepper. Stir in the parsley, chives, and thyme. Add $1/4$ cup of the mayonnaise and toss gently, then add the remaining mayonnaise and toss gently again. Serve on a bed of lettuce or mesclun or on crostini or crackers, garnished with the remaining shrimp and extra herbs. Serves 4 as a main dish with other salads, more if served as an hors d'oeuvre.

Apple Crisp

Some apple crisp recipes call for oats; some don't. But oats add flavor and the crunchiness implied in the word "crisp," so oatey crisps such as this one are surely the best.

6 Northern Spy, Cortland, or Delicious apples, peeled, cored, and sliced
$^1/_3$ cup granulated sugar
$^1/_2$ cup all-purpose flour
1 stick (4 ounces) butter
$^1/_2$ cup firmly packed brown sugar
1 cup rolled oats
1 teaspoon ground cinnamon

1. Preheat the oven to 350° F. Grease a baking dish.
2. Put the apple slices into the prepared dish and sprinkle the granulated sugar on them.
3. Put the flour into a bowl. Cut the butter into several bits and rub them into the flour until the flour mixture looks like coarse crumbs. Stir in the brown sugar, oats, and cinnamon. Rub the mixture a little more with your fingers to make sure that everything is combined.
4. Sprinkle the mixture over the apple slices and bake in the center of the oven for 20 minutes, or until the top is golden and aromatic and the apples are soft. Serve warm.

APPLES, BOYS, AND THE PUBLIC DEBT

Amelia Simmons's American Cookery, *the first book written specifically for American rather than English cooks, begins with a chapter on fruits and vegetables, likely added by someone else. Scholars have not identified the writer, but clearly it was someone who placed a lot of faith in apples:*

"Apples . . . are highly useful in families, and ought to be more universally cultivated, excepting in the compactest cities. There is not a single family but might set a tree in some otherwise useless spot, which might serve the two fold use of shade and fruit; on which 12 or 14 fruit trees might easily be engrafted, and essentially preserve the orchard from the intrusions of boys, &c. which is too common in America. If the boy who thus planted a tree, and guarded and protected it in a useless corner, and carefully engrafted different fruits, was to be indulged free access into orchards, whilst the neglectful boy was prohibited — how many millions of fruit trees were to spring into growth — and what a saving to the union. The net saving would in time extinguish the public debt, and enrich our cookery."

Apple Butter

Apple butter is the easiest preserve to make: there's no peeling and no chance of it not setting because apple skins and cores have lots of pectin — the fruit product that makes preserves gel. Watch and stir as it boils, though — it can stick to the pan if you are not eagle-eyed.

3 pounds McIntosh or other apples
$^1/_2$ cup water
2 cups granulated sugar
$^3/_4$ teaspoon ground cinnamon
$^1/_2$ teaspoon ground allspice
$^1/_4$ teaspoon ground nutmeg or mace

1. After thoroughly washing the apples, break off any stems. Chop each unpeeled apple into 6–8 pieces and put the apples and water into a large pot. Cover and cook over gentle heat, stirring occasionally, for 20–30 minutes or until completely tender.

2. Press the apples, in batches, through a sieve into a bowl, discarding the peels and cores as you go. Returned the sieved apples to the rinsed out pot and stir in the sugar. Bring to a boil, stirring frequently to prevent sticking.

3. After 5 minutes, stir in the cinnamon, allspice, and nutmeg. When the apple mixture looks shiny, mounds on a spoon, and falls off in a flake-shaped dollop rather than drops, it is ready.

4. Pour the apple butter into jars sterilized by having been boiled for 10 minutes. Store in the fridge or eat within 2 weeks. Apple butter does not last as well as jam because proportionately it has less sugar. Serve with toast or popovers, or use as a sauce with ham. Makes about 4 half-pint jars.

A. BLAKE GARDNER

Salad of Massachusetts
Blue Cheese with Roasted Pears & Walnuts

Several cheese makers in Massachusetts make blue cheese. Try this salad with Berkshire Blue from the mountains of the west, Hubbardston Blue Cow or Blue Goat from the hills of Central Massachusetts, or Great Hill Blue from the coast of Buzzard's Bay in the southeast. As for pears, many apple orchards also have a few pear trees. Look for Bartlett pears in September and Boscs in late September and early October. Choose ripe pears that require little cooking. A few orchards also make their own cider vinegar. If you can find it, use it in the dressing. Quantities can be varied to suit your taste and convenience in this recipe. If you add more cheese and walnuts, you have an excellent no-meat lunch or main dish.

DRESSING
2 tablespoons vegetable oil
1 tablespoon cider vinegar
$^1/_4$ teaspoon Dijon mustard

SALAD
1–2 tablespoons butter
3 large ripe Bartlett or Bosc pears, peeled and cored
6 cups washed and dried mesclun or other salad greens
Bunch fresh watercress, washed and dried
Salt to taste
4 ounces Massachusetts blue cheese, crumbled
$^1/_2$ cup chopped walnuts

1. To make the dressing, whisk together the oil, vinegar, and mustard. Set aside.

2. To make the salad, melt the butter in a skillet, then remove from the heat. Slice each pear into 8 wedges and quickly, before they have a chance to brown, toss them in the melted butter. Return the skillet to moderately high heat and sauté the pears for 3–4 minutes, or until they are golden and tender, but not soft or mushy.

3. Mix together the mesclun and watercress. Toss the mixture with the reserved dressing and season with the salt. Divide among 4 salad plates. Arrange some pear slices on top. Scatter the cheese on the pears and sprinkle each serving with some walnuts.

CHAPTER 9

WINE, BEER & CIDER
IN NEW ENGLAND

The English who came to New England in the seventeenth century drank beer as their all-purpose beverage. Even children had beer; it was more nutritious and safer than water, which was often polluted.

As gentlemen, the settlers were also accustomed to drinking wine, and they certainly had wine at the first Thanksgiving in 1621. Undoubtedly, they looked forward to making their own. Vines grew in plenty on the northeastern coast of North America, as the Vikings had noted 600 years previously, naming the land Vinland to mark this striking bounty. But as would-be winemakers discovered, American labrusca and muscadine grapes produce wine that enologists describe as "foxy": having an aroma like animal fur rather than the berry or flower fragrances of wines made from European vinifera grapes. The solution was to grow vinifera vines in New England, but seventeenth-century attempts to do this failed. New England's winters were one problem; its pests were another. Only recently have New Englanders worked their way around these

difficulties and established wineries growing vinifera grapes in Connecticut, Rhode Island, and Massachusetts.

The early settlers also encountered problems making beer. English beer is made from barley. When soaked in water, it germinates; it is then heated and dried to stop growth, thus becoming malt. The work is specialized, and both commercial and home brewers had to buy malt from maltsters. Its value was such that early students at Harvard could pay for their board with malt. Then, too, brewing was chancy. Even professional brewers knew little of the chemistry of the process until the nineteenth century, so brews could go seriously wrong. All this raised the price of beer.

What, then, were the other options? Beer from the plentiful corn and pumpkins of the New World was unsatisfactory, though spruce beer gained some popularity. Tea and coffee did not arrive until the end of the seventeenth century and were costly. Fortunately, by the mid-seventeenth century, English apple trees had found a good home in America. Most varieties were acid: not good for eating but ideal for cider, which became the staple drink of New England. Cider is easy to make, requiring no more than crushing the juice out of apples and allowing the natural yeasts on the skins to start fermentation.

By 1657, New Englanders were also making rum. Eventually, even tiny Nantucket had a distillery and Newport, Rhode Island, had thirty-nine distilleries. The raw material was molasses brought from the Caribbean islands in the ships that took New England's salt cod to feed the slaves on the plantations. By the eighteenth century, rum was both cheap and popular. British taxes on the raw materials were one of the complaints that fueled the Revolution, so it is fitting that Paul Revere is credited with drinking Medford rum before galloping off to warn of the arrival of British troops in 1775.

With so much rum, hard cider, and beer flowing around, drunkenness was a problem, and nineteenth-century New Englanders, especially women, helped lead the temperance movement that culminated in Prohibition. Since its repeal in 1933, cider has mostly been sold in its nonalcoholic form, though some orchards produce both hard cider, which has less than seven percent alcohol, and apple wine, which has more.

As for beer, national brands of German-style beers dominated New England until legal changes in the 1970s permitted brewpubs. Like seventeenth-century taverns, they are allowed to make beer for drinking on the premises only. Microbreweries, making relatively small batches of beer and distributing it locally, appeared at the same time. Now, New England produces a wide variety of British-style beers, ales, and porters, probably closer in style to the beers that the settlers tried to make than the thin brews produced by the giant breweries. Indeed, many microbreweries highlight their

local and historical origins with names such as Smuttynose, Paper City, Buzzard's Bay, and Wachusetts.

As well as dozens of breweries making excellent beer, New England also has about fifteen wineries producing wines from vinifera grapes. Today's growers have succeeded where their ancestors failed because they understand that American vines don't succumb to the native phylloxera louse, whereas European vinifera vines do. To benefit from the vinifera flavors, wineries in both America and Europe now graft European grape varieties onto American rootstocks. As for dealing with the icy New England winters, growers plant cold-resistant grape varieties. Then, too, many wineries are near the sea, which ameliorates the climate. It also draws visitors. With tastings, fairs, musical events, and cooking classes, most wineries are also tourist destinations. For example, Connecticut and Rhode Island have wine trails to guide people from winery to winery.

With winemaking still new to New England, one would guess that there would be few, if any, traditional recipes calling for wine. But old cookbooks tell a different story. In her *American Cookery,* published in Hartford in 1796, Amelia Simmons calls for wine in trifle, syllabub, and mincemeat recipes. She also specifies claret in a beef dish and Madeira in her turtle recipe. Lydia Maria Child also calls for claret with beef in her 1833 book *American Frugal Housewife.* Child, like most cookbook authors, included a section of recipes for invalids, among them wine whey made by separating milk with wine in which rennet had been steeped. The thin wine-and-whey mix was then served to the sick. This wide use of wine indicates its easy availability.

Conversely, we might expect that local drinks would feature often in recipes. Cider certainly appears. Simmons sometimes suggests "rich sweet cider" as an alternative to wine, for example, while nineteenth-century cookbooks had recipes for cider pies and cakes. But beer, "a good family drink," according to Lydia Maria Child, rarely appears except in recipes for Welsh rarebit. Rum, a dessert flavoring in France, is virtually ignored, though frugal Mrs. Child suggested soaking rye in rum and grinding the result to make fake coffee. She also washed her hair in rum and used it in a mixture for cleaning brass — evidence of its lowly place in the hierarchy of drinks. Fannie Merritt Farmer, writing in the 1890s and more influenced by French cooking than earlier writers, gives a lone rum recipe — for a sweet sauce.

All drinks add instant flavor to food, while the acids in wine and cider act as tenderizers. Thus, added to their other charms, they are useful ingredients in the kitchen.

NOVA DEVELOPMENT

Peaches in Red Wine

New England's peaches are at their best in August and early September, when the weather is far too hot for making baked desserts. Chilled peaches in wine are just the thing. Red wine may seem overpowering, but it works well in this recipe.

4 medium-large ripe peaches
Boiling water
3 tablespoons red raspberry jelly
1 cup red wine
4 sprigs fresh mint

1. Make a cut in the skin of each peach. Put the peaches in a large bowl and pour the boiling water over them. Let stand for 1 minute, then carefully remove them one at a time and strip off the skin starting with the cuts. Slice the peaches, then halve the slices if necessary to produce bite-sized pieces. Put them into a bowl and set aside.

2. Put the jelly into a small saucepan over low heat and add $^1/_4$ cup of the wine. Stir until the jelly has melted. Pour the mixture over the reserved peaches and toss gently so all are moistened.

3. Transfer the peaches to 4 sherbet glasses or wineglasses. Pour any remaining jelly mixture over them. Divide the remaining wine among the 4 servings. Place the glasses in the fridge for at least 1 hour or up to 4 hours. Garnish with the mint sprigs and serve.

MORE RECIPES CALLING FOR WINE:

Grilled Shiitakes (see page 44)
Lobster & Cucumber Risotto (see page 54)
Monkfish in Red Peppers with Pernod Mayonnaise (see page 62)
Duck Breasts with Blueberry-Lavender Sauce (see page 84)
Beef Alamode (see page 176)
Partridge with a Pear Sauté (see page 211)
Winter Compote of Dried Fruits with Port (see page 215)

Pears with Beauty Spots

Like beauty spots, the allspice berries dramatize the pale pears and golden syrup of this dessert. Of course, they add their mild spicy flavor, too.

2 cups New England riesling wine
10 allspice berries
$^1\!/_2$ cup granulated sugar
5 large ripe Bartlett or Bosc pears, peeled and cored

1. Mix together the wine, allspice berries, and sugar in a large saucepan. Bring to a simmer, then remove from the heat.

2. Slice each pear into 8 wedges. Drop the wedges into the wine mixture as you work so they don't turn brown. Return to the heat and simmer gently until the pears are cooked, about 3–10 minutes depending on ripeness.

3. Remove the wedges from the liquid and put into a shallow glass serving dish. Boil the liquid until you have only 1 $^1\!/_2$ cups. Pour this liquid over the pears. Serve at room temperature. Be sure to include some allspice berries when you pour the syrup on the pears. They add a little drama to this simple dish, and they can easily be set aside on the edge of the plate.

VINIFERA GRAPES IN NEW ENGLAND

Faced with the unpleasant taste of the labrusca grapes native to New England, growers created many hybrid varieties teaming European grapes with American stock. Among the earliest are the American-French hybrids of labrusca and vinifera grapes, which produced grapes such as Concord, Catawba, and Niagara. Later, French-American hybrids created the seyval blanc, vidal blanc, chancellor noir, and Maréchal Foch varieties. These eliminated the foxy taste of the labrusca grapes, and many good wines, such as Rhode Island's Sakonnet Vineyards' outstanding seyval blanc, are now made from them.

Still, the classic vinifera grapes hold pride of place in the wine world, and as diseases have been controlled over the last thirty years, Riesling and pinot noir, both of which ripen quickly and tolerate cooler weather, have thrived. Today, Connecticut's Haight Vineyards and Hopkins Vineyard produce excellent Rieslings, as does Westport Rivers Vineyard & Winery in Massachusetts.

More recently, geometric analysis of the orientation of vineyards to the sun has shown that planting vines in north-south rows on double trellises and thinning the leaf canopy increases the photosynthesis needed to ripen vinifera grapes, such as cabernet sauvignon, cabernet franc, merlot, and chardonnay, which have not traditionally fared well in New England's relatively short summers. Connecticut wines, such as Chamard Vineyards' Cabernet Franc and Estate Chardonnay and Stonington Vineyards' Chardonnay show that these sun-loving grapes can produce delicious wine, even in New England's climate. In total, New England now makes reliably good wine from about twenty vinifera and French-American hybrid grape types.

Baked Pork Loin with Juniper & Herbs

You must use juniper and bay to give this pork loin its unique flavor. You need plenty of herbs, too, but the amount and choice of these depend on your taste or what you have available. The meat is delicious served hot with mashed potatoes and other vegetables. You may like it even better cold, thinly sliced and served on sandwiches or on a buffet. To serve a crowd, simply buy a bigger piece of pork and adjust the seasonings proportionately, always remembering that moderation in the use of herbs is not what's called for here.

3 cloves garlic
2 whole cloves, chopped
6 small bay leaves, or 3 large bay leaves, halved
6 leaves fresh sage
4 sprigs fresh thyme
12 juniper berries
2 ¹/₂–3-pound piece boneless pork loin
1 cup New England white or red wine
Salt and granulated sugar to taste

1. Choose a baking dish into which the loin will fit with about 1-inch space all around. Peel the garlic and chop only 2 of the garlic cloves. Sprinkle the chopped garlic and cloves on the dish. Add 4 small bay leaves or bay leaf halves, 4 sage leaves, 3 thyme sprigs, and 3 juniper berries, arranging them so they are not all in one spot.

2. Make some tiny incisions in the pork. Cut the remaining garlic clove into thin slivers and stick them in some of the incisions. Put the remaining juniper berries into the other incisions. Place the pork on top of the herbs in the dish and pour the wine over the pork. Cover and keep in the fridge for at least 2 hours or up to 8 hours. Turn the pork three or four times while it is in the marinade, rearranging the herbs as necessary to flavor all parts of the meat.

3. Preheat the oven to 400° F. Remove any herb bits sticking to the top surface of the pork, pat dry, and sprinkle with the salt. Return the pork to the marinade, cover, and bake for 20 minutes. Baste with the marinade and reduce the temperature to 325°. Cover tightly again and cook for 40–45 minutes more.

4. Remove from the oven and let the pork stand for 10 minutes. Strain the liquid in the baking dish into a saucepan and bring to a boil. Boil rapidly for 5 minutes, then taste. Add more salt if necessary. You may also find that 1 teaspoon sugar brings out the flavors.

5. Slice the pork and pour some of the juices over the slices. Garnish with the remaining bay leaves, sage, and thyme. Serve the remaining juices with the pork. Serves 6.

Roast Venison with Cranberries

Today, the venison served in restaurants and much of that cooked at home, comes from farm-raised animals. Nonetheless, it comes to the table trailing the glory of the hunt, raising thoughts of chases through the forest, of woodsmen returning home rich with a store of meat.

One 2 ¹/₂ – 3-pound piece venison leg
¹/₂ teaspoon juniper berries
3 cloves garlic, peeled
¹/₂ teaspoon dried thyme
Several grinds black pepper
2 bay leaves
1 medium onion, sliced

2 cups New England Maréchal Foch or
  pinot noir
¹/₂ cup dried cranberries
Salt and black pepper
3 tablespoons vegetable oil
1 tablespoon all-purpose flour
2 teaspoons butter at room temperature
2 tablespoons cranberry jelly

1. With the point of a sharp knife, make 6–8 incisions, each about ¹/₂ inch deep, spaced over each side of the venison. Set aside 4 juniper berries. Crush together the remaining juniper berries and 2 of the garlic cloves in a small bowl. Mix in the thyme and grind on some black pepper. Push a little of this mixture into the incisions. If you have some mixture left, make an extra incision or two and use it up.

2. Put the bay leaves and half of the onion slices into a baking dish big enough for the venison to fit with a little room to spare. Place the venison on top, then scatter the remaining onion slices over and around it. Make a marinade by coarsely chopping the remaining garlic clove and the reserved juniper berries, then add them to the wine. Stir in the cranberries and pour the marinade over the venison. Let stand for 1 hour in the fridge, then turn it over. Repeat this procedure at least two more times so the venison marinates for at least 3 hours (marinating for 2 hours more is even better).

3. Preheat the oven to 375° F. Remove the venison from the baking dish, pat dry, and season with the salt and black pepper. Heat the oil over moderate heat in a roasting pan. Put the venison into the pan and brown on all sides for 6–8 minutes. Strain ¹/₂ cup of the marinade over the venison, then cover and transfer to the oven. Roast for 40–50 minutes, basting several times with the pan juices. Remove from the pan, place on a serving platter, and cover with tented aluminum foil. Set aside in a warm place.

4. While the venison is cooking, strain the remaining marinade into a small saucepan. Include 2 tablespoons of the cranberries from the marinade and simmer for 10 minutes. Set aside. Mix together the flour and butter into a paste.

5. When you take the venison from the pan, put the pan with all its juices over low heat. Stir in one-fourth of the flour-butter paste. When it has dissolved, add one-fourth more. Proceed this way until all of the paste is used. Stir in the jelly, then the reserved, strained marinade. Season to taste with more salt and black pepper. Boil vigorously for 5 minutes to reduce and thicken the sauce.

6. Serve the venison in slices cut across the grain. Pour some of the sauce over the meat and serve the remaining sauce on the side.

Welsh Rarebit

Welsh rarebit, sometimes called Welsh rabbit, has been appearing in New England cookbooks since at least 1832, when Mrs. N. K. M. Lee anonymously published an alphabetical list of recipes called *The Cook's Own Book: Being a Complete Culinary Encyclopedia.* The recipe, which comes in various forms, originated in Wales, which has been known for its cheese and toast dishes since at least Shakespeare's time.

1 teaspoon butter
8 ounces extra-sharp Vermont Cheddar cheese, sliced or grated
1 teaspoon prepared English or Chinese mustard, or pinch cayenne pepper
$^1\!/_2$ cup pale ale
2 eggs, lightly beaten
4 – 8 slices buttered toast (depending on size)

1. Melt the butter over low heat in a medium saucepan. Add the cheese and heat until the cheese is melted, about 3 – 4 minutes.

2. Stir in the mustard, then stir in the ale. Increase the heat and simmer, stirring constantly, for 2 minutes.

3. Remove from the heat and stir in the eggs. Return to the heat and cook, stirring constantly, until the mixture is thick. Place the toast on plates, pour the rarebit over the toast, and serve immediately.

Broiled Chicken Legs

The beer marinade in this recipe is easy and effective. Try it with pork chops and spareribs as well as chicken.

2 tablespoons tomato paste
One 12-ounce bottle pale ale
1 small onion, chopped
1 clove garlic, chopped
1 teaspoon dried thyme
1 tablespoon granulated sugar
4 chicken legs
Salt

1. For the marinade, mix together the tomato paste, ale, onion, garlic, thyme, and sugar in a small bowl.

2. Put the chicken legs into a shallow bowl and pour the marinade over the chicken. Let stand, turning occasionally, for 3–4 hours in the fridge. (If you want to get a head start, you can marinate the chicken overnight in the fridge.)

3. Preheat the oven to 425° F. Remove the chicken legs from the marinade and season with the salt. Put them in a shallow baking pan. Put the marinade into a small saucepan, bring to a boil, and cook for 2–3 minutes.

4. Pour half of the hot marinade over the chicken. Place the chicken toward the top of the oven and bake for 25 minutes, basting two times with the marinade. Remove the chicken legs from the oven.

5. Turn on the broiler and place an oven rack under it. Baste the chicken with more marinade, then place the chicken under the broiler and broil for 5–7 minutes, or until the skin is brown and crusty. Brush the chicken with the marinade once or twice while broiling. Serve with potatoes or a rice dish and with any leftover marinade, boiled once again.

For outdoor grilling: *Cut the chicken legs in half (or use 8 chicken thighs). Broil over hot coals, basting liberally with the marinade for 20 minutes, or until the juice that exudes when you pierce the thickest part with a skewer is clear, not pink.*

Stout Beef Stew

This simple recipe can be varied by using different kinds of beer. Pale ale gives a lighter flavor. Another variation is to replace one or two of the carrots with rutabaga or sweet potato chunks.

¹/₄ cup all-purpose flour
Salt and black pepper
2 teaspoons dried thyme or oregano
1 ¹/₄ pounds beef, cut into cubes
2–3 tablespoons vegetable oil
1 large onion, chopped
1 clove garlic, chopped
One 12-ounce bottle stout, porter, or other dark beer
1 bay leaf
1 pound carrots, cut into 1-inch pieces
1–2 tablespoons brown sugar

1. Mix together the flour, a seasoning of the salt and black pepper, and thyme in a bowl. Add the beef cubes, a few at a time, and lightly coat with the flour mixture.

2. Heat the oil in a large pot. Add the beef cubes and sauté for 5 minutes, or until they are browned. Add the onion and garlic and cook for 2–3 minutes or until slightly softened. Pour in the beer, stirring to blend in any crusty bits from the bottom of the pot. Add the bay leaf, bring to a simmer, and cook for 1–2 hours, or until the beef is tender.

3. Add the carrots and 1 tablespoon of the sugar and simmer for 30 minutes more, or until the carrots are tender. Taste and add the remaining sugar if you want to soften the flavor of the gravy. Add more salt and black pepper if needed. Serve hot with baked or mashed potatoes.

Cider-Baked Winter Vegetables

Exact amounts of each vegetable do not matter much in this recipe; the important thing is to have a variety and to bake them with apples and cider. This brightly colored dish looks and tastes good with any meat dish and with quiches and other savory pies, too.

1 pound baby carrots or larger carrots, cut into pieces
1/2 small rutabaga, cut into chunks
4 medium parsnips, peeled and cut into large pieces
2 large sweet potatoes, peeled and cut into chunks
1 1/2 teaspoons salt
2 large Cortland or Delicious apples, peeled, cored, and sliced
2 tablespoons vegetable oil
1 large onion, coarsely chopped
2 cloves garlic
1 cup cider
1 teaspoon dried thyme or winter savory

1. Preheat the oven to 375° F. Grease a large shallow baking dish.

2. Put the carrots and rutabaga into a saucepan. Put the parsnips into another pan and the sweet potatoes into a third pan. Cover all of the vegetables with cold water, add 1/2 teaspoon of the salt to each pan and bring to a boil. Cook until the vegetables are just beginning to get tender, though not yet cooked through, about 8–10 minutes for the carrots and rutabaga and about 7–8 minutes for the parsnips and sweet potatoes. Drain in a colander and put the vegetables into the prepared dish. Add the sliced apples.

3. While the vegetables are cooking, heat the oil in a large skillet. Add the onion and garlic and cook for 3–4 minutes, or until they have softened. Pour in the cider, add the thyme, and bring to a boil. Pour the onion mixture over the vegetables. Cover and bake for 20 minutes, or until the vegetables are tender. Serves 6–8.

MORE GREAT RECIPES WITH BEER OR CIDER:
Baked Ham with Cider Sauce (see page 37)
Chicken with Corn (see page 96)
Vermont Cheddar & Potato Soup with Beer (see page 124)

Cider Shortcake

Ingredients for this homey sticky-topped cake are usually on hand. It is good for dessert, and leftovers go down well at breakfast.

CAKE

¹/₂ cup cold butter
2 cups all-purpose flour
1 tablespoon baking powder
¹/₂ cup granulated sugar
1 egg
¹/₂ cup cider
1 Cortland or Delicious apple, peeled,
  cored, and thinly sliced

TOPPING

¹/₂ cup cider
³/₄ cup firmly packed brown sugar
3 whole cloves

1. Preheat the oven to 350° F. Grease an 8-inch cake pan or pie plate.

2. To make the cake, cut the butter into several bits. Mix together the flour and baking powder in a bowl. Rub the butter into the flour mixture until the mixture looks like coarse crumbs. Stir in the sugar and make a well in the center of the mixture. Break the egg into the well, then pour in the cider. Stir quickly to make a very soft dough.

3. Divide the dough into 2 equal portions. Flour your hands and pat one portion into the prepared pan. Set aside 6–8 nicely shaped apple slices. Scatter the remaining slices evenly over the dough in the pan. Flour your hands again and pat the second dough portion on top. (It will probably look raggedy, but it will sort itself out in the baking.) Place the reserved apple slices in a pattern on top and bake for 25–35 minutes, or until golden and a toothpick inserted in the center comes out clean.

4. To make the topping, mix together the cider, ¹/₂ cup of the sugar, and the cloves in a small saucepan. Bring to a boil and boil for 5 minutes. By this time, the mixture will be syrupy. Fish out the cloves.

5. As soon as you take the cake from the oven, sprinkle 1 ¹/₂ tablespoons of the remaining sugar over the top. Trickle on one-third of the cider syrup, using the back of a spoon to spread it over the cake somewhat. Repeat this 4–5 minutes later with another 1 ¹/₂ tablespoons of the remaining sugar and one-third more of the syrup. Repeat this step once more with the remaining sugar and syrup. Let stand for 15–20 minutes. Serve the cake slightly warm. Apple butter is a good accompaniment.

CHAPTER 10

THANKSGIVING

The hundred or so Puritans who struggled off the Mayflower and onto the dry land of what was to become Plymouth, Massachusetts, in December 1620 probably gave heartfelt thanks for their deliverance from four months on the North Atlantic. But they had yet to survive the rigors of a winter harsher than they had known in England and the mistake of planting their crops too early, dooming them to freezing nights and therefore failure.

Fortunately, a second planting was possible, so when they had gathered in the harvest, the settlers who had not succumbed to illness followed their English custom of relaxing from their labors with a harvest feast. Chief Massasoit's Wampanoags, who celebrated each harvest of the year with its own festival, celebrated with them, bringing five deer as a contribution to the meal. The Puritans must have been thrilled. They did not have the wherewithal to hunt deer for themselves because they had come from the Old World, where venison was the perquisite of the aristocracy: an extraordinary luxury. Very likely, the venison was the highlight of their feast.

Back in England, large birds, such as geese, herons, and swans — even peacocks — were traditional festive foods on the holiday tables of the great. They were also used to eating turkeys, which had been introduced to Europe by the Spanish, who brought them from Mexico. There was no shortage of these and other festive birds at the first Thanksgiving because in the fall, flocks of geese, duck, and other wildfowl fly over New England's coast on their way to warmer wintering spots. This phenomenon was not lost on the settlers. One of the two records of the first Thanksgiving, a letter written by Edward Winslow, notes that "Our harvest being gotten in, our governor sent four men on fowling. . . . They four in one day killed as much fowl as with a little help served the company almost a week." Governor William Bradford, who penned the other account of the foods of the first Thanksgiving, noted that "besides waterfowl, there was a great store of wild turkeys."

Turkeys are probably one of the few foods that appeared both then and now. Corn, beans, cranberries, and squash were likely others, but there were no potatoes, bell peppers, or tomatoes — all American crops, but not native to New England. Pumpkins may have been served, but probably not in pie form. There were no apple pies either because apples did not grow in America until settlers brought them later in the seventeenth century. Mincemeat pies were a possibility since the English had long confected meats with dried fruits, spices, and alcohol as a holiday preserve. They could have made cheese, too, using milk from their cows and goats.

Bustle is the other thing shared by the seventeenth-century and twenty-first-century Thanksgivings. While the fowlers dispatched by Governor Bradford were at work, men must have been catching the cod, eel, and bass known to have been served at the feast, and women would have scurried to draw water, tend fires, and prepare grains and vegetables for the big event; it lasted for days, so there was much to do. With all this, the atmosphere at Plymouth in 1621 may well have been less frenetic than today because no one had to fly or drive great distances to get together, nor, settled so far from in-laws, did they have to negotiate which side of the family to visit.

President Lincoln declared Thanksgiving a national holiday in 1863 and fixed the date as the last Thursday in November. But it had long been a New England tradition: "the great puritan holyday" according to Emily Dickinson's brother, Austin, proclaimed each year by the governors of the states and therefore falling on different days. Marriages then were often celebrated at home, and Thanksgiving was a favorite time for weddings because the family was already gathered and in the mood for festivity.

Having a good time with family and close friends lights up Thanksgiving, while the traditional foods infuse it with memories of all the Thanksgivings we have ever known — and

of that first one eaten on the edge of a vast continent. There must be turkey, cranberries, and corn. There must be lots of vegetable dishes, preferably featuring vegetables native to America. There must be pies. Something a little different is often welcome; radical inventions rarely so.

With all of this to think of, ease of preparation is crucial — and it is traditional. Those first Thanksgiving cooks had the barest of equipment and probably boiled most things they ate, including the turkeys, which were toughened by lives of foraging at the forest edge and in the cornfields. Today's cooks have the technology to produce more elaborate dishes, but it is best used to spread the burden of cooking over a longer period. Good mincemeat needs time to mature, so it should be made weeks, preferably months, before. Cranberry sauce and pastry for pies can be made days ahead and stored in the refrigerator. The fourth Thursday in November is late for fresh vegetables in New England, so Thanksgiving is a good time for frozen or canned varieties; often they taste better than vegetables trucked in from distant places. The pies can be cooked a day or two before and stored in a cool pantry or on the back porch.

The goal is to rejoice in the success of the year's work, not to exhaust yourself with more hustle and bustle.

Oyster Stew

Oysters appeared in many forms on the tables of nineteenth-century New England. They were served scalloped or fried, made into a chowder or stew, or even tucked into the stuffing for the Thanksgiving turkey. Avid harvesting of the native oyster beds made oysters a luxury, but oyster stew survives as one of the traditional ways to begin Thanksgiving dinner. Fresh oysters make the best oyster stew, but shucking them is time-consuming. Canned oysters are a good second choice and also taste good. Keep portions small; oyster stew is rich.

2 dozen fresh oysters, or two 8-ounce cans oysters
1 cup milk
1 ¹/₂ cups heavy cream
Salt and white pepper
1–2 tablespoons butter (optional)
1 tablespoon finely chopped fresh parsley, or ³/₄ teaspoon dried fines herbes
Oyster crackers

1. If you are using fresh oysters, line a sieve with a coffee filter and place it over a saucepan. Shuck the oysters over the saucepan, letting their juice — a crucial ingredient — drip through the filter, which traps bits of shell and sand. (You could do this a couple of hours ahead of the meal, adding the oysters to the strained liquid and keeping the pan covered in the fridge until a few minutes before serving time.)

2. About 10 minutes before serving time, put the pan with the oysters and oyster liquid over medium heat and bring to a simmer. Simmer (don't boil) for 2–3 minutes, or until the oysters are slightly opaque and creamy beige.

3. Remove the oysters from the liquid. Add the milk and cream and boil briskly for 3–4 minutes or until slightly thickened. Season lightly with the salt and white pepper. Before serving, return the oysters to the pan, add the butter if you are using it, and simmer for 1 minute more to reheat. Add the parsley at the last moment.

4. Put 3–4 oysters into each soup bowl and pour on the broth. Add 3–4 oyster crackers to each serving. Have more oyster crackers on the table. Serves 6. This recipe can be multiplied for a larger party.

Roast Turkey with Two Stuffings & Giblet Gravy

Everybody has a favorite part of Thanksgiving dinner, and often the stuffings upstage the turkey. The two stuffings here are both traditional: sage and onion came to New England with settlers from Britain, and it remains popular on both sides of the Atlantic. Potato stuffings feature in Polish and German and eighteenth-century New England cooking, but the one given here is French Canadian. It is a family recipe from Dorothy Johnson of New Salem, Massachusetts. It comes from her great-grandmother, who left Canada to work in the mills of Holyoke in the nineteenth century. Dorothy generally cooks a twenty-two-pound turkey and uses almost ten pounds of potatoes to make the mashed potatoes that go into the stuffing; she bakes any excess stuffing in a casserole. The version below is scaled to fit a smaller bird.

Cooking a turkey is not hard, but when you have a whole Thanksgiving dinner to prepare, the experience can be stressful. The following group of recipes steps you through the process. Brining the turkey before cooking makes it tender and flavorful; this is step one. Making stock for the giblet gravy is step two, and you take both these steps the day before. You can also make the two stuffings — steps three and four — a day ahead. Or, simplify matters and make just one stuffing; both recipes are sufficient for a whole bird. The flavored butter is another potential do-ahead item — see step five. This leaves you only with the task of stuffing the bird and buttering its breast on the morning of the big day. Cranberry sauce is a do-ahead item, so that's out of the way. That just leaves the gravy to be finished, the vegetables to be done, the first course to be fixed. . . .

BRINE

5 quarts water
1/2 cup granulated sugar
1 cup salt
3 bay leaves
1 tablespoon allspice berries
One 12–14-pound turkey, giblets removed

TURKEY

1 stick (4 ounces) butter
2 cloves garlic, crushed
1/2 teaspoon ground allspice
1 medium onion, peeled

GIBLET GRAVY

Turkey giblets
1 carrot, halved
1 large stalk celery, halved
1 medium onion, halved
1 bay leaf
1 sprig fresh thyme, or 1/2 teaspoon dried thyme
1/2 teaspoon black peppercorns
Salt to taste
5 cups water
2 tablespoons all-purpose flour
2–3 teaspoons Worcestershire sauce

SAGE-ONION STUFFING

2 large onions, chopped
1 large sprig fresh sage
2 cups water
2 tablespoons chopped fresh sage
6 tablespoons peanut or other
   light-flavored oil
One 16-ounce package stuffing crumbs

SAUSAGE-POTATO STUFFING

1 pound pork sausage
1 large onion, chopped
$^1/_2$ cup chopped celery
1 $^1/_2$ tablespoons dried mixed herbs or
   parsley
6 cups mashed potatoes (about 3 $^1/_2$–4
   pounds unpeeled)

1. To make the brine, mix together the water, sugar, salt, bay leaves, and allspice berries in a large pot (preferably stainless steel). Bring to a boil and simmer for 10 minutes. Let cool. Strain out the bay leaves and allspice berries. Wash the turkey inside and out. Put it into the pot and pour the cooled brine into the cavity and then over the turkey. Let stand for 24–36 hours in the fridge. (Depending on the size of the pot and the turkey, the turkey may not be completely immersed. In that case, turn it over several times so all parts, especially the breast, spend time in the brine.)

2. To start the gravy, put the giblets, carrot, celery, onion, bay leaf, thyme, peppercorns, salt, and water into a large saucepan. Simmer for 1–2 hours to make stock. Strain the stock and chill until the turkey is prepared. If you like, strip the meat from the neck and add it to the stock.

3. To make the sage-onion stuffing, put the onions, sage sprig, and water into a large saucepan and simmer for 20 minutes, or until the onion is soft. Discard the sage. Put the onion mixture into a large bowl and add the chopped sage. Stir in the oil and crumbs. If the mixture does not cohere, add more water.

4. To make the sausage-potato stuffing, crumble the sausage and brown in a skillet for 2–3 minutes. Add the onion and celery and cook for 4–5 minutes more. Sprinkle with the herbs and stir in the potatoes.

5. To prepare the turkey, first make the flavored butter by mashing it in a bowl with the garlic and allspice. Remove the turkey from the brine and pat dry with paper towels. Stuff both cavities, using the same stuffing in each one or putting sage and onion in one and sausage and potato in the other. Seal the neck cavity by folding the flap of skin underneath the bird. Seal the large cavity by blocking it with the peeled onion.

6. Gently separate the skin from the breast. Spread about half of the flavored butter directly on the breast, underneath the skin. Pull the skin gently back over it. Spread the remaining flavored butter over the skin of the turkey, then put the turkey in a roasting pan that is heavily greased with oil. Take a large piece of heavy-duty aluminum foil and tent it loosely over the pan.

7. To cook the turkey, preheat the oven to 425º F. Put the turkey into the oven and roast for 25 minutes. Lift the foil and baste thoroughly. Reduce the temperature to 375º and roast for 2 hours more, basting well every 10–15 minutes. Remove the tent of foil for the last 30 minutes so the turkey can brown. If it seems slow about doing this, increase the temperature to 425º again and baste every 5 minutes. To test for doneness, insert the point of a sharp knife into the thickest part of the thigh and observe the juice that runs out. If pink, cook longer; if clear, the turkey is ready. A leg that moves when wiggled is another sign of doneness. Remove from the oven and let stand in

a warm spot for 10 minutes, then transfer to a platter for carving by someone other than the person who is finishing the giblet gravy and sorting out the vegetables.

8. If you have made both stuffings, you will have leftovers to cook. Put the sausage-potato stuffing in a greased casserole, cover, and bake for the last 30 minutes of turkey cooking time. If you have any leftover sage-onion stuffing, either bake it in a greased and covered casserole while the turkey is cooking and keep it warm for serving or form it into balls or patties and lightly fry in oil.

9. To finish the giblet gravy, discard all but 3 tablespoons of the fat from the roasting pan. Off the heat, stir the flour into the remaining fat, then stir in 1 cup of the giblet stock. Set the pan over low heat and gradually add the remaining giblet stock, stirring frequently, until it simmers. Add the Worcestershire sauce and simmer for 4–5 minutes. If the gravy is thicker than you would like, thin it with broth from the vegetables or with water or canned chicken broth. Season to taste with some salt and black pepper. Serve all!

Cranberry-Lime Sauce

This quick sauce can be made at least a week ahead of Thanksgiving and kept in a jar in the fridge. Its tart, fresh taste makes a vibrant contrast to the heavier dishes of the meal.

1 cup apple jelly
3 cups fresh cranberries (12-ounce bag)
1/4 teaspoon freshly grated nutmeg
2 limes

1. Put the jelly into a large saucepan and warm over low heat until it has melted. Stir in the cranberries, bring to a simmer, and cook, uncovered, until the cranberries have popped. Add the nutmeg and stir occasionally until you have a thick, lumpy sauce, about 10 minutes. Remove from the heat and let cool.

2. Scrape the zest from 1 of the limes and chop. Stir 1/2 teaspoon of the chopped zest into the cooled cranberry mixture. Squeeze the juice from half of the lime and add 1 tablespoon of the juice to the mixture. Taste and add more zest and juice if you would like.

3. Scrape long thin strips of zest from the remaining lime for a garnish.

Portabellas with Hazelnut Stuffing

Many people enjoy the stuffing almost more than the turkey. This recipe calls for packaged stuffing crumbs to make a meatless stuffing for portabella mushrooms. For vegetarians, choose large portabellas and serve them as a main dish at Thanksgiving or at any time. Alternately, use smaller mushroom caps and serve them on the side. After Thanksgiving, this recipe is a good way to use up the last of a package of crumbs.

5 tablespoons olive oil
$^1/_3$ cup hazelnuts
4 large well-shaped portabella mushroom caps
Salt
$^1/_2$ cup grated carrot
1 cup packaged stuffing crumbs
$^1/_2$ boiling water
4 tablespoons grated sharp Vermont Cheddar cheese

1. Preheat the oven to 350° F. Brush a baking sheet with some of the oil.

2. Put the hazelnuts into a pie plate and bake for 10 minutes, or until the skin looks dark, though not quite black. Tip them onto a clean, cloth kitchen towel. Fold the towel over them and rub vigorously to loosen the skins. If a few bits of skin stick to a nut or two, it's no problem, but if a lot of skin remains, scrape it off with a knife. Coarsely crush the nuts and set aside.

3. Cut the stems from the mushrooms. Cut off and discard the end of each stem, which usually has soil on it, but wipe the top parts of the stem with damp paper towels. Chop the stems. Also wipe the mushroom caps with damp paper towels.

4. Place the mushroom caps gill-side down on the prepared baking sheet and sprinkle with the salt. Brush the caps with some of the oil and bake for 10 minutes, or until the edges sizzle a bit.

5. While the mushroom caps are baking, heat the remaining oil. Add the chopped mushroom stems and carrot and gently cook for 4–5 minutes. Mix in the crumbs, pour in the boiling water, and stir to combine. Add a little more water if necessary to make the stuffing cohere. Stir in the reserved toasted hazelnuts.

6. Remove the mushroom caps from the oven and turn the caps gill-side up. Divide the stuffing into 4 portions and spread each portion on top of a mushroom. Sprinkle with the cheese. Return to the oven and bake for 5–8 minutes more, or until the cheese has melted and the stuffing is thoroughly heated. Serve hot.

Creamy Pearl Onions

Many people love pearl onions more than any other vegetable on the Thanksgiving table. They can be dotted in with the succotash or in a dish of peas. Or, they can appear as a separate dish such as in this recipe.

1 pound pearl onions, unpeeled
1 ¹/₂ tablespoons butter
1 ¹/₂ tablespoons all-purpose flour
1 ¹/₂ cups milk
1 large leaf fresh sage, or 1 bay leaf
Salt and white pepper

1. Put the onions in a large saucepan and cover with water. Bring to a boil and cook for 3–4 minutes, then drain and run cold water over them. Cut off the root end of the peel, then strip off the skin or squeeze the onion slightly and it will just pop out. Set aside. (You could do this a day ahead of time and keep the peeled onions covered in the fridge.)

2. Melt the butter in a medium saucepan over low heat. Off the heat, stir in the flour to make a smooth paste. Stir in ¹/₄ cup of the milk, then increase the heat to medium and stir in the remaining milk. Cook, stirring constantly, until the sauce has thickened.

3. Add the reserved onions and sage leaf. Season lightly with the salt and white pepper and simmer over very low heat, stirring frequently to prevent sticking, until an onion feels tender when pierced with a fork, about 5–10 minutes depending on the size of the onions. Discard the sage before serving. Serve hot.

HARRIET BEECHER STOWE ON AMERICAN VEGETABLES

After the success of her novel Uncle Tom's Cabin, *Connecticut-born Harriet Beecher Stowe traveled widely in Europe and admired the careful presentation of food in England and France, often complaining that in America, abundance had bred "slovenly and wasteful" food habits. Nonetheless, she wrote warmly of the pleasures of American vegetables. Here she describes returning from abroad to an array that sounds like a Thanksgiving spread:*

"I sat down at once to a carnival of vegetables: ripe, juicy tomatoes, raw or cooked; cucumber in brittle slices; rich, yellow sweet potatoes, broad Lima beans, and beans of other and various names; tempting ears of Indian corn steaming in enormous piles, and great smoking tureens of savoury [sic] succotash, an Indian gift to the table . . . sliced eggplant in delicate fritters; and marrow squashes of creamy pulp and sweetness: a rich variety, embarrassing to the appetite and perplexing to the choice."

Succotash with Ham

The word "succotash" comes from the Narragansett word *msickquatash*, an original dish from Native Americans, who often added meats, including squirrel, bear, or venison to make a sustaining stew. On December 21, the people of Plymouth, Massachusetts, celebrate Forefathers' Day, a commemoration of the Pilgrims' landing at Plymouth Rock, with an authentic succotash made of salt beef and pork boiled with dried beans, dried corn, and turnips. It's a meal in itself. For a side dish with turkey and all the trimmings, the simpler succotash of later days is best. In summer, it could be made with fresh green beans and corn just stripped from the cob, but by November, New England's corn and beans are long past, so this simple recipe calls for frozen baby lima beans and corn cooked with a little cream and ham for flavor.

1 tablespoon vegetable oil
One 6-ounce $^1/_2$-inch thick ham slice, cut into $^1/_2$-inch cubes
$^1/_2$ cup chopped onion
One 10-ounce package frozen baby lima beans, thawed
2 cups fresh or canned corn kernels
$^1/_2$ cup light cream
Salt and black pepper to taste

1. Heat the oil in a large saucepan. Add the ham and onion and cook for 1 minute. Add the lima beans and corn, then stir in the cream. Season with the salt and black pepper. Cover and simmer for 5–6 minutes, or until the vegetables are cooked through. Serves 8.

Sautéed Red Bell Peppers & Baby Corn

This dish adds dazzle to the Thanksgiving table. It is blessedly easy, and though not traditional to New England, it does combine two new-world crops: corn and bell peppers.

2 tablespoons vegetable oil
$^1/_2$ cup chopped onion
2 large red bell peppers, deveined, seeded, and cut into $^1/_4$-inch strips
1 can baby corn on the cob, drained
Salt and black pepper to taste

1. Heat the oil in a skillet. Stir in the onion and cook for 1–2 minutes or until wilted. Add the pepper strips and cook, stirring occasionally, for 2 minutes.
2. Add the corn to the onion-pepper mixture. Season with the salt and black pepper and cook for 3–4 minutes, or until the corn is heated through. Serve hot.

Squash & Apple Gratin

Think of spices as magic. They work wonders, but like the broom borrowed by the sorcerer's apprentice, they can get bossy and dominate the dish if used wantonly. In this gratin, a little allspice adds sparkle. Though it has flavor notes of cloves, pepper, and nutmeg, allspice is not a spice mixture. It comes from an aromatic bush native to the Caribbean — hence its old name, Jamaica pepper. Allspice and chili peppers are the only spices that European explorers, eager to reach the spice islands of the East, actually found in the New World.

1–2 butternut squash (about 3 pounds total)
2 medium-large Cortland or Golden Delicious apples, peeled and sliced
1–2 tablespoons granulated sugar
1 tablespoon water
³/₄ teaspoon ground allspice
Salt and black pepper to taste
1–2 teaspoons milk (optional)
³/₄ cup bread crumbs (made from day-old bread)
1 tablespoon melted butter
¹/₂ cup chopped walnuts

1. Preheat the oven to 375° F. Grease a baking dish. (You can prepare the squash ahead of time.)

2. With a heavy cleaver, cut off the fat end of the squash and discard. Cut the remaining squash into 5–6 chunks and place in the prepared dish. Cover and bake for 45–60 minutes, or until the squash is tender.

3. While the squash is cooking, toss the apple slices with the sugar and water in a small saucepan. Cover and cook over low heat for 10 minutes or until tender but still holding their shape. (Cortland apples are best for this dish because they stay white when exposed to air.)

4. Let the squash cool to a workable temperature, then strip off the skin, which will come away easily. Mash by hand or in a food processor the squash, allspice, salt, and black pepper. (You should have a smooth puree about as thick as mashed potatoes. If it is thicker, add the milk.)

5. Preheat the oven to 350° F. Grease a shallow baking dish. Put half of the squash mixture into the prepared dish. Spread the cooked apple slices on top and cover with the remaining squash. Toss together the bread crumbs and butter and sprinkle them on the gratin. Bake for 10 minutes, then sprinkle on the walnuts and bake for 5 minutes more or until heated through. Serve hot.

Parker House Rolls

In the nineteenth century, Boston's Parker House hotel set the trend for elegance and luxury, hiring European cooks and bakers at wages far higher than the going rate. A German baker is credited with creating these rolls, still made in-house at the Omni Parker House using the following recipe. They are a good choice for a New England feast.

6 cups bread flour
$1/4$ cup plus 3 tablespoons granulated sugar
$1/4$ cup plus 3 tablespoons vegetable shortening
$1/4$ cup plus 1 $1/2$ tablespoons dry milk powder
1 $1/2$ teaspoons salt
2 packages active dry yeast
2 $1/4$ cups water, warmed to 110° F
1 stick (4 ounces) butter, melted

1. Put the flour, sugar, shortening, milk powder, and salt into the bowl of an electric mixer or other mixing bowl. Beat or rub the shortening into the flour mixture.

2. Dissolve the yeast in the warm water. Make a well in the center of the flour mixture and add the yeast mixture. Using a dough hook attachment of the electric mixer and a dough beater or wooden spoon if not, mix until the dough is smooth, about 5 minutes with an electric mixer and 10 minutes or more by hand. The dough should be soft, almost sticky, and the amount of water necessary to achieve this can vary depending on humidity and the dryness of the flour. If your dough is stiff, add more water, 2 tablespoons at a time.

3. Cover the bowl with plastic wrap and let the dough rise in a draft-free spot for about 1 $1/2$– 2 hours or until doubled in bulk. When the dough has risen, punch down, then separate into 24 balls. Let stand for 15 minutes.

4. Flatten each ball of dough and brush with some of the melted butter. Stretch each roll to about double its length. Fold one end so it just slightly overlaps the other to approximate a semicircle. (If you fold it precisely in half to make a neat semicircle, the rolls tend to spring open in the oven.) Place on a buttered baking sheet in rows, with the widest part of each semicircle just touching the widest part of the roll in the next row. Cover with plastic wrap and let stand for 20 minutes.

5. Preheat the oven to 400° F. Bake the rolls until golden brown, about 15–20 minutes. Remove from the oven and brush the tops with the remaining melted butter. Serve hot.

Pumpkin Chiffon Pie with a Gingernut Crust

This is an airier adaptation of the traditional pumpkin custard pie.

5 ounces gingernut cookies (1 ¹/₂ cups crumbs)
1 stick (4 ounces) butter, melted
1 package unflavored gelatin
¹/₄ cup water
1 cup cooked or canned pumpkin
3 eggs, separated
1 cup milk
³/₄ cup firmly packed light brown sugar
¹/₂ teaspoon ground ginger
¹/₂ teaspoon ground nutmeg
1 teaspoon ground cinnamon
3 tablespoons dark rum

1. Preheat the oven to 350° F. Grease a 9-inch pie plate.

2. Crush the cookies, either by pulsing in a food processor or by placing in a plastic bag and beating them up with a rolling pin. Mix together the crumbs and melted butter in a bowl, then evenly line the base and sides of the pie plate with the mixture. Bake for 12–15 minutes or until crisp and slightly dark. (Keep your eye on the crust for the last few minutes to prevent burning.) Let cool and set aside.

3. Stir together the gelatin and water in a cup. Place the cup in a saucepan of warm water over low heat and stir until the mixture looks clear, not grainy. Keep it warm in the pan of water while you proceed.

4. Mix together the pumpkin, egg yolks, milk, sugar, ginger, nutmeg, and cinnamon in a large saucepan. Bring to a simmer over moderate heat, stirring constantly. Remove from the heat and thoroughly stir in the warm gelatin mixture and the rum. Let chill in the fridge for 1 hour, or until it begins to set.

5. Whisk the egg whites to stiff peaks, then fold them into the pumpkin mixture. Pour the filling into the reserved pie shell, letting it mound in the center and swirling it to make an attractive pattern. Return to the fridge for 4 hours to finish setting. Serve chilled. Serves 6–8.

Apple Streusel Pie

A deep-dish, two-crust apple pie remains a favorite on New England's Thanksgiving tables. Variations include apple-cranberry pie, apple-raspberry pie, and this streusel-topped pie.

PASTRY

1 ¹/₃ cups all-purpose flour
¹/₄ cup vegetable shortening
¹/₄ cup cold butter
2 tablespoons cold water
1 teaspoon granulated sugar

FILLING

5–6 large apples, peeled, cored, and cut
*   into thick slices (Northern Spy, Baldwins,*
*   or Cortland)*
¹/₃ cup granulated sugar
Grated zest of half a lemon

TOPPING

¹/₂ cup all-purpose flour
¹/₄ cup cold butter
¹/₂ cup firmly packed light brown sugar
¹/₂ teaspoon ground cinnamon

1. Preheat the oven to 425° F. Grease a 9-inch deep-dish pie plate.

2. To make the pastry, put the flour into a large bowl. Add the shortening and toss it about with a fork to break it into lumps. Cut the butter into several bits and rub them into the flour mixture until it looks like fine crumbs. Make a well in the center of the flour mixture and add the cold water. Pull the mixture together. If it is too dry to form a rollable pastry, add more cold water, 1 tablespoon at a time, until you can shape the mixture into a ball.

3. Flour a pastry board or work surface and a rolling pin. Put the ball of pastry in the middle and flatten it into a disk. Roll into a 12-inch circle. Fit the pastry into the prepared pie plate, lifting it over the rolling pin to make it easy to handle. Trim off the excess and chill in the fridge.

4. To make the filling, toss together the apple slices, sugar, and lemon zest. Set aside.

5. To make the topping, put the flour into a bowl. Cut the butter into several bits and rub them into the flour until the mixture has pea-sized lumps in it. Stir in the sugar and cinnamon.

6. Remove the pie shell from the fridge. Put the apple mixture into the shell, then sprinkle the streusel on top. It doesn't matter if some chunks of apple peek through. Bake for 10 minutes, then reduce the temperature to 375° and bake for 20–25 minutes more, or until the top is golden. Serve warm.

Mincemeat

Mincemeat is one of the best recipes to make with children. They love sniffing the spices and stirring them into the dark and glistening dried fruit. Since mincemeat is not cooked until it goes into a pie, there is no risk of burns. This chapter includes a Mincemeat Lattice Pie (see recipe on page 163), but don't think of mincemeat as a pie filling only. Pack it into the cores of apples before you bake them or stir a cup of mincemeat into recipes for scones, cookies, and quick breads. And Mincemeat Ice Cream is a terrific holiday dessert (see recipe on page 228).

¹/₄ pound suet or butter, frozen
3 pounds tart apples, peeled and grated
One 15-ounce package dark raisins
One 15-ounce package golden raisins
One 12-ounce package currants
1 pound firmly packed brown sugar
Grated zest and juice of 1 medium orange or 1 large lemon
1 whole nutmeg, grated, or 2 teaspoons ground nutmeg
¹/₂ teaspoon ground cloves
¹/₂ teaspoon ground mace
1 teaspoon ground cinnamon
1 teaspoon ground ginger
³/₄ cup rum or brandy

1. Grate the suet or butter on the coarse blade of a grater or in a food processor fitted with a grating blade. (Freezing makes this easier, and it also prevents the fat from blending into the other ingredients; it should stay in small fragments.)

2. Mix together the grated suet or butter, apples, raisins, golden raisins, currants, and sugar in a large covered container. Stir in the zest and juice, nutmeg, cloves, mace, cinnamon, and ginger, then stir in the rum. Cover and place in the fridge. Stir again the next day.

3. Proceed like this for 1 week. Add more of any ingredient you like, making especially sure to spice the mincemeat to your taste. Pack into sterilized jars. (To sterilize jars, boil them empty in a large pot of water for 10 minutes.) Store in a cold spot at least 1 month before using. Mincemeat ages well and is best made once a year, for use as needed. Makes 6–7 pints.

WHERE'S THE MEAT?

Mincemeat has fallen on evil days. The mincemeat that you buy in jars from the store is an excessively sweet mush, tasting of unidentifiable spices. Naturally, most people don't like it. Others assume that mincemeat contains meat and avoid it because they don't fancy meat mixed with sugar. But mincemeat almost never contains meat. The name is a holdover from the past.

In medieval England, farmers had to slaughter most of their animals in late fall because they could not feed them through the winter. Fall was also the season for hunting, so in November and early December, there was generally more meat than could be consumed; in contrast, late winter would see a dearth. Preserving some of the plenty was therefore essential. Salting and smoking were the usual methods, but when trade with the East brought sugar, spices, and dried fruits to England, a more glorious way to put by meat was to mix it with these luxuries — all of which have some preservative effects. Add alcohol and a form of fat, two more preservatives, and you have a long-lasting supply of the best pie filling ever invented. Since mincemeat was made late in the year, it became a staple for Christmas, and by the seventeenth century, mincemeat pies meant merrymaking. The Puritans detested frivolity on a religious holiday, so they famously forbade the pies in their colony.

Fortunately, mincemeat survived the ban. In American Cookery, *the first cookbook written specifically for Americans, Amelia Simmons explains the advantages of making a batch of mincemeat pies and storing them. "Weeks after, when you have occasion to use them, raise the top crust and with a round edg'd [sic] spoon, collect the meat in a bason [sic], which is warm with additional wine and spices to the taste of your circle, while the crust is also warmed like a hoe cake, put carefully together and serve up, by this means you can have hot pies through the winter." Her recipe calls for calves feet, minced meat, and suet, and meat remained in many nineteenth-century recipes from New England. You may still find it included in the occasional recipe in community cookbooks. Often the choice is venison, suggesting that hunters' families may find this old form of mincemeat as useful as their forbears did. Meat had disappeared, however, from English recipes much earlier. In* The Boston Cooking-School Cookbook, *published at the end of the century, Fannie Farmer offered four mincemeat recipes: one with beef and suet, an English mincemeat that has only suet, a mincemeat without liquor, and an economy version made with crackers and molasses. Clearly, thrift was not the rule for the holidays, however, as Miss Farmer pointed out, "For Thanksgiving and Christmas pies, Puff Paste is often used for rims and top crusts."*

Today, mincemeat is confected from a base of apples (or occasionally green tomatoes), with raisins and other dried fruits, sugar, spices, rum, or brandy with butter, or better yet, suet — the last reminder of the meaty mincemeats of yore. Once made, mincemeat keeps for months, and homemade mincemeat converts mincemeat doubters into mincemeat fans.

Mincemeat Lattice Pie

A lattice-topped mincemeat pie looks alluring, and should you want to add a little more rum at the last minute, you can just pour it into the openings in the lattice.

1 recipe Mincemeat (see recipe on page 161)
1 ¹/₂ cups all-purpose flour
¹/₄ teaspoon baking powder
2 teaspoons granulated sugar
6 tablespoons cold butter
¹/₃ cup vegetable shortening or lard
¹/₄ cup cold water
1 tablespoon cream

1. Prepare the mincemeat recipe.

2. Preheat the oven to 425° F. Grease a 9-inch pie pan.

3. Mix together the flour, baking powder, and 1 teaspoon of the sugar in a mixing bowl. Cut the butter into several bits and coat with the flour. Add the shortening in bits and toss them, too.

4. Rub both fats into the flour mixture with your fingers or a pastry blender until it looks like coarse crumbs. Make a well in the center and add ¹/₈ cup of the cold water. With your fingers, stir the mixture, pulling it together into a dough. If necessary, add more water until you get a workable, not sticky, dough.

5. Flour a cold pastry board and a rolling pin. Divide the dough into 2 portions, one about twice as big as the other. Keep the smaller portion in the fridge while you roll the larger portion into a 12-inch circle and fit it into the prepared pan. Fill it with the prepared mincemeat. Do not trim off the edges at this point. Roll out the smaller portion of dough into a rectangle and cut it into ³/₄-inch strips. Arrange the strips across the pie, weaving them in an under-over fashion to form the lattice. (Re-roll the bits to make the shorter strips if necessary, but don't re-roll more often than you must.)

6. Now fold the ragged edges of the bottom layer of dough over the ends of the lattice strips, using just enough to make a neat edge. Brush the dough with the cream. Sprinkle with the remaining sugar and bake for 20 minutes or until golden. Cool on a wire rack. Serve warm.

Marlborough Pie

Marlborough pie, sometimes called Marlborough pudding, is actually a tart filled with apple custard. It was a nineteenth-century Thanksgiving favorite, especially in Massachusetts. Such pies trace back to England, from whence settlers brought them to New England, adapting the idea to American ingredients such as pumpkin — hence the pumpkin custard pies of tradition. An early ancestor of Marlborough pie comes from Robert May's *The Accomplisht Cook* of 1660. He called it simply "A Made dish of Butter and Eggs," but as a cook who prided himself on working for the aristocracy, he worked on the grand scale, calling for "fine minced pippins" and twenty-four egg yolks. Marlborough pie has aristocratic connections, too. Almost certainly, it is named for the Duke of Marlborough, a military hero of the early eighteenth century, an era when naming dishes after the great was the fashionable thing to do.

3 – 4 large apples (about 2 pounds), peeled and cored (Northern Spies or Cortland)
Grated zest and juice of half a lemon
³/₄ cup granulated sugar
3 eggs, lightly beaten
1 tablespoon rum (optional)
¹/₂ teaspoon ground nutmeg, or large pinch ground mace
4 tablespoons butter
¹/₂ cup milk or half-and-half
1 baked 9-inch pie shell

1. Preheat the oven to 425° F. Grate the apples. (You should have 1¹/₂–2 cups grated apple.) Quickly mix together the grated apple, lemon zest, and juice, then stir in the sugar. Add the eggs, rum, and nutmeg and mix together well.

2. Melt the butter in a small saucepan, then stir it into the apple mixture. Add the milk and pour the mixture into the pie shell. Place in the center of the oven and bake for 15 minutes. Reduce the temperature to 350° and bake for 15–20 minutes more, or until the filling looks puffed and a toothpick inserted in the center comes out clean. Cool on a wire rack. Serve warm. Serves 6.

Cranberry Crumb Tart

When New Hampshire native Jim Dodge took over the kitchens of the Museum of Fine Arts in Boston, he transformed the ho-hum offerings of the Museum's café and restaurant by offering inventive and vibrant food. This tart is adapted from his recipe.

PASTRY	FILLING
1 ¼ cups all-purpose flour	*1 stick (4 ounces) cold unsalted butter*
¼ teaspoon kosher salt	*¾ cup all purpose flour*
1 teaspoon granulated sugar	*¼ teaspoon baking powder*
1 stick (4 ounces) cold unsalted butter	*1 ½ cups granulated sugar*
¼ cup whipping cream	*3 cups fresh cranberries (12-ounce bag)*

1. Preheat the oven to 425° F. Lightly grease a 9-inch quiche dish or pie pan.

2. To make the pastry, on a large work surface, mix together the flour, salt, and sugar with your fingers, then form the mixture into a ring 14 inches wide. Cut the butter into ½-inch slices and put them in the empty center of the ring. Press the butter into the work surface with the heel of your hand. You will notice how brittle, cold, and firm the butter is. Continue to work it until it becomes smooth, but still cool. Use both hands to push the flour into the butter in the center of the ring. Once you have closed the ring and covered the butter, use your fingertips to gently pinch flour into the butter, each time lifting your hands a few inches and dropping the ingredients to keep the mixture cool and light in texture. Continue blending until they form a coarse meal.

3. Form a well in the mixture. Add the cream and gently blend with your hands until the dough comes together. Press the mixture into the work surface with a gentle kneading motion. Roll into an 11-inch circle. Fold in half and unfold over the prepared pan. Center the dough in the pan. Lift the edges so the dough falls into the bottom of the pan. Press the dough into the sides and trim the edge against the rim of the pan. Place in the fridge.

4. To make the filling, cut the butter into 1-inch cubes. Put the butter cubes, flour, baking powder, and 1 cup of the sugar into a bowl and mix until it forms large clumps. Pinch one or two of the clumps; if you pinch into solid butter, keep mixing. Set aside.

5. Put the cranberries into the chilled pie shell and sprinkle with the remaining sugar. Top with the reserved crumb mixture and bake in the center of the lower rack for 35 minutes, or until the top is golden brown and the fruit bubbles a little around the edges. Serves 6–8.

Turkey Pilaf with Sausage & Bell Pepper

Turkey leftovers can be solitary pleasures — bits eased off the carcass while getting a drink from the fridge, or a sandwich of turkey, stuffing, and cranberry sauce scarfed in front of the TV. But when turkey makes a second appearance at the family table, a vibrant new presentation appeals more than a re-run of Thanksgiving dinner. Sausage, bell peppers, and dried cranberries light up this pilaf. As in all leftover dishes, exact quantities are not important; add more or less turkey, sausage, and vegetables depending on what you have or like. Omit the dried cranberries or substitute raisins if you prefer. Be sure, however, to keep a 2:1 ratio of rice to liquid: 2 cups of water or stock to 1 cup of rice.

1 cup basmati or other long grain rice
2 cups cold water
1 teaspoon vegetable oil
$^1/_2$ pound sweet Italian sausage or breakfast sausage, cut into bite-sized pieces
$^1/_2$ pound hot Italian or Portuguese sausage, cut into bite-sized pieces
1 cup chopped onion
1 clove garlic, chopped
1 large red or green bell pepper, deveined, seeded, and cut into $^1/_2$-inch dice
3 plum tomatoes, peeled, seeded, and chopped, or 1 cup diced canned tomatoes
2 cups turkey or chicken stock or water
1 bay leaf
1 teaspoon dried thyme
Salt and black pepper to taste
2 tablespoons dried cranberries (optional)
2 cups large-cubed cooked turkey

1. Mix together the rice and cold water in a bowl. Let stand while you prepare the vegetables.

2. Heat the oil in a skillet over moderate heat and brown all of the sausage, without necessarily cooking them through. Transfer the sausage to a plate and set aside.

3. Stir the onion and garlic into the fat in the skillet. Cook for 2 minutes, then stir in the bell pepper and tomatoes. Drain the rice and stir it into the mixture. When it is glistening and colored, pour in the stock, add the bay leaf, thyme, salt, and black pepper, and simmer for 10 minutes.

4. When much of the liquid has evaporated, stir in the cranberries, turkey, and the reserved sausage. Cover, turn the heat as low as possible, and cook for 8–10 minutes more, checking once or twice to make sure that the pilaf has not dried out. If it shows signs of drying, add more stock or water. Serves 4–5, but can be doubled for a larger group.

MORE TURKEY LEFTOVERS

The best turkey leftover dishes team mild-flavored turkey with big flavors or zingy tastes. Bacon adds the richness and flavor edge in a turkey club sandwich. The fruity vinaigrette does the job in the Turkey & Zucchini Salad with Raspberry Vinaigrette (see recipe on page 85). You can make a Thanksgiving version of that recipe by substituting cider vinegar for the raspberry vinegar and dried or fresh cranberries for the raspberries. Here are three more ideas for turkey leftovers:

Turkey-Celery Soup*: In 6 cups stock made from the turkey carcass or from chicken bouillon cubes, cook 1 small bunch celery (each stalk chopped into $^1/_2$-inch pieces), 1 cup chopped onion, and 1 garlic clove. After 15 minutes, add 2 cups diced turkey. Season to taste and simmer for 5 minutes until everything is hot and tender.*

Red Flannel Turkey Hash*: Fry 1 chopped onion and 2 cups cooked potatoes in vegetable oil. Season with dried sage or thyme and salt and black pepper. Add 1–2 cups turkey bits and 1 cup diced cooked beets. Dust on some ground allspice, then cook, stirring frequently, until hot.*

Curried Turkey Salad*: Mix together $^3/_4$ cup mayonnaise, 2 teaspoons curry powder, and 1–2 drops Tabasco sauce in a bowl. Toss in 2 cups turkey cubes, then add $^1/_3$ cup golden raisins or dried apricots snipped into bits and 1–2 tablespoons chopped fresh cilantro. Serve on lettuce leaves.*

A. BLAKE GARDNER

CHAPTER 11

PARTY TIME

As the nights lengthen, the Spirit of Parties awakes, stretches its limbs and looks around for fun. Soon, its geniality inspires potlucks and dinner parties, brunches, suppers, and get-togethers. So what if everybody is busy? With the party spirit at work, all sorts of friendly gatherings can be tucked in around the great feasts of fall and winter.

Of course, summer has its parties, too: backyard barbecues and picnics at the beach or a lake. These summery occasions notwithstanding, parties seem quintessentially wintry events. Perhaps it is the fun of dolling yourself up in your nicest clothes and venturing forth, all wrapped up, into the dark night to gather around a friendly table. Perhaps it's the crunch of the snow as you walk up a driveway or the bright lights of cars and street lamps that add a festive touch. Whatever is at work, the calendar makes clear that the traditional holidays that prompt festivities cluster around the harvest months, the turn of the year, and the coming of spring. Although summer sees some historic commemorations, May, June, and July have few holidays compared to the other months of the year, while August has none at all. These hot-weather months prompt wanderlust. New Englanders vacation at the shore or in the mountains; they may even go to Europe or pack everybody in the car and drive to distant states. But when the school year starts in September, they are back at home, ready to work, and ready, also, to recount sagas of the summer's exploits.

Trading stories over food and drink is one reason for getting together with pals. But as the leaves fall and the snows come, a deeper need presses. In the cold and dark, the need to cluster together for warmth and safety wells up from the past, when to be alone in winter was to be in danger. Today, most of us live securely in warm homes, linked to the outside world by telephones and computers. Still, it only takes an ice storm to bring down the power lines to remind us of the harshness of winter and the importance of human warmth and companionship. All the more reason then to confront the chill and the dark: brighten the house with flowers and candles, deck the table with a cloth and platters of tasty food, pull the corks on bottles of wine, and open the door to guests.

Winter holidays and festivals fuel the partying urge. Included in this chapter are recipes for these holidays, as well as hors d'oeuvres, entrées, and desserts for brunches, potlucks, and other parties. Even though Thanksgiving and Christmas dominate, winter also brings New Year's Eve, Hannukah, Kwanzaa, Chinese New Year, and Valentine's Day. Often the foods of the day recall the meaning of the festival. At Kwanzaa, for example, some African-American families choose dishes from Africa, the Caribbean, or other regions of the African Diaspora. At Chinese New Year, people focus on long foods, such as noodles, to symbolize long life and tangerines or oranges, whose golden color signals wealth and prosperity. On Valentine's Day, candies and desserts say "sweets to the sweet."

ICE

Today, ice is a party staple, but it used to be a luxury requiring forethought and muscle. As Henry David Thoreau explained, "While yet it is cold January, and snow and ice are thick and solid, the prudent landlord comes from the village to get ice to cool his summer drink; impressively, even pathetically wise, to foresee the heat and thirst of July now in January . . . . He cuts and saws the solid pond, unroofs the house of fishes, and carts off their very element and air, held fast by chains and stakes like corded wood, through the favoring wintry air, to wintry cellars." Thoreau was reflecting on living on Walden Pond in Concord, Massachusetts, in 1854, by which time the lakes of Massachusetts and the Kennebec and Penobscot rivers in Maine were ice suppliers, not just to the southern states, but to the world.

Frederick Tudor, known as the Ice King of Boston, pioneered this trade. In 1805, he was sending ice to Martinique, and by 1812, he held the British government monopoly of the ice trade to Jamaica. In 1833, he contracted to ship ice 16,000 miles to Calcutta, then capital of British India. Eventually, Tudor's ships also carried ice from Boston to Bombay, Madras, Singapore, Hong Kong, and Yokohama. Despite the distance, Tudor sold ice cheaply because his profit came from the goods that he imported in the returning vessels.

Tudor was not the only ice supplier. In 1844, the Wenham Lake Company sent two shiploads of ice from Boston to England. A sample that they presented to Queen Victoria impressed her so much that the Palace ordered a regular supply. The company prospered, sending ice carts around London twice a day. Then in 1846, a mild winter reduced supplies from New England at the very moment that Norwegians were getting into the business. The company solved this problem by buying the right to rename Lake Oppegaard in Norway as Lake Wenham so they could legally market its ice under the Massachusetts name.

Refrigeration ended New England's ice trade. But its heritage is still with us. While melting glaciers etched the region's lakes and ponds, ice harvesters widened them by damming their outlets. These ice ponds had shallow margins so ice formed early. Today, waterlilies pack the edges: a home to frogs, herons, kingfishers — even the occasional osprey.

Caramelized Onion & Rosemary Minipizzas

Many supermarkets sell frozen bread dough, and it is fine for these tiny pizzas if you don't want to make your own dough. Sweet onions, such as Vidalias, Walla Wallas, or Oso Sweets, caramelize much more easily than regular onions. They make a base on which to add toppings: smoked bacon, olives, or whatever your imagination suggests.

MINIPIZZAS
1 package active dry yeast
1 cup lukewarm water
3 cups bread machine flour or all-purpose flour
2 teaspoons salt
6 tablespoons olive oil
2 pounds sweet onions, sliced
1 egg, beaten
³/₄ cup sour cream
¹/₄ teaspoon dried rosemary
¹/₂ teaspoon dried thyme
Salt and black pepper to taste

TOPPINGS
4 strips thick-cut smoked bacon, half-cooked and cut into small bits
15 grape tomatoes or cherry tomatoes, halved
20 pitted black olives
¹/₃ cup roasted red pepper strips (homemade or from jar)

1. To make the minipizzas, mix together the yeast and ¹/₂ cup of the lukewarm water. Let stand for 5 minutes or until slightly frothy.

2. Mix together the flour and 1 teaspoon of the salt in a warmed bowl and drizzle 1 tablespoon of the oil over the mixture. Make a well in the center and add the yeast. Add the remaining water and knead until the dough is smooth and does not stick to your hands or the bowl, about 10-15 minutes by hand or 6–7 minutes with an electric mixer. Cover with plastic wrap and let stand in a draft-free spot until the dough has doubled in bulk, about 1 ¹/₂–2 hours.

3. Punch down the dough and knead for 1 minute, then set aside for 15 minutes or until it has relaxed, allowing you to pull and shape it. (If using purchased dough, simply let it rise once, punch down, and let it relax, then proceed from this point.)

4. While the dough is rising, heat 3 tablespoons of the oil in a large skillet over low heat. Stir in the onions and sprinkle them with the remaining salt. Cook very gently, uncovered, stirring occasionally, for 40–60 minutes, or until they are tawny and slightly sticky.

5. While the onions are cooking, mix together the egg, sour cream, rosemary, and thyme. Season lightly with the salt and black pepper. Set aside.

6. Preheat the oven to 425º F. Grease 3 baking sheets or line with baking parchment.

7. Divide the dough into walnut-sized balls, then pull or thinly roll out into small disks. Place on the prepared baking sheets and cover with plastic wrap or a clean cloth as you go. Let the disks stand for 20 minutes.

8. Brush each disk with a $^1/_2$-inch border of the remaining oil. Add 1 teaspoon of the reserved egg mixture to each disk and top with 1 teaspoon of the caramelized onions.

9. To make the toppings, add the bacon bits to half of the pizzas, then add tomato halves. Use the pitted olives and roasted pepper strips on the remaining pizzas. (You also could top all of the pizzas with one topping, doubling the amount specified, or top with other tidbits of your choice.) Bake in the top half of the oven for 10 minutes or until golden. Serve as appetizers. Makes 30–40 minipizzas.

Basket of Crispy Skate & Peppery Shrimp with Lemon Cocktail Sauce

Skate is an undervalued but delicious and versatile fish. It has ridges, which are actually elongated flakes, and this recipe takes advantage of that by using them as thin strips, perfect for dipping into cocktail sauce (or a salsa if you prefer). They team well with the peppery shrimp.

LEMON COCKTAIL SAUCE

$^{1}/_{2}$ cup finely chopped shallot or red onion
$^{1}/_{4}$ cup tomato paste
2 cups canned or diced fresh tomatoes
Grated zest and juice of 1 large lemon
1 teaspoon salt or more to taste
$^{1}/_{2}$ cup prepared horseradish
2 teaspoons Worcestershire sauce
1 tablespoon granulated sugar
Few drops Tabasco sauce (optional)

CRISPY SKATE

$^{1}/_{2}$–$^{3}/_{4}$ pound skate wings
$^{1}/_{4}$ cup milk
1 cup uncooked Cream of Wheat cereal
Peanut or canola oil

PEPPERY SHRIMP

1 teaspoon coarsely ground black pepper
1 teaspoon sea salt
1 teaspoon Chinese five-spice powder
1 teaspoon ground ginger
2 tablespoons light-flavored oil
$^{3}/_{4}$ pound cooked shrimp without shells

1. To make the sauce, mix together the shallot, tomato paste, tomatoes, lemon zest and juice, salt, and horseradish in a large saucepan. Bring to a boil and cook, stirring frequently, for 6–7 minutes.

2. Stir in the Worcestershire sauce and sugar and cook for 1 minute more. Remove 1 teaspoon, let it cool, then taste. Add more salt or sugar if necessary and a few drops of Tabasco if you want a fiery taste. The sauce at this point is quite chunky. You can serve it this way, or if you prefer it smoother, put it into a blender or food processor and pulse a few times until it is the consistency you like. The yield is about 1 pint. Leftovers keep in the fridge for 2–3 weeks.

3. To make the skate, lay the fish flat and cut into strips following its natural divisions. This gives you many thin pieces. Place the pieces in the milk, then dip them, a few at a time, in the Cream of Wheat. Spread them on a tray and let dry for a few minutes, or longer if more convenient.

4. Pour the oil into a skillet until it is $^{1}/_{4}$ inch deep. Heat until it is just trembling, then add the skate pieces and cook for 2 minutes, turning so they crisp. Cook, in batches, so you do not have to crowd the pan. Transfer to a basket lined with paper towels or napkins.

5. To make the shrimp, mix together the black pepper, salt, five-spice powder, and ginger in a small bowl. Set aside.

6. Heat the oil in another skillet. Add the shrimp and cook for 2 minutes or until hot. Remove from the pan and toss with the reserved spice mixture. Add the shrimp to the basket of skate and serve with the cocktail sauce.

Leek, Potato & Red Pepper Casserole

Scrambling eggs and making home fries calls for last-minute attention. This egg and potato casserole tolerates waiting a little better, so it's a good choice when you have guests for brunch — and equally good for a no-meat supper on a busy evening.

2 cups ¹/₂-inch cubed potatoes
¹/₂ teaspoon salt
4 medium-to-large leeks
¹/₃ cup water
¹/₂ cup roasted red pepper strips (homemade or from jar)
2 tablespoons olive oil
³/₄ cup all-purpose flour
¹/₂ teaspoon baking powder
4 eggs, lightly beaten
1 cup milk
1–2 cups grated sharp Vermont Cheddar cheese
1–2 teaspoons dried oregano to taste
Salt and black pepper to taste

1. Preheat the oven to 400° F. Generously oil a 9 x 13-inch baking dish.

2. Put the potatoes into a medium saucepan and cover with cold water. Add the salt and bring to a boil. Cook for 10 minutes or until just tender. Drain and set aside.

3. Trim the coarse outer layers and green leaves from the top of the leeks. Make a 4-inch cut lengthwise, open the layers, and rinse under cold water to remove any grit or soil. Slice into ¹/₂-inch circles and put into a large saucepan with the water. Season with salt. Cover and gently cook for 5–6 minutes, or until the leeks are slightly tender but not too soft. Spread the leeks in the prepared baking dish and scatter about one-third of the red pepper strips over them.

4. Heat the oil in a skillet over high heat. Toss in the potato cubes and cook, turning them, until they have taken color and are slightly crisp. Put about one-third of the potatoes into the baking dish with the leeks.

5. Mix together the flour and baking powder in a large bowl. Make a well in the center and add the eggs. Mix the flour into the eggs, then add ¹/₂ cup of the milk and beat until smooth. Stir in the remaining milk, the cheese, and oregano. Season with the salt and black pepper.

6. Pour half of the egg mixture over the vegetables in the baking dish. Scatter on the remaining potatoes, distributing them evenly, then pour on the remaining egg mixture. Some of the potato cubes should be exposed. Scatter on the remaining red pepper strips and bake in the center of the oven for 20–25 minutes, or until a knife blade inserted in the center comes out clean. Serve hot.

Curried Chicken Salad with Grapes & Salted Almonds

Curried chicken has a long history in New England, dating back to at least 1833, when Lydia Maria Child included it in her *American Frugal Housewife*. This version has a long ingredient list, which can seem daunting, but it is easy to make and always greeted with cries of acclaim. It's good also on sandwiches or served as a first course with salad greens. If you don't have time to poach your own chicken, buy a couple of chickens from the supermarket rotisserie, skin them, and cut up the meat. If you don't have time for the chicken salad, just make the salted almonds — perfect with drinks.

SALTED ALMONDS

1 cup whole blanched almonds
$^1/_2$ cup slivered almonds
1 teaspoon unsalted butter
1 teaspoon sea salt

CHICKEN SALAD

3 pounds skinless chicken breast and thighs
1 teaspoon black peppercorns
1 teaspoon salt
2 bay leaves
1 teaspoon dried thyme or mixed herbs
3 tablespoons light-flavored oil
$^3/_4$ cup chopped onion
1 clove garlic, chopped
1 teaspoon finely chopped fresh gingerroot
$^3/_4$ cup coarsely chopped celery
1–2 tablespoons curry powder to taste
15–20 dried apricots, each cut into 4 pieces
2 cups halved and seeded green grapes, plus red and green grape clusters for garnish
2 cups mayonnaise
2 tablespoons chopped fresh cilantro or parsley
1 English cucumber, washed and thinly sliced

1. Preheat the oven to 300° F. To make the almonds, put the whole almonds into a shallow baking pan and put the slivered almonds into another baking pan. Toast the whole almonds for 10–15 minutes, or until they are a light fawn color. Stir the butter into them and sprinkle with the salt. Let cool, then wrap in aluminum foil. Toast the slivered almonds for 15 minutes, or until they are the color of toffee, but check to make sure they don't burn. Set aside.

2. To make the chicken salad, put the chicken into a large saucepan and add enough water just to cover. Add the peppercorns, salt, bay leaves, and thyme. Bring to a simmer and cook for 30–40 minutes, or until the chicken is tender. Remove the chicken from the broth and let cool. (Save the broth for another use, such as making soup.)

3. While the chicken is cooling, heat the oil in a large skillet. Add the onion, garlic, and ginger-root. Cover and soften for 4–5 minutes over low heat. Add the celery and cook for 1–2 minutes only so the celery remains crisp. Stir in the curry powder and cook for 30 seconds more.

4. When the chicken is cool, cut it into bite-sized pieces. Remove the skillet from the heat and stir the chicken pieces, apricot pieces, reserved toasted slivered almonds, and the halved grapes into the curried mixture. Then stir in the mayonnaise and one-third of the cilantro. Add more salt if necessary.

5. Mound the salad on a serving dish. Sprinkle with the whole salted almonds and the remaining cilantro. Surround with the cucumber slices and add some grape clusters here and there. Serves 8–12.

Beef Alamode

As its name suggests, beef alamode originated in France, but recipes for it appear in every cookbook used by New Englanders from the settlers' arrival in this country to the turn of the twentieth century. All specify a large piece of round or rump beef weighing up to fifteen pounds, and all direct the cook to make holes in it and stuff the holes with a spiced and herbed mixture of bread crumbs and suet. Cooked in a large kettle on an open hearth, beef alamode could have bubbled away all day. Its demise was no doubt hastened by the nineteenth-century arrival of cooking stoves, which were often too small for huge pots and kettles. Smaller beef pot roasts became popular instead. But beef alamode, the bigger, older cousin of pot roast, is worth making when you have a crowd to feed. You can take advantage of its long cooking time to get an early start and to work on other dishes, and though it will not produce the rosy slices admired by lovers of rare beef, it will yield plenty of well-flavored meat and a delicious gravy.

1/4 teaspoon ground cloves
1 teaspoon ground allspice
1 teaspoon ground cinnamon
1/4 teaspoon black pepper
2 tablespoons dried thyme
4 ounces white suet, grated (or butter)
3 cups bread crumbs (made from day-old bread)
1/2 cup chopped fresh parsley

2 cloves garlic, chopped
4 ounces breakfast or sweet Italian sausage
1 cup hot water or broth
One 8–12-pound steamship round of beef
Salt
1 medium onion, sliced
2 carrots, sliced
2 bay leaves
1 bottle red wine

1. Stir together the cloves, allspice, cinnamon, black pepper, and 1 tablespoon of the thyme in a small bowl. Mix together the suet, bread crumbs, parsley, garlic, and the remaining thyme in a large bowl. If the sausage is in a skin, remove it, then crumble the sausage. Add the sausage to the bread crumb mixture and rub it in, then add about half the spice mixture. Pour in the hot water and mix to form a stuffing.

2. The beef round generally comes rolled and tied. In the center, there is a space. Make 3–5 more spaces by cutting out chunks of meat. Reserve these chunks for another use, such as a beef soup or stew. Fill the spaces using about half of the stuffing mixture.

3. Season the meat with the salt and rub with the remaining spice mixture. Line a large roasting pan with a clean kitchen towel, leaving the ends hanging over the sides. Put the meat onto the cloth. Tuck the onion, carrots, and bay leaves around it and pour in the wine. Cover the pan and place the ends of the cloth over the lid. Put on low heat and simmer as gently as possible for 4–5 hours. Check occasionally and top up with more wine or water as needed.

4. Preheat the oven to 350º F. While the beef is cooking, put the remaining stuffing in a baking dish and bake for 20 minutes or until crusty on top. Keep warm.

5. Let the meat stand for 20 minutes after you have turned off the heat. Remove from the pan by lifting it with the ends of the cloth and place on a serving platter. Pour off 3 cups of the

accumulated liquid and bring to a rapid boil in a saucepan. Taste for seasonings, add more salt and black pepper if needed. Remove excess fat from the surface of the sauce by pouring it through a fat-removing pitcher with a low-slung spout or strain it off with a spoon or paper towel.

6. Slice the meat and serve with the sauce and the baked stuffing. Serves 8 or more, depending on the size of the beef.

Cornish Game Hens Stuffed with Lemon & Herbs

Though their name suggests their origin in Cornwall, the final bit of crossbreeding that created Cornish game hens occurred in the United States when Indian game fowl, valued for their white meat and deep breasts, were developed into Yankee game hens and crossed with Plymouth Rock hens. A little flock of these minichickens, roasted gold and perched on a bed of rice or vegetables, such as Sugar Snap Peas & Potatoes on page 94 or Cider-Baked Winter Vegetables on page 146 looks festive for a dinner party. A good stuffing makes them tasty, and while large appetites can perhaps handle a whole bird, they are meatier than they look and a half of a bird is plenty for most people.

Four 1-pound Rock Cornish game hens
1 ¹/₂ teaspoons salt, divided
2 cups bread crumbs (made from day-old bread)
1 cup chopped fresh parsley
2 tablespoons snipped fresh chives
1 teaspoon dried thyme or oregano

2 large lemons
Freshly grated black pepper
5 tablespoons butter, melted
1 tablespoon water
Salt and black pepper
Bunch fresh watercress or arugula, washed

1. Preheat the oven to 425° F. Grease a large roasting pan. Remove the giblet package from the hens and wash the hens inside and out. Pat dry with paper towels. Rub the inside of each hen with ¹/₄ teaspoon of the salt.

2. For the stuffing, mix together the bread crumbs, parsley, chives, and thyme in a bowl. Scrape the zest from one of the lemons with a zester and finely chop. Add half of the zest, ¹/₂ teaspoon of the salt and a grating of the black pepper to the bread crumb mixture. Toss the mixture, then add the remaining zest, another grating of black pepper, and the juice of the lemon and mix well. Drizzle in 3 tablespoons of the melted butter and the water and mix to combine.

3. Divide the stuffing into 4 portions and stuff the hens, filling the cavities about three-fourths full. Tie the legs together with string and place them close together in the prepared pan. Season with more salt and black pepper, squeeze the juice of the remaining lemon over them, then brush the breasts with the remaining butter. Cover with tented aluminum foil and roast for 25 minutes.

4. Remove the foil and roast for 20 minutes more, basting once or twice with the pan juices. Test for doneness by inserting a skewer into the thickest part of the thigh. If the juice runs clear, the hens are ready; if it is pink, continue cooking for a few more minutes. Remove from the oven and let stand for 5 minutes.

5. Place the hens on a large platter and surround with the watercress. If you plan to serve half a hen to each person, split the hens before placing them on the platter.

Latkes with Applesauce

The Jewish holiday Hanukkah falls in December. It commemorates the Jewish victory over the Syrian Greeks in 165 B.C. When the Jews returned to their Temple, they discovered only enough consecrated oil to keep the lamp burning for one day. It took eight days to get more, but miraculously, the oil lasted so the lamp never went out. Today, Jews celebrate by lighting one candle a day for eight days and by eating potato pancakes called latkes. The significant emblem is not the potatoes, but the oil in which they are cooked. Latkes are often varied by adding herbs or other vegetables, including Jerusalem artichokes or sweet potatoes. Here is the basic version, along with a recipe for applesauce, the most popular accompaniment.

APPLESAUCE	LATKES
2 pounds McIntosh apples (about 5–7)	*4–5 medium Yukon Gold potatoes*
1 tablespoon water	*1 medium onion, chopped*
2–4 tablespoons granulated sugar to taste	*Salt and black pepper to taste*
1 teaspoon butter	*$^1/_4$ cup all-purpose flour*
	1 egg, lightly beaten
	Olive or vegetable oil

1. To make the applesauce (which can be made as much as 1 day ahead of time), peel, core, and slice the apples. Put them in a medium saucepan with the water. Cover and cook over low heat for 8–10 minutes, stirring occasionally.

2. When the apples have softened and collapsed into a puree with some solid bits, stir in the sugar and butter and cook until the sugar has dissolved and the butter has melted. Let cool to lukewarm or cold if you like.

3. To make the latkes, peel and grate 4 of the potatoes. You should have about 4 cups of grated potatoes. If necessary, grate the remaining potato to get this amount. Let stand for 15 minutes. By this time the liquid will have seeped from the potatoes. Strain the potatoes through a sieve, then squeeze thoroughly, a handful at a time, to remove as much liquid as possible.

4. Put the squeezed potatoes into a large bowl and stir in the onion. Season with the salt and black pepper, tossing well to make sure that all parts are seasoned. Stir in the flour and when absorbed, stir in the egg.

5. Preheat the oven to 275º F. Line a large ovenproof platter with 2–3 paper towels and place in the oven. Pour enough oil into a large skillet to make a $^1/_4$-inch layer, then heat. Using a $^1/_4$-cup measuring cup, scoop portions of the potato mixture and drop them into the hot oil. Flatten them a bit with a spatula and press in the sides to form vaguely round portions. Fry for 3 minutes per side, or until each side is nicely golden. When the latkes are cooked, transfer them to the paper-lined plate. Repeat with the remaining potato mixture. Serve with the applesauce.

Chicken & Peanut Stew

In 1966, Maulana Karenga created a celebration of African-American culture, calling it Kwanzaa, a Swahili word that means "first fruits of the harvest." He chose Swahili because it is widely spoken in Africa and thus emphasizes that African-Americans come from all over that continent. The celebration, which begins on December 26 and lasts for seven days, focuses on the seven principles of unity, self-determination, collective work, collective economics, purpose, creativity, and faith. Each day celebrants light a candle in a candelabra called a kinara to honor one of the principles. Finally, there is a great feast, the Kwanzaa Karamu, with speeches, music, dancing, storytelling — and lots of food. The dishes come from Africa, the Caribbean, South America, the southern states of the U.S., and other places where people of African heritage have lived. This stew is from Nigeria, the ancestral home of many African-Americans. Whether you celebrate Kwanzaa or not, it is a dish worth knowing: easy, flavorful, and a winner with lovers of peanut butter.

6 chicken thighs and 2 chicken breast halves, or one 3-pound chicken
4 teaspoons ground ginger
1 teaspoon salt
¼ cup peanut or canola oil
1 ½ cups coarsely chopped onion
2 cloves garlic, chopped
2 cups canned or diced fresh tomatoes
2 tablespoons tomato paste
1 tablespoon chopped fresh gingerroot
½ teaspoon deseeded chopped serrano chili, or cayenne pepper to taste (optional)
2 cups hot chicken broth or water
¾ cup smooth peanut butter
Ground red pepper to taste
¼ pound cooked shrimp (optional)
Selection of small dishes: quartered hard-boiled eggs, sliced cucumber, chopped fresh
*   tomatoes, avocado slices, roasted peanuts, fresh or canned pineapple cubes, fried*
*   plantain, sliced bananas*

1. Cut each chicken piece into large chunks and trim off excess skin and fat. Mix together the ginger and salt and rub into the chicken pieces.

2. Heat the oil in a large saucepan or stew pot and brown the chicken, a few pieces at a time. Transfer the pieces to a plate and add the onion and garlic to the pan. Gently cook for 3–4 minutes, then add the tomatoes, tomato paste, gingerroot, and the serrano chili if you are using it. Mix well and simmer for 5 minutes, then pour in the hot broth. Return the chicken to the pan and simmer for 15 minutes.

3. Remove 1 cup of the liquid from the pan. Mix it with the peanut butter in a small bowl, then stir the mixture into the pan. Taste and add salt if necessary and red pepper to taste if you want a hotter stew. Simmer for 20 minutes more, uncovered, so the sauce thickens. If you want to use the shrimp, chop into pea-sized bits, discarding the tails. Stir them in the last 5 minutes of cooking time.

4. Serve with rice, potatoes, or sweet potatoes. Have on hand the selection of the small dishes.

Chinese-Style Whole Fish
with Mushroom & Ginger Sauce

The lunar New Year celebrated by the Chinese and many other Asian communities falls in late January or early February. The most lavish festival of the Chinese year, it is preceded by a flurry of housecleaning and business settlements so everyone can begin the year with a fresh start. Much food preparation also takes place ahead of time. Hams, ducks, and sausages are likely to hang in any convenient spot, and all the meat and vegetables are precut, so that no one has to risk cutting off their New Year luck by using knives or scissors. Many foods also have symbolic meanings. Sticky rice cakes are popular because the word for them also means "year." A whole fish symbolizes prosperity because the Chinese word for fish sounds the same as the word for "abundance." The fish must be served whole to symbolize plenty, and when the diners have eaten one side, they must not turn the fish over to reach the underside — that would be turning abundance away; they must lift out the bone to reach the flesh below. This recipe comes with an easy sweet and sour ginger sauce. It's good also with fish fillets.

MUSHROOM & GINGER SAUCE

4 shiitake mushrooms, washed and thinly sliced

3 tablespoons finely chopped scallion

¹/₃ cup white vinegar

1 teaspoon hot bean paste, or pinch red pepper flakes

2 tablespoons soy sauce

¹/₂ cup coarsely chopped pickled ginger

¹/₃ cup granulated sugar

1 cup water

1 tablespoon cornstarch

2 tablespoons water

FISH

One 2–2 ¹/₂-pound whole sea bass or other fish

3 tablespoons rice wine or dry sherry

1 tablespoon minced fresh gingerroot

2 cloves garlic, minced

2 tablespoons cornstarch

¹/₂ teaspoon salt

1 tablespoon oil, plus more oil for frying

¹/₂ cup water

2 scallions, chopped

1. To make the sauce, which can be made a day ahead and reheated immediately before serving, put the mushrooms, scallion, vinegar, hot bean paste, soy sauce, pickled ginger, sugar, and the 1 cup water into a large saucepan and simmer for 5 minutes.

2. Meanwhile, stir together the cornstarch and the 2 tablespoons of water in a bowl to make a smooth paste. Stir in ¹/₃ cup of the hot liquid from the pan. Off the heat, add the cornstarch mixture to the mushroom-ginger mixture. Return to the heat and stir constantly until it returns to a boil and thickens. Set aside.

3. To make the fish, wash inside and out and scrape from the head toward the tail with a knife to remove any remaining scales. Make cuts 1 ¹/₂ inches apart, slashing from the skin down to the bone on both sides of the fish. Put the fish into a shallow dish. Mix together the rice wine, ginger-

root, and garlic in a small bowl and pour over the fish. Marinate for 30 minutes, basting with the liquid so the flavorings penetrate into the slashes. Remove the fish and pat dry with paper towels.

4. Mix together the cornstarch, salt, the 1 tablespoon of oil, and the water in a shallow dish. Place the fish in this mixture and turn over so it is lightly coated. Pour enough oil into a large skillet to come $1/2$ inch up the sides of the pan. Heat over high heat until ripply. Taking care to protect your hands with oven mitts and standing out of the range of spatters, gently place the fish in the oil. Cook on one side for 2 minutes, then using a broad spatula, turn over and immediately lower the heat. Cook for 6–7 minutes more, or until the flesh of the fish is white and opaque.

5. While the fish is cooking, reheat the reserved mushroom-ginger sauce. As soon as the fish is cooked, transfer to a warm serving dish and spoon the sauce over it. Garnish with the scallions and serve immediately.

JANE MCWHORTER

Noodles with Pork, Shrimp & Vegetables

At Chinese New Year, long foods symbolize long life, so long noodles are always served. This dish could accompany Chinese-Style Whole Fish with Mushroom & Ginger Sauce (see recipe on page 182), or serve it for supper any time. It lends itself to variations: chicken or beef instead of pork, for example, kale or bok choy instead of spinach, scallops instead of shrimp. It could be garnished with a thin two-egg omelette, cooked without turning, then cooled and cut into thin strips.

4 quarts water
1 tablespoon salt
12 ounces linguine or other long noodles
1 teaspoon cornstarch
3 tablespoons soy sauce
1/3 cup rice wine or dry sherry
4 tablespoons chopped scallion
1 teaspoon minced fresh gingerroot
1 clove garlic, chopped
1 cup water

2 center-cut pork chops (about 8–10 ounces)
2 stalks celery
1 small onion, chopped
2 carrots, peeled
One 8-ounce can sliced water chestnuts, well rinsed
1/4 pound cooked shrimp
6–8 cups loosely packed baby spinach leaves or other tender greens, washed
2 tablespoons sesame or vegetable oil

1. Put the 4 quarts water into a large saucepan and bring to a boil. Add the salt. Drop in the linguine and cook according to package directions until tender but not soggy. Drain. Cover with cold water, swishing around so the linguine doesn't stick together. Drain again and set aside.

2. Stir together the cornstarch and soy sauce in a large bowl. When smooth, add the rice wine, 2 tablespoons of the scallion, the gingerroot, and garlic. Stir in the 1 cup of water.

3. Cut the meat from the pork chops into $1/8$-inch slices, then cut the other way so you have $1/8$-inch strips. Stir the strips into the soy sauce mixture.

4. Cut the celery into $1/8$-inch strips and pile on a large plate, then pile the onion on the plate. Cut the carrots into long thin strips, then halve them and pile on the plate. Add the water chestnuts to the plate. Finally add the shrimp and spinach to the plate.

5. Heat the oil in a large sauté pan and stir in the pile of onion. Cook for 1 minute, stirring constantly, then add the pork mixture and stir briskly. When the pork has lightly browned, add the celery, carrots, and water chestnuts, then the spinach. Finally, add the shrimp and the reserved linguine. Toss the mixture in the pan over high heat, making sure that the pork, shrimp, and vegetables get thoroughly mixed with the linguine. Add extra soy sauce or water if necessary. Dish onto a large warmed platter and sprinkle with the remaining scallions. Serve immediately.

Calico Beans

These green, white, and dark red beans get their name from the multicolored patterns typical of calico. This dish is good for a potluck because it travels and reheats without coming to grief.

¹/₄ pound lean bacon, cut into 1-inch pieces
2 cups chopped onion
1 pound fresh ground beef
2 cups canned or home-cooked pea or navy beans
2 cups canned or home-cooked kidney beans or baked beans in tomato sauce
1 package frozen lima beans, thawed
Salt to taste
1 teaspoon dried oregano or Italian seasoning
2 tablespoons white vinegar
¹/₂ cup firmly packed brown sugar
¹/₂ cup tomato ketchup

1. Preheat the oven to 350° F. Put the bacon pieces in a large pot over moderate heat and cook until the fat runs a little, but remove while still undercooked and not yet golden. Set aside.

2. Add the onion and beef and cook until the onion is tender and the beef is browned. Drain off the fat.

3. Add the pea beans, ¹/₂ cup of the liquid from the pea beans, the kidney beans, and lima beans. Season with the salt.

4. Mix together the oregano, vinegar, brown sugar, and ketchup in a bowl and stir it into the bean mixture. Transfer the bean mixture to a baking dish. (If it is more convenient, you can prepare up to this point and cook up to 1 day later, keeping the dish in the fridge until you are ready.)

5. Cover and bake for 30 minutes. Uncover and check to make sure that the beans have not dried out. If they have, stir in a little water. Scatter the reserved bacon bits on top and bake for 10–15 minutes more, or until the bacon has browned. Serve with rice or potatoes.

Cranberry Bread Pudding
with Cranberry-Cinnamon Sauce

This rich bread pudding is treat-yourself food. The recipe comes from Chris Freeman, Chef at the Wauwinet Hotel in Nantucket, where guests can order individual puddings for breakfast. This version is perfect for brunch or for dessert — with ice cream if you want to go completely over the top. You have to start several hours ahead of cooking time, but the pudding reheats easily, so this is a good dish to make when you want to get some of the work out of the way.

PUDDING

1 ¹/₂ cups fresh cranberries
1 cup granulated sugar
2 eggs, plus 2 egg yolks
1 cup light cream or half-and-half
2 teaspoons pure vanilla extract
¹/₄ teaspoon ground cinnamon
¹/₄ teaspoon ground allspice
5 cups torn crustless brioche, challah, or
  Portuguese Sweet Bread

SAUCE

1 cup jellied cranberry sauce
¹/₂ teaspoon ground cinnamon
¹/₂ cup water

1. To make the pudding, about 4 hours before you want to serve the pudding (or the night before if you want it for breakfast or brunch), coarsely chop the cranberries and toss with ¹/₂ cup of the sugar. Let stand, covered, until they are juicy.

2. Whisk together the eggs, cream, vanilla, cinnamon, allspice, and the remaining sugar in a large bowl. Add the torn bread and stir well. Let stand for 2 hours or longer. (You can let the mixture stand overnight in the fridge if you like.)

3. Preheat the oven to 350º F. Grease a baking dish.

4. Pour the mixture into the prepared dish and bake for 45–60 minutes, or until a knife inserted in the center come out clean. (To make individual puddings, bake for 30 minutes in ramekins set in a pan of water.)

5. To make the sauce, mix together the cranberry sauce, cinnamon, and water in a small saucepan over moderate heat. Drizzle a little on the pudding and serve the remaining sauce on the side.

To make Cranberry-Raisin Bread Pudding: *Substitute 1 loaf of raisin bread, crusts removed, for the breads called for in the recipe above. Omit the cinnamon and add only ¹/₄ cup granulated sugar to the egg and milk mixture because raisin bread is already sweet.*

Honey Delectation

Choose a fragrant wildflower or clover honey made by a local beekeeper for this elegant dessert, or pick any flavorful honey, except buckwheat, which is too strong. If you have a heart-shaped or other pretty mold, use it to make this for Valentine's Day. If you enjoy dessert wines, serve this with a glass of Sauternes — they taste divine together.

1 package unflavored gelatin
³/₄ cup water
³/₄ cup wildflower honey
2 eggs, separated, or 4 teaspoons pasteurized egg whites
1 cup heavy cream

1. Stir together the gelatin and water in the top of a double boiler over simmering water. Cook, stirring frequently, until the gelatin has dissolved. Stir in the honey. When the mixture is warm, lightly beat the egg yolks in a bowl and add 1 cup of the warm honey mixture, then return the egg mixture to the honey mixture. Continue to cook, stirring frequently, until the mixture is very hot, though not simmering, and slightly thickened, about 10–15 minutes. Let cool in the fridge, until it begins to thicken and look gelatinous.

2. Beat the egg whites in a bowl until stiff. (In this dessert, the egg yolks are cooked, but the egg whites are not. Since they pose a tiny hazard to children or people with weak immune systems, you could substitute the pasteurized egg whites reconstituted with ¹/₄ cup of water instead of the fresh egg whites.) Beat the cream in a bowl until stiff. Rinse a mold in cold water, shake off the excess, but do not dry the interior. (This helps the dessert emerge from the mold later.)

3. Fold the cooled honey mixture into the egg whites. When it is well mixed, fold in the whipped cream until thoroughly blended. Pour the mixture into the prepared mold or pour into individual sherbet cups. Swirl the top surface if using sherbet cups. Place in the fridge for 4 hours to set.

4. Bring to room temperature for serving. To unmold, loosen the edge of the dessert from the mold using a palette or other round-bladed knife. Fill a large bowl with hot water. Dip the mold in it for 20–30 seconds, taking care that no water touches the dessert. Place a serving dish on top of the mold. Put one hand firmly on the serving dish and the other firmly on the bottom of the mold, then tip the mold over, giving it a sharp shake.

Boston Cream Pie

Boston cream pie is a cake not a pie, and it is filled with custard not cream. Early versions were made in small pie pans and split for filling. Now cream pies are baked in two layers. A dusting of confectioners' sugar used to be the customary finish, but the Parker House Hotel in Boston replaced this with a thin layer of chocolate frosting, and that, too, has become traditional. In either form, Boston cream pie has the charm of simplicity. It's cake to take to a potluck or to serve with tea or coffee.

CAKE

1 stick (4 ounces) unsalted butter at room temperature
³/₄ cup granulated sugar
2 teaspoons pure vanilla extract
2 teaspoons rosewater (optional)
2 eggs
2 ¹/₂ cups cake flour, sifted
1 tablespoon baking powder
¹/₂ cup milk

CUSTARD FILLING

1 teaspoon unflavored gelatin
1 tablespoon hot water
1 ¹/₄ cups milk
2 teaspoons pure vanilla extract
4 egg yolks
¹/₄ cup all-purpose flour
¹/₂ cup granulated sugar
³/₄ cup whipping or heavy cream

FROSTING

¹/₂ cup confectioners' sugar
2 tablespoons butter
1 tablespoon rum, brandy, or crème de cacao
  (optional)
4 ounces chocolate

1. Preheat the oven to 350º F. Lightly grease two 9-inch layer cake pans and line with baking parchment or waxed paper.

2. To make the cake, cream the butter and sugar together in a large bowl until they are pale and soft. Add the vanilla, the rosewater if using, and the eggs, one at a time, beating after each addition. Beat in 1 ¹/₄ cups of the flour and the baking powder. When well blended, beat in the remaining flour, then beat in the milk.

3. Divide the mixture between the 2 prepared pans, smoothing it out. Bake in the center of the oven for 20 minutes, or until a toothpick inserted in the center comes out clean. Cool on a wire rack for 10 minutes, then remove from the pans, strip off the baking parchment, and finish cooling before filling.

4. To make the custard filling, mix together the gelatin and the hot water in a cup or small bowl. Stand the cup or bowl in a pan of hot water to keep it warm. The gelatin should look clear and remain liquid while you work on the custard. Reheat, still standing in the pan of hot water, if necessary to reliquefy it.

5. Bring the milk to a simmer in a small saucepan. Add the vanilla. Stir the egg yolks and flour into a smooth paste in a large saucepan, then mix in the sugar and pour in the simmering milk. Cook over very low heat, without letting the mixture boil, stirring constantly until it thickens into a smooth custard with the density of pudding. Stir in the gelatin mixture, then pour into a bowl and cool in the fridge. Whip the cream and fold it into the custard filling.

6. Put one cake layer onto a serving plate and spread with the custard filling. Add the other layer. (You can sift confectioners' sugar on top at this point if you don't want frosting.)

7. To make the frosting, sift the sugar into a bowl and cream with the butter. Stir in the alcohol if you are using it. Melt the chocolate over a saucepan of simmering water, then stir it into the butter mixture. Spread the frosting on top of the cake. The sides are not usually frosted, though often the frosting is allowed to drip down here and there.

CHAPTER 12

COLD WEATHER FUN

Beside the interstate, a red-tailed hawk perches on a bare branch. The sky is brilliant and the day cold, so the hawk puffs its creamy breast and sits still and stoic, as if hired to count the ski-topped cars speeding north to the slopes. Realistically, though, it is watching for a movement that betrays a mouse or some other morsel hidden in the frozen grass.

Ice fishermen share its interest in life below the surface. They get out early on winter weekends, bringing dogs and children to keep them company and pulling sleds loaded with electric augers for piercing the ice and red-flagged tip-ups that signal a pickerel or bass on the hook below. As they spread out across the lake, the scene looks like a Dutch painting of winter. Beneath a luminous sky, some walkers have ventured forth to marvel at the thickness of the ice. The fishermen hunch on their stools, while children in bright pom-pommed hats bounce to keep warm, and dogs caper in happy mischief. In one corner, teenagers with hockey sticks whiz around on skates; in another, a couple enjoys a moment of dalliance. And if

the weather is at its coldest cold, there may be a fire, right there on the ice, drawing people, their hands outstretched, to its glow.

Fish fresh out of the lake taste delicious dipped in cornmeal and fried, but most ice fishermen are out for sport, so they generally use their fires for warmth, letting the fish slither back into their holes. Historically, though, for Native Americans and settlers alike, ice fishing was winter work providing valuable food.

Similarly, skating, skiing, and snowshoeing were not pastimes but practical ways of getting around snowy terrains. Skates were developed by the Dutch so they could skim down their canals and rivers. They were unknown in England until the mid-seventeenth century, by which time many colonists in New England had probably already adopted them from the Dutch settlers of neighboring New York.

Native Americans invented snowshoes using wooden frames and rawhide strips so they could get around the forests to hunt animals, who were hampered by heavy snows. Settlers quickly saw the benefits of this racquetlike footgear. State militias and the U.S. Army used to be kitted with snowshoes. New England's foresters and maple sugar farmers still sometimes wear them for working in snowbound woodlands.

As for skis, the earliest written account of skiing comes from the Viking sagas, and archeologists have found 4,000-year-old skis in Scandinavia and Siberia. Like the snowshoeing Native Americans, these northern Europeans traveled, hunted, and fought on their winter footgear, but skiing did not become a sport until the mid-nineteenth century, when Norwegians started ski racing. Soon, Norwegian miners had brought ski competitions to California. In New England, the first ski club was organized at Dartmouth College in Hanover, New Hampshire, in 1909, indicating that the sport was already popular then. Today, of course, every mountainous area of New England has its ski resorts, while cross-country

skiers — free of the need of lifts — head off on sun-dappled forest trails.

No one comes back from either form of skiing — or from skating, ice fishing, or snowshoeing — without an appetite, so ski resorts have dozens of restaurants, some alpine in inspiration, others modeled on British pubs, French bistros, or New England inns of yesteryear. But whatever culinary tradition they draw from, all agree that the food has to be eaten within sight of a giant fireplace ablaze with roaring logs - and it has to be hearty. New England fare, such as thick soups, fish fillets, steaks and chops followed by puddings and pies, comes into its own in these settings. A fondue, recalling the après-ski foods of Switzerland, may be welcome, and chili is very acceptable. But after cold weather fun, the charms of light contemporary food fade beside the pleasures of comforting traditional fare.

Not French Onion Soup

French onion soup made from browned onions and packed with cheese and bread is popular in winter sport resorts, but it is time-consuming to make at home, and the cheese topping makes it heavy. This onion soup is lighter and easier to make, and it does a perfect job of warming you up on a cold day. It also helps when you have a cold.

1 $^1/_2$ pounds onions, peeled and sliced (about 6 onions)
6 cups cold water
1 bunch fresh parsley
1 teaspoon salt
1 tablespoon cornstarch
$^1/_3$ cup cold water
Salt and white pepper to taste

1. Put the onions, the 6 cups cold water, 10 parsley sprigs, and the 1 teaspoon salt into a large saucepan. Bring to a boil. Reduce the heat to simmer and cook for 20 minutes, or until the onions are tender. Remove the parsley and discard.

2. If you want a smooth soup, let the mixture cool slightly, then puree, in batches, in a food processor or pass through a food mill. Return the puree to the pan. If you want a chunkier soup, simply proceed to the next step.

3. Mix the cornstarch and the $^1/_3$ cup cold water into a paste in a small bowl. Stir in $^1/_2$ cup of the soup, then add the mixture to the pan. Return to a simmer, stirring occasionally, and cook until the soup has thickened slightly. Repeat this step if you would like a thicker soup. Taste for seasonings and add more salt if necessary and the white pepper to taste.

4. While the soup is cooking, chop the remaining parsley. You should have at least 1 cup. Just before serving, stir almost all of the parsley into the soup. Before cooking darkens the bright flecks of green, ladle the soup into bowls and sprinkle each serving with a little more parsley. Serve hot.

Cheese Fondue

In the United States, the popularity of cheese fondue, a dish of the European alps, grew with that of skiing, but surprisingly fondue was served in Boston long before New England's mountains were striped with ski slopes. Its purveyor was Jean-Baptiste Gilbert Payplat, a Frenchman known as Julien, who opened the first restaurant in Boston in 1794. He called it a Restorator, and compared to the taverns of the time, it was elegant. Its fame attracted Claude Anselme Brillat-Savarin, soon to be the author of the classic of gastronomic literature, *The Physiology of Taste*, but at the time living near Hartford, Connecticut. Once in Boston, he received Julien's recipe for consommé, offering in return his recipe for fondue, a mixture of eggs, Swiss cheese, and butter, which soon became a favorite late-night supper of Boston's gentlemen. Brillat-Savarin advised, "With it drink your best wine, and you will see wonders." The Swiss-style wine and cheese fondue popular in ski resorts is a cousin to this dish, and no less wonderful: an ideal meal for a group of friends who have been out in the cold. Children think it's fun, too.

2 cups white wine
2 cloves garlic, halved
1 pound Gruyère cheese or Jarlsberg cheese
1 pound Emmenthaler cheese
2 tablespoons cornstarch
⅓ cup kirsch
Chunks of white and whole wheat bread

1. Put the wine into a fondue pot or large saucepan over medium heat. Add the garlic and simmer for 3–4 minutes, then discard the garlic.

2. Grate the Gruyère and Emmenthaler into a bowl or cut into small cubes and toss both cheeses with the cornstarch. Add the cheese, 1 cup at a time, to the wine and stir until it has melted. Repeat until all of the cheese has been used, and the mixture is thick. Immediately before serving, stir in the kirsch.

3. If using a fondue pot, place it over its burner turned down low and set it in the center of the table. If using a saucepan, set it over a warmer, powered with a tea light, or simply set it on a heated serving tray. Place the bread in a basket on the table. To eat the fondue, everybody takes some bread on the end of a fork and dips it into the cheese mixture.

Swordfish with Rapini, Lemon & Pine Nuts

The firm flesh of swordfish and the vibrant flavors of rapini, lemon, and pine nuts make this tasty dish a good choice for a winter evening. Rapini, also called rabes or broccoli rabe, looks like a thinner, leafier form of broccoli. It's an Italian favorite, as are the other ingredients of this dish.

¹/₃ cup pine nuts
3 – 4 tablespoons olive oil
2 tablespoons freshly squeezed lemon juice
1 ¹/₂ – 2 pounds swordfish, 1-inch thick
1 large bunch fresh rapini
3 tablespoons all-purpose flour
¹/₄ teaspoon salt
¹/₄ teaspoon black pepper
3 tablespoons chopped fresh parsley
2 – 3 cloves garlic, chopped (to taste)
1 lemon, cut into slices or wedges for garnish

1. Preheat the oven to 325° F. Put the pine nuts into a shallow baking pan and toast for 5–7 minutes or until golden. (Watch them at the end of the toasting time; they can burn in a heartbeat.) Remove from the oven and increase the temperature to 425°.

2. Mix together 1 tablespoon of the oil and the lemon juice in a shallow dish. Cut the swordfish into 4 serving pieces (or leave it whole if you prefer) and place in the oil mixture. Turn to baste both sides and let stand in the dish for 10 minutes, turning once or twice.

3. Wash the rapini and trim 1 inch from the stems. Discard any overly large or ragged leaves. Bring a saucepan with 2 inches of water to a boil. Put the rapini into the pan, stalks down with the leafy tops above the water level. Cover and cook for 3–4 minutes. Drain well and set the rapini aside.

4. Mix together the flour, salt, and black pepper in a shallow bowl. Dip the swordfish in the flour mixture so that both sides are coated. Heat 1 tablespoon of the oil in a large shallow ovenproof pan and cook the swordfish for 2 minutes. Turn it over carefully and immediately put the pan into the oven and bake for 8 minutes.

5. While the swordfish is cooking, add half of the reserved pine nuts to the parsley and chop together to make a coarse mixture. Set aside.

6. Five minutes before the swordfish is ready, heat 1 tablespoon of the oil in a large skillet and add the garlic. Gently cook for 1 minute, then add the reserved rapini and season lightly with more salt. Toss it in the pan over moderately high heat. Add the remaining pine nuts and cook the rapini for 4 minutes or just long enough to heat through.

7. Transfer the rapini to 4 dinner plates or one large platter. Position pieces of the swordfish on top. Scatter the reserved parsley mixture on the swordfish. Garnish with the lemon slices or wedges at the side. Serve hot.

Pork Chops with Parsnip & Apple Mash

Today, pork is much leaner than it used to be, so cooking can dry it out. In this recipe, a crumb coat protects the pork chops, holding both moisture and flavor in the meat. It also contrasts pleasantly with the soft mash of parsnips, potato, and apples.

PORK CHOPS

1 ½ cups dried herb-flavored bread crumbs
  (type used for stuffing)
4 large center-cut pork loin chops, each
  ¾ inch thick
Salt and white pepper
1 teaspoon dried thyme or oregano
1 egg, beaten with 1 tablespoon milk
2 tablespoons light-flavored oil

PARSNIP & APPLE MASH

1 large potato, peeled and cut into chunks
1 teaspoon salt
1 pound parsnips, peeled and cut into
  1-inch pieces (about 4 large)
2 McIntosh or Cortland apples, peeled,
  cored, and sliced
2–3 tablespoons milk
Black pepper (optional)

1. Preheat the oven to 375º F. Lightly grease a baking dish.

2. To make the pork chops, crush the bread crumbs with a rolling pin or in a food processor until they are fairly fine. Put them on a plate.

3. Season the chops with the salt and white pepper and sprinkle with the thyme. Dip each chop first in the egg mixture, then in the crumbs. Press the crumbs firmly onto the meat and place the chops in the prepared dish. Let stand in the fridge for 15 minutes.

4. Heat the oil in a skillet and cook the chops for 2 minutes per side. Put them back into the baking dish and bake for 18–25 minutes, depending on thickness, timing this so that the chops go in the oven a few minutes after you put the potato chunks on to cook.

5. To make the mash, put the potato chunks in a large saucepan and cover with cold water. Add the salt and bring to a simmer. Cook for 3–4 minutes, then add the parsnips and cook for 10 minutes more. Add the apple slices and cook for 5 minutes more, or until everything is tender. Drain thoroughly and mash, adding the milk only if necessary to make a smooth mixture. Taste for seasonings and add the black pepper if you like and more salt if necessary.

6. Check the chops while the vegetables are cooking. If the juice comes out clear when you pierce the chops with a knife point, they are ready. If the mash is not yet done, keep the chops warm by covering the dish with aluminum foil and placing in a warm spot near the stove.

7. To serve, pile mounds of the mash on 4 plates and rest 1 chop against each. Accompany with a green vegetable, such as Brussels sprouts, broccoli, or rapini. Serve hot.

Braised Lamb Shanks with Rosemary & Potatoes

This slow-cooked braise is perfect winter food: comforting and tasty. The recipe accommodates your needs: make it ahead and reheat if you like; add more carrots for a one-dish meal; double up on lamb shanks if they are small or appetites are large. They have a big bone that contributes mightily to the flavor, but makes them a bit less substantial than they look.

Two 1-pound lamb shanks
2 cloves garlic, slivered
$^1/_2$ teaspoon dried rosemary
Salt
1 tablespoon vegetable oil
2 medium-large onions, coarsely chopped
2 cups chicken broth or water
6 carrots
1 bay leaf
6 large potatoes, peeled and cut into $^1/_2$-inch slices

1. Lamb shanks are covered with a silvery skin. Make incisions all over the skin so that it does not tighten onto the meat in cooking. Stick some of the garlic slivers and rosemary into the incisions. Rub the surface with the salt.

2. Preheat the oven to 350° F. Heat the oil over low heat in a roasting pan and braise the lamb shanks, turning often, for 10–15 minutes, or until the exterior is golden brown. Add the onion and the remaining garlic to the pan and pour in the broth. Halve 2 of the carrots. Add these carrots, the bay leaf, and a seasoning of salt to the pan. Cover and bring to a simmer, then transfer to the oven.

3. Gently cook the shanks for 2 hours, reducing the temperature if necessary to keep them just simmering. Turn the shanks over in the liquid three or four times.

4. Cut the remaining carrots into thin disks. When the lamb has shrunk from the bone, remove the halved carrots and bay leaf from the pan and discard. Remove and set aside 1 cup of the cooking liquid. Put the sliced carrots into the pan, then place the sliced potatoes on top so they cover most of the meat and carrots. Sprinkle on the remaining rosemary, then pour on the reserved cooking liquid.

5. Return to a simmer on top of the stove, then return to the oven and cook for 40–50 minutes more, or until the potatoes are tender. Uncover and let the surface brown for 10 minutes. Serve immediately or reheat for later.

Codfish Cakes

Today, the majority of New Englanders have never tasted homemade codfish cakes made from salt cod, yet they used to be staple breakfast and supper fare, often served with baked beans, especially in the winter. One reason why codfish cakes have become so much less common is that salt cod tastes stronger than fresh fish, and for many people, it is an acquired taste. Then, too, it must be soaked before being cooked, so if you want codfish cakes, you must get the fish in water many hours ahead of time. Today, salt cod is getting some attention again. Chefs are putting it on their menus, sometimes in traditional codfish cakes, sometimes in one of the many dishes brought by Portuguese, Italian, and Caribbean immigrants. Some chefs even salt their own cod, but for home cooks, the excellent Canadian salt cod packed in wooden boxes and stocked by most supermarkets works well.

$^1/_2$ *pound salt cod*
4 medium-large potatoes, peeled and cut into chunks
1 tablespoon chopped fresh parsley
$^1/_4$ *teaspoon ground allspice or nutmeg*
Black pepper to taste
4 tablespoons all-purpose flour
Bacon fat or vegetable oil

1. Rinse the cod under cold running water for 5 minutes. Put it into a bowl and cover with plenty of water. Let stand for 12–30 hours, changing the water three to four times during this period. (The longer you soak the fish, the milder it will taste. Salt cod aficionados prefer the shorter soaking times.)

2. Drain the cod and put it into a saucepan. Cover with water and bring just to a simmer over low heat. As soon as it simmers, turn off the heat and cover. Let the cod stand in the water for 15 minutes, then drain and flake, removing any bones (though usually there are none).

3. While the fish is cooking, boil the potatoes in lightly salted water in a large saucepan for 20 minutes or until tender. Drain and mash. Add the flaked cod, parsley, allspice, and black pepper.

4. When the potato mixture is cool enough to handle, shape it into small cakes, roughly 2 inches wide x $^3/_4$ inch high. Shake the flour over a plate, then dip both sides of each cake in the flour.

5. Heat enough bacon fat or oil (or a mixture) to cover a skillet by $^1/_8$ inch. Fry the codfish cakes for 4–5 minutes per side or until completely golden. Serve hot with Baked Beans (see recipe on page 202). Makes 10–12 codfish cakes.

Chicken Breast Clementine in a Hazelnut Crust

Clementines arrive in New England in time for Christmas and disappear again by the end of January. Most are imported from Spain, though the fruit was originally developed in Algeria by a priest, Father Clement, hence its name. In this recipe, clementines combine with hazelnuts to give flavor to boneless, skinless chicken breasts.

8 boneless skinless chicken breast halves
4 clementines or tangerines, or 2 small oranges
1 clove garlic, finely chopped
2 teaspoons dried thyme
3 tablespoons olive oil
1 cup hazelnuts or sliced almonds
²/₃ cup all-purpose flour
1 egg, beaten with 2 tablespoons milk
Salt and black pepper

1. Chicken breasts have a white, ribbonlike membrane along the side. In cooking, this shrinks, pulling the meat into an ugly shape, so it is best to remove it by slicing the meat away from it with a sharp knife, then pulling it out. Flatten the breasts by beating them several times with the flat side of a cleaver and place in a large shallow bowl.

2. Grate the zest from 2 of the clementines. Sprinkle the zest, garlic, and 1 teaspoon of the thyme over the chicken. Squeeze the juice from the clementines and pour it on the chicken. Add 2 tablespoons of the oil and turn the breasts over several times. Cover and place in the fridge for 2 hours (or longer if more convenient), turning once or twice to marinate the chicken.

3. Preheat the oven to 325° F. Skin the hazelnuts by placing them in a shallow baking pan and roasting them for 6–7 minutes, by which time you should see some of the skins loosening. Tip the nuts into a clean cloth, fold it over them, and rub vigorously. The loose skins will have mostly come off. If any scraps remain, scrape them off with a knife. If some nuts remain unskinned, return them to the oven for a few more minutes, then try again.

4. Return all of the skinned nuts to the oven for 3–4 minutes, or until they are golden and fragrant. Coarsely chop, either in a food processor or by putting them in a plastic bag and beating them with a cleaver or rolling pin until they look like very coarse crumbs.

5. Put ¹/₂ cup of the flour on a plate, the egg mixture in a shallow bowl, and the crushed hazelnuts mixed with the remaining flour and thyme on another plate. Season the chicken with the salt and black pepper, then dip the chicken first into the flour, then into the egg mixture, and then into the hazelnut mixture.

6. Preheat the oven to 400° F. Grease a large shallow baking dish. Put the coated chicken into the prepared dish and place in the fridge for 15–20 minutes.

7. Sprinkle the remaining oil over the chicken and bake in the top third of the oven for 12 minutes, or until the juice that runs when you pierce the breast with a skewer is clear, not pink,

and the crust is golden. (If the chicken is ready but the crust is still pale, remove the breasts from the oven and turn on the broiler. When it is hot, briefly broil the chicken for 1 minute or just long enough to color the crust.)

8. Slice the remaining clementines. Place 1 chicken breast on each plate and garnish with the sliced clementines. Serves 8.

To make Chicken Breast Clementine in an Almond Crust: *Substitute 1 cup chopped or slivered almonds for the hazelnuts. Put the almonds into a shallow baking pan and toast at 325° F for 10 minutes, or until they are toffee-colored and fragrant. Stir them once or twice while they are toasting. Crush until they look like very coarse crumbs, then proceed as directed in the recipe.*

Chili with Colored Peppers & Cinnamon Corn Bread

Nineteenth-century New England housewives made the juicy tomatoes of summer into chili sauces by stewing them down with mustard and cayenne pepper, but chili con carne was invented on the cattle trails of the West, where cooks dealt with tough meat by cutting it into small pieces, dosing it with hot pepper, and cooking the daylights out of it. An early recipe from the 1896 *Manual for Army Cooks* told soldiers how to make chili in their mess kits by squeezing soaked hot peppers onto steak and rice. Today, chili is not so simple, nor is it solely a western dish. Every region has a favorite version, often alarming chili purists, who campaign against using beans, tomato products, and commercial chili powders. Nevertheless, New Englanders generally include all three. Quite often, they also add vegetables, such as corn or bell peppers. Beef, pork, venison, and sausage are all good in chili, as is tempeh. Ground meat is usual, but diced meat works better because it does not disintegrate. Chili is best when cooked slowly, and it takes well to reheating, so it's a perfect do-ahead meal to have on hand when you return from a day outdoors. No wonder that this dish from the hot Southwest has become such a favorite in the cold Northeast!

CHILI WITH COLORED PEPPERS

$1/2$ pound sweet Italian sausage or breakfast sausage
1 tablespoon vegetable oil
1 large onion, chopped
1–3 cloves garlic, chopped (to taste)
$1 1/2$ pounds lean stew beef, cut into 1-inch pieces
4–6 tablespoons chili powder (to heat tolerance)
1 teaspoon cumin seeds
1 tablespoon dried oregano
1 cup crushed canned tomatoes, or one 8-ounce can tomato sauce
2 cups beef or chicken broth or water
Salt to taste
2 cups canned or homecooked kidney or pinto beans, drained and rinsed
1 yellow or orange bell pepper, deveined, seeded, and cut into $1/2$-inch dice
1 red bell pepper, deveined, seeded, and cut into $1/2$-inch dice

CINNAMON CORN BREAD

¹/₂ stick (2 ounces) butter
1 cup yellow cornmeal
1 cup all-purpose flour
1 tablespoon granulated sugar
1 teaspoon chili powder
1 teaspoon ground cinnamon
2 teaspoons baking powder
1 egg
¹/₂ cup milk
One 11-ounce can whole kernel corn

1. To make the chili, if the sausage is in skins, remove it and cut the sausage into 1-inch pieces. Heat the oil in a large pot. Add the sausage and cook until it has browned on all sides, then stir in the onion and garlic. Reduce the heat, cover, and cook, stirring occasionally, for 4–5 minutes, or until the onion is tender.

2. Add the beef to the pot, stirring occasionally, until browned. Sprinkle 4 tablespoons of the chili powder over the meat and stir well. (Use the additional chili powder only if you want a hot chili.) Mix in the cumin seeds and oregano, then the tomatoes, broth, and salt. Cover and simmer for 1 hour, stirring frequently. You can work to this point up to 1 day ahead.

3. Twenty minutes before serving, add the beans and both bell peppers and simmer until serving time.

4. Make the cornbread while the chili is cooking. Preheat the oven to 400° F. To make the corn bread, put the butter into an 8-inch square baking pan and let it melt.

5. Thoroughly mix together the cornmeal, flour, sugar, chili powder, cinnamon, and baking powder in a large bowl. Whisk together the egg and milk in another bowl. Swirl the melted butter around the baking pan to grease the sides, then pour it into the egg mixture.

6. Make a well in the center of the flour mixture. Add the egg mixture and the corn, including ¹/₂ cup of its liquid. Stir to combine, adding enough additional milk to make a dough with a soft dropping consistency. Put the dough into the prepared pan and bake for 20 minutes, or until a toothpick inserted in the center comes out clean. Cool on a wire rack.

7. To serve, cut the corn bread into squares and place in serving bowls. Pour the chili over or around them and serve. Serves 6.

Baked Beans

Boston is called "Bean Town" because time was when baked beans were staple fare, regularly made on Saturday evening and eaten for both Saturday supper and Sunday breakfast, often with codfish cakes — a custom widely shared throughout New England, though rare today. Still baked beans remain favorite fare, especially at buffet meals, and especially when a ham is also on the menu. Recipes vary widely. In Maine, people prefer a local bean, such as yellow-eyed peas. Many people prefer the lighter flavor of maple syrup to molasses. A chunk of salt pork in the bottom of the bean pot used to be traditional. Now bacon bits may replace it, or there may be no meat at all, as in this recipe. It comes from Jeffrey Paige, Chef of The Creamery Restaurant at Canterbury Shaker Village in Canterbury, New Hampshire. He adapted it from a recipe developed by Shaker sisters in the 1930s, when they made weekly batches of baked beans and delivered them to townspeople in nearby Concord.

1 pound navy or pea beans
1 large onion, diced
2 tablespoons Dijon mustard
$^1/_4$ cup firmly packed dark brown sugar

$^1/_3$ cup firmly packed light brown sugar
$^1/_4$ cup molasses
1 teaspoon salt or to taste

1. Discard any discolored beans. Cover the beans with plenty of cold water and soak overnight or for 6–8 hours.

2. Drain the beans and cook over medium heat in enough fresh water to cover by 1 inch. Bring to a simmer and cook until just tender, about 45 minutes, but may be longer if the beans are old or the soaking time was short. Drain the beans and set aside the cooking liquid.

3. Preheat the oven to 325° F. Mix together the drained beans, onion, mustard, dark and light brown sugars, molasses, and salt in a bean pot or deep-lidded casserole, Add enough of the reserved cooking liquid to just cover the beans and stir to blend everything. Cover and bring to a simmer on top of the stove, then bake for 2 hours, checking every 30 minutes to make sure the beans don't dry out. Add more of the reserved cooking liquid if this seems likely.

4. Once the beans are thoroughly tender, uncover and cook for 20 – 30 minutes more if you like a slightly crusty top. Serve with Codfish Cakes (see recipe on page 197).

To make Baked Beans with Pork: *Rinse off any crusted salt on a 3-inch square of salt pork with cold water. Score the skin two to three times in each direction, then place it in the center of the bean mixture before you put it into the oven.*

To make Baked Beans in Tomato Sauce: *Omit the dark and light brown sugars from the recipe. Add 1 bay leaf, 1 cup canned tomato sauce, 2 tablespoons vegetable oil, and, optionally, a few drops Tabasco sauce. Mix these ingredients with the onion, mustard, molasses, and salt and cook as directed. Remove the bay leaf before serving.*

Eggnog Tapioca Pudding

Tapioca pudding compels attention. The little balls of tapioca give you pause, while the creamy context soothes the mind. This eggnog version of an old favorite is especially good when made with large pearl tapioca.

1/2 cup large or small pearl tapioca
2 cups cold water
1 1/4 cups milk
4 egg yolks
1/2 cup granulated sugar

1/2 teaspoon pure vanilla extract
1/2 cup cream
1/4 teaspoon ground nutmeg (preferably freshly grated)
1–2 tablespoons rum to taste

1. Put the tapioca into a large saucepan and cover with the cold water. Cover and bring to a boil. Immediately take the pan from the heat and let stand for 1 1/2–2 hours, by which time the pearls will have swollen into a jellylike mass. Stir in the milk, breaking up the mixture, and bring to a simmer. Cook for 10–15 minutes, stirring frequently, or until the tapioca pearls are tender. (Bite one to test it. Large pearl tapioca takes longer to become tender than small pearl.) The mixture should be thick.

2. Meanwhile, in the top of a double boiler or in a large bowl set over a pan of simmering water, whisk together the egg yolks, sugar, and vanilla. Stir in the cream and cook for 5–10 minutes, stirring frequently, until thick enough to coat the back of a wooden spoon. When you can draw your finger across it and leave a path, it's ready.

3. Pour the thickened tapioca, 1/8 teaspoon of the nutmeg, and 1 tablespoon of the rum into the egg mixture. Stir until very thick, only about 2–3 minutes. Stir in the remaining rum. Spoon the pudding into a serving bowl or individual dishes and sprinkle with the remaining nutmeg. Serve at room temperature or chilled.

NUTMEG

Connecticut is called the Nutmeg State, but nutmegs don't grow there. They grow in Indonesia and the Caribbean island of Granada. Like other nuts, the nutmeg sits inside a shell, which is itself encased in a lacy fiber. This hard fiber is mace, a spice that tastes a little like nutmeg, but it is more potent and used in smaller amounts. In the nineteenth century, when a grating of nutmeg was the finishing touch to many punches, neguses, and other drinks, a pocket nutmeg grater was just the thing to ensure that there was always a fragrant fresh supply; once ground, nutmeg quickly loses its flavor. Of course, if you had inadvertently purchased a wooden nutmeg, you were out of luck. Wooden nutmegs became a byword for something fraudulent, and Connecticut was called the Nutmeg State because it reputedly made wooden nutmegs for export.

Indian Pudding

Indian pudding sounds like a Native American dish adopted by European settlers. In fact, all of the ingredients, except the corn, are old-world foods, and the pudding is a variation on English wheat- or oat-based puddings. When settlers arrived from England, they adapted their recipes to corn, which they called "Indian meal" to distinguish it from other meals; to them, "corn" meant any grain, most particularly wheat. Since they made their pudding out of Indian meal, it became Indian pudding. It's rib-sticking food, and especially delectable when served hot with a dollop of vanilla ice cream.

$^1/_2$ stick (2 ounces) butter
$^1/_2$ cup molasses
$3\ ^1/_2$–4 cups milk
$^1/_2$ cup yellow cornmeal
1 teaspoon ground ginger
$^1/_2$ teaspoon ground cinnamon
$^1/_4$ teaspoon salt
1 egg, beaten
Vanilla ice cream

1. Preheat the oven to 350º F. Grease a soufflé dish and a $^1/_2$-cup measuring cup with a little of the butter. Put the molasses into the cup and set aside.

2. Bring 3 cups of the milk to a simmer in a large saucepan. Off the heat, stir in the cornmeal. Reduce the heat and replace the saucepan. Gently cook for 5 minutes, stirring constantly, until the mixture has thickened. Sift the ginger and cinnamon onto the mixture through a sieve or sprinkle it carefully over the whole surface so it doesn't form lumps. Whisk in. Stir in the salt and the reserved molasses (which will pour easily out of the greased cup). Lightly beat together the egg and $^1/_2$ cup of the milk and stir it into the mixture.

3. Pour the mixture into the prepared dish and bake for 20 minutes, then stir. Reduce the temperature to 325º and bake for 50–60 minutes more, stirring after 30 minutes. If the pudding seems stiff, add $^1/_2$ cup of the milk (or more if necessary).

4. When the pudding has a brown, thickened top and is as thick as oatmeal, but not stiff, remove it from the oven. It will thicken more as it cools. Should it get thicker than you like, stir in the remaining milk. Serve warm with the ice cream. Two alternate toppings for Indian pudding are whipped cream or maple syrup.

Carrot & Apricot Cake

Carrot cake is made with oil rather than butter or shortening, and for this reason, stays moist for several days, especially when topped with the traditional cream cheese frosting. Recipes vary. In this version, apricots add succulence and fruit flavor.

CAKE

20 dried apricots, quartered
$1/2$ cup cold water
1 $1/2$ cups light-flavored oil
4 eggs
1 cup firmly packed dark brown sugar
$1/2$ cup raisins
2 cups grated carrots (about 4 carrots)
1 teaspoon ground ginger
$1/2$ teaspoon ground mace
1 teaspoon ground cinnamon
3 cups all-purpose flour
1 tablespoon baking powder

FROSTING

One 8-ounce package cream cheese at
    room temperature
$1/2$ stick (2 ounces) butter at room
    temperature
$1/4$ teaspoon pure vanilla extract
Few drops lemon oil to taste
1–2 teaspoons fresh lemon juice
1 cup confectioners' sugar

1. Preheat the oven to 350º F. Grease a 9 x 13-inch baking pan. Line it with baking parchment if you want to take the cake out of the pan; if you plan to serve it from the pan, this is unnecessary.

2. To make the cake, put the apricots and cold water into a small saucepan. Bring to a simmer and cook for 5 minutes or until tender. Let cool to lukewarm.

3. Mix together the oil, eggs, and sugar in a large bowl. Add the raisins, carrots, apricots (including the liquid), ginger, mace, and cinnamon and mix well. Combine the flour and baking powder and stir it thoroughly into the mixture.

4. Turn the batter into the prepared pan and bake in the center of the oven for 30–35 minutes, or until a toothpick inserted in the center comes out clean. Cool on a wire rack. If you have lined the pan and want to remove the cake, run a knife around the sides and then invert it after it has cooled for 30 minutes. Strip the paper from the base of the cake and let it finish cooling completely before frosting.

5. To make the frosting, blend together the cream cheese, butter, vanilla, lemon oil, and lemon juice in a bowl. Sift the confectioners' sugar onto the mixture and blend in. Be sure that the cake is cool before frosting the top. Cut the cake into squares and serve.

Anadama Bread

New England legend has it that this bread was created by a fisherman who was annoyed with his wife, Anna, for failing to get the job done. "Anna, damn her," he muttered as he worked, so Anadama became the name of the bread. Whether the tale is true or not, it's generally agreed that Anadama comes from Massachusetts, most likely from the fishing town of Gloucester. It's a hearty bread, drawing its appeal from the mixture of cornmeal and wheat flour and the sweetening of molasses. But while all Anadama recipes have these ingredients, exact quantities vary. The following recipe makes a firm but tender loaf, excellent with soup and good for sandwiches.

1 package active dry yeast
¹/₂ cup warm water
2 tablespoons light vegetable oil
¹/₂ cup molasses
1 ¹/₂ cups hot water
4 cups bread flour or bread machine flour
1 cup yellow cornmeal
¹/₂ cup wheat germ (optional)
2 teaspoons salt
1 tablespoon butter, melted

1. Mix together the yeast and warm water in a small bowl. Let stand for 5 minutes or until slightly frothy.

2. Pour the oil into a ¹/₂-cup measuring cup and swirl it so it greases the cup, then tip the oil into a large bowl. Measure the molasses in this greased cup and add it to the oil; you will find that it pours out of the cup cleanly. Add the hot water to the molasses mixture. Let stand until lukewarm.

3. Mix together the flour, cornmeal, wheat germ (if using), and salt in a large bowl. Make a well in the center and add the yeast mixture, then the lukewarm molasses mixture. Mix thoroughly and then knead until the dough comes away from the bowl and does not stick to your hands, about 5–6 minutes using an electric mixer or 10–12 minutes working by hand.

4. Cover the bowl with plastic wrap and let stand in a draft-free place until the dough has doubled in bulk, about 1 ¹/₂ hours. Punch down the dough and knead a few times more.

5. Grease two 9 x 5 x 2-inch loaf pans. Put the dough into the pans and cover with plastic wrap. Let rise until doubled in bulk, about 1 hour.

6. During this rising time, preheat the oven to 375° F. Bake the loaves for 25 minutes, or until the bottom sounds hollow when rapped sharply. Brush the butter over the top of the hot bread to give a shiny finish. Cool on a wire rack. Makes 2 loaves.

CHAPTER 13

ONCE A YEAR

Every holiday comes around only once a year, but when we say "Christmas comes but once a year," we make a special appeal to generosity, forgiveness, festivity, extravagance — all qualities that light up the darkness.

Of course, religious tradition plays a part in all this, but other things are going on, too. Christmas comes at the end of the year, so there's a reflective undertone to the holiday. With a new year coming up, it's a time to look back on pleasures and successes and let go of what cannot be helped.

More dramatically and like all festivities that fall in the dark of winter, Christmas incites us to frolic, to gather together, and to laugh in the face of cold. There can be few New Englanders who have not shoveled snow in order to get out to a party or to cut a Christmas tree, even when it was crusted with ice. As for stringing lights around rooflines and yards and stationing Santas and reindeers on housetops and lawns, the custom thrives in New England, especially in country districts, where people defy the darkness most vividly, cheering the way of those who have to drive deserted roads on the ice-cold nights of the darkest months.

Illuminating the house for Christmas takes time and ingenuity, and so does Christmas baking. Many hours go into shaping cookies and baking breads and cakes. Often they are Christmas specialties, made only once a year, their annual appearance making them all the more welcome. But for the cook, rarely made specialties can be daunting, freighting Christmas baking with worries about whether the breads and cakes will rise as they should, whether the cookies will be as beautiful and aromatic as those of yore.

Why bother then? Since Christmas baking demands time and provokes anxiety, why not buy stuff from the store? Of course, everybody makes some purchases, but they still bake and cook. Time and anxiety are not a problem; they are the point, maybe even the main point: a way of acknowledging the importance of the dishes that make Christmas special to each family and a way of passing Christmas traditions on to another generation.

Yet with all that Christmas now entails, it's surprising to realize that Christmas as we know it in New England was invented only fairly recently. The seventeenth-century Puritan and Quaker settlers reacted against the high jinks of the traditional English Christmas and the ceremony of Anglican customs. Christmas was purely religious, they insisted. On December 25, therefore, people attended to business as usual, at least until the end of the eighteenth century, when the first sign of today's Christmas appeared as a Christmas cookie recipe in Amelia Simmons's *American Cookery,* a book published in Connecticut.

Nearly fifty years were to pass before Connecticut declared Christmas a public holiday in 1845, the first New England state to do so. By that time, New Englanders had become enthusiastic about the holiday. As fervent Puritanism waned, some adopted the festivities of Episcopalian churches and homes. Others knew of the Christmas trees of England, a tradition brought by Queen Victoria's husband from Germany and eagerly promoted by the Queen. Yet others were influenced by the Dutch traditions of neighboring New York, where Santa Claus brought gifts and housewives baked their traditional *koekjes* — cookies as English speakers were to call them. Gradually, children began hanging stockings at the chimney, expecting to find in the morning an orange in the toe, along with candies, nuts, and even some toys. In 1846 Emily Dickinson wrote that she "found an abundance of candy in my stocking," but she doubted — so she said — that it had "the anticipated effect on my disposition, in case it was to sweeten it." As for foods, Thanksgiving dishes, such as oyster stew, turkey, and pie, were putting in second appearances at Christmas,

with goose, duck, wine jellies, and English steamed puddings as alternatives.

Immigrants later added more variety to the holiday. Traditionally, many Roman Catholics abstained from meat before Christmas. Today, this custom remains in a celebratory fish dinner on Christmas Eve. Italians call it the Feast of Seven Fishes, because at its most elaborate, they serve seven courses of fish or seafood. Poles call their meal *wigilia,* which means "vigil" in English, because its celebrants await the birth of Jesus by keeping an empty place at the table. For Franco-Americans, Christmas Eve spells *Le Réveillon,* a banquet of Quebecois dishes, typically *tourtière* (a pork and beef pie) and *cipaille* (a stew of mixed meats baked under pastry). Desserts include doughnuts, maple sugar pie, and bûche de Noël, a chocolate-frosted cake decorated as a Yule log.

It's easy to see that these hearty dishes bring warmth to northern winters. In contrast, many Puerto Rican families of New England are not necessarily committed to the roast turkey, which probably remains the most typical Christmas dinner of the region. Instead they sometimes roast pork with garlic and oregano. They continue celebrating until Three Kings' Day on January 6, the traditional time for giving presents. There is always plenty of food around, including sweet specialties, such as candied fruits, Spanish nougat, and arroz con dulce, a dense rice pudding crisscrossed with sprinkled cinnamon.

Notwithstanding this variety, New Englanders share a common pleasure in a grand Christmas feast, featuring a splendid main dish, followed by special desserts, usually something traditional, with fruits, nuts, and candies on hand throughout the holiday.

Apple-Stuffed Roast Goose with Roast Potatoes

Many people roast a turkey for Christmas, but since the holiday comes on the heels of Thanksgiving, others like to choose something different. Goose is both festive and delicious. As water birds, geese have a large body cavity, perfect for keeping them afloat — and for stuffing — but it makes them look bigger than they really are, so buy the heaviest goose you can find. It is a good choice for 6–8 people.

APPLE STUFFING
1 cup chopped onion
2 cups water
2 medium apples, peeled, cored, and diced
¼ cup light-flavored oil
3 cups packaged herb-flavored bread crumbs

ROAST GOOSE WITH ROAST POTATOES
One 10–12-pound goose
3 teaspoons salt
1 medium onion, peeled
1 tablespoon melted butter
8 large potatoes, peeled and quartered

1. To make the stuffing, put the onion and water into a medium saucepan and simmer for 10 minutes. Add the apples and simmer for 5 minutes more. Add the oil.

2. Mix together the bread crumbs and apple mixture in a bowl. If the mixture is too dry, add a little hot water until it coheres.

3. Preheat the oven to 425° F. To make the goose, remove the neck and giblets from the inside. Pull out the pieces of fat from the interior and put them into a baking dish large enough to take the potatoes in a single layer. Wash the goose inside and out. Rub the cavity with the salt, then fill it with the stuffing. Put the whole peeled onion at the mouth of the cavity and put the goose into a large roasting pan. (The pan should be large enough to make basting easy and at least 2 inches deep so it will hold the plentiful fat that comes from the goose.) Brush the legs with the melted butter. Prick the breast in several places to enable the fat to run out. Place a sheet of aluminum foil over the goose, folding it round the edges of the pan so it covers the drumsticks but leaves the breast exposed.

4. Put the goose into the oven. Baste every 10–15 minutes by lifting the foil from the drumsticks so you can baste them and then replace the foil. After 30 minutes and when the fat is sizzling in the pan, reduce the temperature to 375°. Continue roasting and basting for 1 hour more, or until the breast is golden. Loosely recover the whole bird with foil and cook, basting once or twice for 30 minutes more, or until the drumstick moves slightly when wiggled and the juice looks only faintly pink. Transfer the goose to a warmed carving dish, cover lightly with a clean cloth, and let stand in a warm spot for 10–15 minutes before carving.

5. Start the roast potatoes after the goose has cooked for 1 hour. Put the baking dish, holding the fat from the goose cavity, into the oven. Let the fat melt. At the same time, boil the potatoes in lightly salted water for 10 minutes. They should be slightly softened but not tender. Drain.

6. Remove the baking dish from the oven and discard any crisped or unmelted bits of fat. Add the potatoes, turning them to coat. Put the potatoes in the oven and baste once or twice, turning

occasionally to brown all sides. (Use the fat from the goose for basting.) The potatoes are ready when they are golden and crisp on the outside and tender inside, about 30–45 minutes. If necessary to brown them, increase the temperature to 400° and place high in the oven.

7. To carve the goose, remove the wing close to the body of the bird. (The wing is virtually meatless, so save it for making soup or give it to someone who likes gnawing on bones.) Remove the legs at the thigh, then cut the leg in two. Carve the breast into long thin slices, starting at the neck and working toward the tail. Scoop some stuffing from the cavity and serve with the slices of goose. Serve the potatoes separately in a warmed serving dish. Serves 6–8.

NOVA DEVELOPMENT

Partridge with a Pear Sauté

Partridge is one of the birds listed in the Christmas carol "On the First Day of Christmas." The carol refers to the old English custom of serving birds for feasts — a custom that the settlers brought to New England. Large birds, such as swans, herons, and geese, were the most splendid dishes, but smaller birds, including sparrows and blackbirds, were made into pies. Partridge was especially welcome because it was considered more digestible than some other birds. America does not have European partridges, but several similar birds, including the bobwhite, are called partridge. Most partridges that you buy are chukar partridges raised on farms. They have little fat, so they are best cooked with moist ingredients to keep them tender. If they are the main focus of a meal, serve one bird per person; half a bird per person if you have many other dishes.

PARTRIDGES
Four 12-ounce partridges
Salt
2–3 tablespoons softened butter
2 tablespoons vegetable oil
3 slices lean bacon, cut into ¹/₂-inch pieces
¹/₂ pound kielbasa or sweet Italian sausage, cut into ¹/₂-inch pieces
1 medium onion, coarsely chopped
2 carrots, grated
8 cups Savoy cabbage, cut into 2-inch strips
Salt and black pepper
1 cup New England riesling or gewürztraminer or other white wine

PEAR SAUTÉ
3 large ripe firm Bosc pears
1 ¹/₂ tablespoons butter
1 tablespoon dark or light brown sugar
Several grinds of black pepper

1. To make the partridges, rinse them inside and out and pat dry with paper towels. Rub a little of the salt into the cavity of each bird. Loosen the skin from the breast and spread some of the butter directly on the breast meat.

2. Heat the oil in a large sauté pan over medium heat. Add the bacon and sausage and gently cook for 5 minutes or until browned. Remove from the pan and set aside.

3. Place the partridges in the pan breast-side down and brown for 4–5 minutes, turning to brown the breast and legs. Remove the birds from the pan and loosely tie their legs together to help them hold their shape. Set aside.

4. Add the onion and carrots to the pan and cook for 1–2 minutes. Stir in the reserved bacon and sausage, then the cabbage, stirring to mix everything and seasoning lightly with the salt and black pepper. Pour in the wine and let it sizzle. Stir, then shape hollows in the vegetables. Sit the reserved partridges in these hollows. Cover and cook over low heat, checking frequently and basting with the pan juices, for 50–60 minutes.

5. To test for doneness, wiggle the legs (they should feel loose) or insert a tester into the thickest part of the thigh; the juice that runs out should be clear, not pink. Quite possibly, the partridges will need 5–15 minutes more before they are done.

6. To make the sauté, peel and core the pears. Thickly slice, then cut across the slices at 1-inch intervals to make chunks. Melt the butter in a skillet over moderate heat, then toss in the pears and cook for 2 minutes. When they are coated with the butter, sprinkle with the sugar and reduce the heat. Gently cook until tender, about 2–4 minutes if the pears are ripe, longer if they are hard. Do not let them get mushy. Grind on the black pepper.

7. Serve the partridges in the cabbage mixture, with the pears on the side. Serves 4–8, depending on appetites.

Tourtière

When French-Canadians emigrated from Quebec to New England, they brought their Christmas foods with them. *Tourtière,* a meat-filled pie, is vital for the festive meal on Christmas Eve. It puts in a second appearance on New Year's Eve, too. Indeed, it's good on any wintry evening.

FILLING
1 ¹/₂ cups ¹/₂-inch diced potatoes (1 large potato)
2 medium onions, chopped
¹/₄ teaspoon salt
1 tablespoon vegetable oil
1 pound ground beef
1 pound ground pork
1 clove garlic, chopped
¹/₂ teaspoon ground cinnamon
¹/₄ teaspoon ground cloves
1–2 tablespoons fines herbes or poultry seasoning to taste
Salt and black pepper

PASTRY
2 cups all-purpose flour
1 teaspoon baking powder
¹/₄ teaspoon salt
¹/₂ cup cold lard or vegetable shortening
¹/₂ stick (2 ounces) cold butter
¹/₄ cup cold water

1. To make the filling, put the potatoes, onions, and the ¹/₄ teaspoon salt into a large saucepan with enough cold water to just cover. Bring to a boil and cook for 12–15 minutes, or until the potatoes are just tender.

2. While the potatoes and onions are cooking, heat the oil in a skillet. Add the beef and pork, crumbling it as you add. Sprinkle on the garlic, cinnamon, cloves, and fines herbes and season with the salt and black pepper. Cook, stirring frequently, for 3–4 minutes, or just until the meat has lost its pinkness.

3. Add the potato mixture to the meat and stir to combine. There should be enough liquid with the potatoes to make a moist though not sloppy mixture. If not, add a little water. Taste the mixture and add more seasoning or herbs if it is too bland. In particular, be sure to add enough black pepper to give it a zing. Let cool.

4. Preheat the oven to 425° F. Grease a 9-inch deep-dish pie pan.

5. To make the pastry, mix together the flour, baking powder, and salt in a large bowl. Cut the lard and butter into several bits and quickly rub them into the flour mixture until it looks like coarse crumbs. Make a well in the center and add the cold water. Pull the mixture together to form a dough, adding more water, 1 teaspoon at a time, if necessary.

6. Flour a work surface. Divide the dough into 2 portions, one somewhat larger than the other. Roll out the larger portion first and fit it into the prepared pie pan, leaving a little pastry overlapping the edge. Roll out the other portion. Put the filling into the shell, spreading it into an even layer. It should come level with the top of the dish. Place the rolled out dough on top. Make several slashes in the top to vent the steam. Dampen the edges of the pastry with water and crimp them together with your fingers.

7. Bake the tourtière for 15 minutes, then reduce the temperature to 375º and bake for 15 minutes more, or until the pie is golden. Serve hot with vegetables. Serves 6.

Winter Compote of Dried Fruits with Port

Bright cranberries scattered on top give this compote a festive look. The choice of fruit and precise quantities don't matter much, though the best compotes include a variety of ingredients. While you could bundle all of the fruit into one pan, the compote tastes better when the fruits are cooked separately because each then preserves its own flavor.

1/2 cup dried cranberries
1/2 pound dried apricots (about 1 1/2 cups)
1/2 pound pitted prunes (about 1 1/2 cups)
1/2 pound dried figs (about 2 cups)
1/4 pound dried apples (about 1/2 cup)
2 ounces dried mango or peach (2 large slices)
1 1/2 cups ruby port
2 whole cloves
1 bay leaf
One 2-inch cinnamon stick
2 tablespoons granulated sugar

1. Put the cranberries, apricots, prunes, figs, apples, and mango into separate saucepans and add enough cold water just to cover. Cover and simmer until all of the fruits are tender, about 7–15 minutes, depending on the dryness of the fruit. Drain all of the fruit, setting aside the juice from the apricots, apples, and mango. Put all of the fruit, except the cranberries, into a large serving bowl.

2. Put the port and 1 cup of the reserved juice from the apricots, apples, and mango into a large saucepan. (If you don't have a cupful, make up the difference with water.) Add the cloves, bay leaf, cinnamon stick, and sugar and simmer for 5 minutes.

3. Remove the cloves, bay leaf, and cinnamon stick with a slotted spoon. Pour the warmed juices over the fruit and scatter the cranberries on top. Serve with butter cookies. Serves 6–8.

Amelia Simmons's Christmas Cookey

The Dutch settlers of New York and Pennsylvania brought Christmas cookies to America in the seventeenth century. This cookie is based on the first published recipe, titled simply "A Christmas Cookey," which appeared in Amelia Simmons's *American Cookery* in 1796. In her preceding recipe, called simply Cookies, she calls for only a quarter pound of butter and 2 large spoonsful of powdered coriander to 2 ¹/₂ pounds of flour, while the Christmas Cookey has a whole pound of butter and "a tea cup of fine powdered coriander seed" to 3 pounds of flour, so it is much richer and more flavorful. Coriander is now used in curry powder and pickling spice, but in the past, it was a favorite in baked goods and not surprisingly: its slightly orangey aroma and flavor are delicious. In her instructions, Amelia Simmons writes "cut or stamp into shape and size [as] you please." I usually use moon- and star-shaped cutters and sprinkle the cookies with sugar to give them sparkle.

1 ¹/₂ *cups all-purpose flour*
¹/₂ *teaspoon baking powder*
³/₄ *cup granulated sugar*
3 *teaspoons ground coriander*
1 *stick (4 ounces) unsalted butter at room temperature*
¹/₃ *cup of milk*
Sparkling crystalized sugar, pearl sugar, or silver dragees (optional)

1. Preheat the oven to 350° F. Grease 2 baking sheets and dust with flour or line with baking parchment.

2. Mix together the flour, baking powder, sugar, and coriander in a bowl. Cut the butter into several bits and rub them into the flour mixture until it looks like coarse crumbs. Rub the mixture through your fingers a few more times to blend in. Make a well in the center and add a little less than ¹/₃ cup of the milk. Pull the mixture together to make a dough. Add the remaining milk if necessary to achieve a soft, rollable dough.

3. Flour a pastry board and a rolling pin. Roll out the dough until it is ¹/₄ inch thick. Using cookie cutters or a sharp knife, cut the dough into whatever shapes you please. Sprinkle with the sparkling or pearl sugar if you have it. Place the cookies on the prepared baking sheets and bake for 16–20 minutes or until lightly golden. Cool on wire racks. Makes about 2 dozen cookies.

AMELIA SIMMONS & AMERICA'S FIRST COOKBOOK

When Amelia Simmons published her tiny book in 1796 she gave it a giant title: American Cookery, or the Art of Dressing Viands, Fish, Poultry and Vegetables and the Best Modes of Making Pastes, Puffs, Pies, Tarts, Puddings, Custards and Preserves and all Kinds of Cakes from the Imperial Plumb to Plain Cake, adapted to this country and all grades of life. *The final words are crucial: Simmons was the first to address the needs of American women cooking American ingredients such as corn, cranberries, turtle, watermelons, squash and Jerusalem artichokes —foods that went unmentioned in the English cookbooks that Americans had been using previously.*

American Cookery *has the first recipe for pumpkin pie, now a Thanksgiving staple, as well as the first published recipe for a Christmas cookie. Calling for more butter, sugar, and spice than other cookies, it also includes pearlash — a woodash preparation that produces potassium carbonate when mixed with liquid, thus acting as a raising agent. This American invention, the precursor of baking powder, was then unknown in Europe.*

Though her book was an immediate success, nothing is known of Amelia Simmons except what can be deduced from it. She had it printed in Hartford, Connecticut, with later editions in Connecticut, Vermont, and New Hampshire, so she was likely a New Englander. She describes herself as "An American Orphan," and in the Preface writes feelingly of the implications, including the likelihood of being "reduced to the necessity of going into families in the line of domestics." Probably, then, she was a servant. Certainly she hoped the recipes in her book would become a stock in trade for "the poor solitary orphan" who, lacking "parents, brothers or riches," had to support herself.

But though we can only conjecture about Simmons's life, American Cookery *reveals much about her personality. Thrifty and practical, she springs from her pages with the briskness and energy of a bright New England day. Her directions are clear and her language vivid. For a raspberry cream, she says, the cream should be boiled "two or three wallops." For cakes, the eggs must be "well beat or whipped into a raging foam." It's no surprise, then, that her recipes continued to appear in American cookbooks until the beginning of the twentieth century or that* American Cookery *is still fun to read today.*

A. BLAKE GARDNER

Gingerbread Cookies

The tradition of making gingerbread goes back to the early Middle Ages, and every European country has a traditional form with many variations in the spices. This dough must be chilled before rolling, but it is easy to work with. It makes crisp cookies that you can cut and decorate as Christmas trees or gingerbread people. You can also make gingerbread stars — just the thing for dipping, one point at a time, into a cup of tea.

$^1/_2$ cup molasses
1 stick (4 ounces) butter at room temperature
$^1/_2$ cup firmly packed dark brown sugar
2 cups all-purpose flour
1 tablespoon ground ginger
$^1/_4$ teaspoon ground cloves
$^1/_4$ teaspoon white or black pepper
$^1/_2$ teaspoon ground cinnamon
$^1/_2$ teaspoon baking soda
Red and green frosting, raisins, silver dragées, sprinkles, crystallized cherries

1. Lightly grease a $^1/_2$-cup measuring cup and pour the molasses into the cup. Cream the butter and sugar together in a large bowl until it is smooth and light.

2. Mix together the flour, ginger, cloves, pepper, cinnamon, and baking soda in a bowl. Mix about half of the flour mixture into the butter mixture. Add the molasses, then mix in the remaining flour mixture. Shape the dough into 2 disks or rectangles, wrap each in plastic wrap, and chill for 2 hours or longer if more convenient.

3. Preheat the oven to 350° F. Cover 2 baking sheets with baking parchment or aluminum foil. Lightly flour a work surface and a rolling pin. Working with one piece of the dough at a time (and keeping the other one cool), roll out until $^1/_4$ inch thick. Cut out gingerbread people (or other shapes) with your cutter and transfer onto the prepared baking sheets. If you like, use raisins or silver dragées for eyes and buttons, slices of crystallized cherry for mouths, or dust with heatproof sprinkles. Bake for 8–12 minutes depending on the size of the cookies, then cool on wire racks.

4. If you want to tie the cookies on the tree, make a hole by wiggling a toothpick in them as soon as they come out of the oven. To frost the cookies, wait until they have cooled completely, then outline their shapes and make faces and buttons with red and green frosting. Makes 12–18 gingerbread people, depending on the size of your cutter. (The recipe can be doubled if you want more. In that case, shape it into 4 portions before rolling, and roll one portion at a time, keeping the others chilled. The dough is also good for gingerbread stars or other smaller cookies, with a yield of about 2 dozen.)

Mint Chocolate Chip Cookies

The original chocolate chip cookie came from the Toll House Inn in Whitman, Massachusetts, in the 1930s when the owner discovered that little chunks of chocolate do not self-destruct when baked in cookie dough. She had used Nestle's chocolate, so the company began making chocolate chips and now carries the Toll House cookie recipe on its packages. This version was an experiment that seemed less than successful because although deliciously minty, they did not look especially pretty — not until they were hung on the tree, when the glow of the lights shining through the pink peppermint bits transformed them.

1 stick (4 ounces) butter at room temperature, or $^1/_2$ cup vegetable shortening
$^1/_2$ cup granulated sugar
$^1/_4$ cup firmly packed brown sugar
1 egg
1 $^1/_2$ cups all-purpose flour
$^1/_2$ teaspoon baking soda
1 cup chocolate chips
$^1/_2$ cup crushed candy canes or Starlight mints

1. Preheat the oven to 325° F. Grease 3 baking sheets and dust with flour or line with baking parchment.

2. Cream the butter and both sugars together in a large bowl until smooth and light. Blend in the egg and mix well. Mix in the flour and baking soda, then stir in the chocolate chips. Set aside 3 teaspoons of the crushed candy canes and stir the remaining canes into the dough. (To crush, put them in a plastic bag and whack them a few times with the rolling pin. Ideally you should have some chunky bits and some powder.)

3. Drop the dough by teaspoonsful onto the prepared baking sheets, taking care not to space them close together because they spread; do not try to fit more than 9–10 on a sheet. Sprinkle with the reserved crushed candy canes and bake in the center of the oven for 10 minutes. Check frequently because they brown very quickly in the last 2–3 minutes of baking time.

4. Cool on a wire rack. If you want to hang the cookies, the time to make a hole is now, while the cookies are still hot and soft. Wiggle a toothpick or skewer in an appropriate place not too close to the edge. As the cookies cool, they crisp. When they are lukewarm, about 5–6 minutes after coming out of the oven, remove from the baking sheets with a palette knife or spatula. Cool completely and store in an airtight container. Makes about 30 cookies.

A Christmas Tree of Cinnamon Rolls

These cinnamon rolls baked in a Christmas tree shape can be decorated with simple white frosting swirls and silver dragées, or you can cover them with frosting and candies or with nuts or crystallized fruit.

CINNAMON ROLLS
1 package active dry yeast
1/3 cup warm water
3 cups all-purpose flour
1/2 teaspoon salt
*1 stick (4 ounces) butter at room
   temperature*
1/4 cup granulated sugar
2 eggs, lightly beaten
1/4–1/2 cup lukewarm water

FILLING
2 teaspoons ground cinnamon
1/2 teaspoon ground allspice
*1 cup firmly packed maple sugar or light
   brown sugar*

FROSTING & DECORATION
1 cup confectioners' sugar
1–1 1/2 tablespoons fresh lemon juice
*Silver balls and dragées or dried fruits or
   small candies*

1. To make the rolls, mix together the yeast and warm water in a small bowl. Let stand for 5 minutes or until slightly frothy.

2. Mix together the flour and salt in a large bowl. Cut the butter into large pieces and toss them in the flour mixture. Briefly rub the butter in with your fingers until the mixture looks like coarse crumbs. Stir in the sugar. Make a well in the center of the mixture and add the yeast and eggs. Mix and add the lukewarm water as needed to form a mixture soft enough to knead into a smooth dough that does not stick to the sides of the bowl or your hands. Kneading takes about 10 minutes by hand or 3 minutes with an electric mixer. Form into a ball and place in the bowl. Cover with plastic wrap and a kitchen towel and let stand until doubled in bulk, about 2 hours.

3. Punch down the dough and slap it on the counter. Knead for 2–3 minutes by hand, then shape into a rectangular block and place on a lightly floured surface. Try rolling it with a floured rolling pin. If it doesn't want to roll out and shrinks back into its original shape, cover, and let stand for 10 minutes. When it is ready, roll into a 10 x 17-inch rectangle.

4. Preheat the oven to 400° F. Grease a large baking sheet and dust with flour or line with baking parchment.

5. To make the filling, mix together the cinnamon, allspice, and sugar in a small bowl. Sprinkle the mixture over the dough, leaving a 1-inch border unsprinkled on one long edge. Starting at the other long edge, roll the dough over and over, jelly-roll fashion, pressing firmly as you go to get a tight roll. Press the unsprinkled border firmly to enclose all of the filling. Cut it into pieces by taking a length of 18-inch sewing thread or dental floss and placing it under the roll where you want to make the first cut. Cross the two ends of the thread over the top of the roll and squeeze until the thread cuts through the dough. Or, use a serrated knife and a gently sawing motion to cut. Make 15 rolls.

6. Typically, you will find that the rolls cut from the ends of your roll of dough are smaller than those cut from the middle. Take one of the small rolls and place it near the top and in the center of the prepared baking sheet. This is the top of the tree. Make the rest of the tree by placing a row of 2 smaller rolls underneath, followed by 2 rows of 3 rolls and 1 row of 4 rolls, using bigger rolls as you work downward. Use the remaining 2 rolls to make a tree trunk by placing them in 2 rows of 1 roll under the final row.

7. The rolls should only just touch each other; it helps to tuck the tail end of the spiral into the interior of the tree shape rather than on the edge. Let the rolls stand for 20 minutes, then bake for 18 minutes or until golden. Cool on a wire rack.

8. To make the frosting, mix together the sugar and 1 tablespoon of the lemon juice until you have a frosting that is smooth and spreadable but not too runny. Either pipe or spread the frosting on the tree, then decorate using silver balls and dragées, colorful dried fruits, such as cherries, apricots, and pineapple pieces, or small candies, such as satin cushions or M&Ms.

Chocolate Yule Log

A chocolate-covered roll cake, often decorated with pine branches and tiny mushrooms of marzipan or meringue, is a popular Christmas confection in most of the U.S. and Europe. Its origin is the French bûche de Noël, and the cake is especially dear to New England's Franco-American community. It is not hard to make, and it is fun to assemble. Make the frosting and filling before you make the cake so you can cover it as soon as it cools and thus prevent it from drying out. The filling in this version is flavored with coffee; for an almond version, replace the coffee with a few drops of almond extract; for a peppermint version, use a few drops of peppermint extract. You could also use a chocolate-flavored cake rather than a yellow cake, and occasionally recipes call for a covering of ganache — chocolate and cream. Buttercream is more typical, however, and is both more subtle in flavor and easier to spread.

CHOCOLATE BUTTERCREAM

3 egg yolks
1/3 cup granulated sugar
1/4 cup light corn syrup
1 stick (4 ounces) butter at room temperature
1 tablespoon instant coffee powder
1 tablespoon warm water
4 ounces semisweet or bittersweet chocolate, melted
1–2 tablespoons brandy, Kahlúa, or Irish cream liqueur (optional)

COFFEE FILLING

1 stick (4 ounces) butter at room temperature
3/4 cup confectioners' sugar
1 tablespoon instant coffee powder
1 tablespoon warm water

CAKE

1/2 stick (2 ounces) unsalted butter
3 eggs
3/4 cup granulated sugar
1 teaspoon pure vanilla extract
1 1/4 cups cake flour
1/2 teaspoon baking powder
1 teaspoon confectioners' sugar
Small Christmas ornaments

MARZIPAN MUSHROOMS

4 ounces almond paste
2 tablespoons light corn syrup
1/4 cup confectioners' sugar
1–2 teaspoons cocoa powder

1. To make the buttercream, beat the egg yolks in a large bowl with an electric mixer until very pale and tripled in bulk. Mix together the sugar and corn syrup in a small saucepan and heat over low heat, stirring constantly, until the sugar has dissolved. Bring to a rapid boil. Pour the mixture in a thin stream into the eggs, stirring constantly. Immediately, beat with an electric mixer until the mixture is cool.

2. Add the butter to the egg mixture, 1 tablespoon at a time, and beat until it is mixed in before adding more. Mix together the coffee powder and warm water. Add the coffee mixture and

2 ounces of the melted chocolate to the egg mixture. Beat in, then add the remaining chocolate and the brandy if you are using it. Keep in the fridge, but return to room temperature before spreading on the cake.

3. To make the coffee filling, beat the butter until it looks pale. Sift the sugar into it and beat again until it is silky. Mix together the coffee powder and the warm water and beat it into the mixture. Set aside.

4. Preheat the oven to 375º F. Line a 10 x 15-inch jelly-roll pan with baking parchment. To make the cake, melt the butter in a microwave or over low heat, taking care it never gets really hot. Let cool without congealing.

5. Whisk together the eggs, granulated sugar, and vanilla in a large bowl with an electric mixer until they form a pale cloudy bulk. Carefully fold in the cooled melted butter. Stir together the flour and baking powder, then sift about one-fourth of the mixture onto the egg mixture. Fold in, then sift on and fold in another one-fourth. Proceed like this until all of the flour has been folded in. Pour the batter into the prepared pan and bake for 14–16 minutes, or until the cake springs back when you press it lightly.

6. With a knife, loosen the cake from the edges of the pan, then turn it out onto a wire rack. Strip off the baking parchment. While the cake is still warm, place it on a clean, cloth dish towel. Have the long edge of the cake closest to you, then roll the towel and the cake up so that the towel is inside the cake. (Rolling the cake at this point makes it easier to reroll later.)

7. When the cake is cool, unroll it and remove the towel. Spread the reserved coffee mixture inside, then reroll. (If the cake cracks, you can squeeze it together as you roll it. Don't worry about it; any flaws will be covered with the buttercream.) Make a diagonal cut about 2 inches down. Transfer the main part of the cake to a serving dish. (An oval dish works well.) Position the small piece of the cake on the edge of the large roll so it looks like a log with a side branch. Cover the cake with the buttercream. Give it a barklike look by drawing a fork over it. Also cover the ends with frosting and draw circles with your fork to look like tree rings.

8. To make the marzipan mushrooms, break the almond paste into little pieces in a small bowl. Add the corn syrup and mix well. Sift on the confectioners' sugar and mix until you have a smooth paste. Dust a work surface with more confectioners' sugar and roll out the marzipan into a $^3/_4$-inch diameter cylinder. Break off 10 pieces and roll into grape-sized balls. (These will become mushroom tops.) Roll the remainder a little thinner and break into 10 bits for stalks. Shape the balls into mushroom tops, making an indentation underneath. Fix the stalk bits into the indentations. Chill for 1 hour or longer if you like or until firm.

9. To make brown mushrooms, dust them with the cocoa and rub it in with your finger. To make speckled mushrooms, sift on the cocoa. Arrange the mushrooms on and around the log. Surround with pine twigs. Sift on a little of the confectioners' sugar for snow. Add small Christmas decorations, such as tiny colored balls, birds, snowmen, or whatever takes your fancy.

Cranberry-Almond Wreath

This wreath-shaped sweet bread conceals a filling of cranberry sauce and almond paste. It is delicious for holiday brunches or teas because it is flavorful, but not too rich.

WREATH

1 package active dry yeast
¹/₃ cup warm water
¹/₂ cup milk
¹/₂ stick (2 ounces) butter
2 tablespoons granulated sugar
1 egg, beaten
2–2 ¹/₂ cups all-purpose flour
¹/₂ cup jellied or whole cranberry sauce
6 ounces almond paste
2 tablespoons cream
1 tablespoon granulated sugar
2 tablespoons milk

DECORATION & FROSTING

¹/₄ cup sliced almonds
2 tablespoons dried cranberries
¹/₃ cup warm water
1 tablespoon granulated sugar
1 cup confectioners' sugar
Cold water

1. To make the wreath, put the yeast and the warm water into a large bowl. Let stand for 10 minutes or until slightly frothy.

2. Heat the milk, butter, and the 2 tablespoons sugar in a small saucepan until the butter has melted. Let cool to lukewarm, then mix in the egg.

3. Add 2 cups of the flour to the yeast and mix in. Add the egg mixture and continue mixing until you have a dough. If it is sticky and soft, add as much of the remaining flour as necessary to achieve a kneadable consistency. Knead until it is smooth and does not stick to your hands or to the side of the bowl, about 15 minutes by hand or 6–7 minutes with an electric mixer. Roll it into a ball and set it in a greased bowl until doubled in bulk.

4. Line a baking sheet with baking parchment or grease and dust with flour. Flour a work surface and a rolling pin. Punch down the dough and knead it on the surface for 1 minute. Cover with plastic wrap and let stand for a few minutes, then roll it into a strip measuring 5 x 27 inches.

5. Spread the cranberry sauce down the center of the strip, leaving a 1¹/₂-inch border on each side. Roll the almond paste into a sausage shape as long as the dough. Place it in the middle of the strip, on top of the cranberry sauce. Fold one side of the dough over the almond paste. Brush it with 1 tablespoon of the cream. Fold the other side over and press together.

6. Working carefully, turn the roll over and transfer it, seam-side down, to the prepared baking sheet, turning the ends to meet each other. Form a circle by tucking one end inside the other, taking care to trim off any unnecessary dough. Brush with the remaining cream and press to make them attach. Cover with plastic wrap and let stand in a draft-free spot until puffy and risen, about 30–45 minutes.

7. Preheat the oven to 400º F. Bake the wreath for 10 minutes. Reduce the temperature to 375º and bake for 10 minutes more. Let cool on the baking sheet set on a wire rack for several minutes, then remove from the sheet and let cool to room temperature. (This is where using baking parchment is a big help; you can slide the wreath right off and onto the cooling rack.)

8. As soon as the wreath comes out of the oven, boil the 1 tablespoon sugar and the milk together in a small saucepan until it is very bubbly. While the wreath is still hot, brush the surface with this mixture, which will give it a shine.

9. Preheat the oven to 300º F. To make the decorations, put the almonds into a baking pan and toast for 10 minutes or until golden. Soak the cranberries in the warm water in a small saucepan for 15 minutes. Add the granulated sugar and simmer for 5 minutes, or until the cranberries have plumped. Drain and set aside.

10. To make the frosting, sift the confectioners' sugar into a bowl. Make a well in the center and stir in the cold water, 1 teaspoon at a time, until it is spreadable. Drizzle the frosting over the wreath, taking care to mask where you joined the ends together. Let the frosting run down the sides. While it is moist, decorate with the toasted almonds and the reserved cranberries. (Since the cranberries are sticky, the easiest way to place them is with a toothpick.) If you like, you could add a ribbon or Christmas ornament — another way of disguising the join.

Italian Butter Nut Cookies

Every year Julia Melchionda of Wallingford, Connecticut, makes these cookies for her family, which now includes a great-grandchild. This is one of her recipes.

1 stick (4 ounces) butter at room temperature
1/2 cup granulated sugar
2 eggs, separated
4 tablespoons evaporated milk
1 teaspoon pure vanilla extract
2 teaspoons lemon zest
2 teaspoons orange zest
2 1/2 cups all-purpose flour
1 cup sliced almonds or chopped walnuts or pecans
18 whole crystallized cherries

1. Cream the butter and sugar together in a large bowl until pale and smooth.

2. Mix together the egg yolks, milk, vanilla, and both zests in a small bowl. Add the egg mixture to the butter mixture. Mix in the flour and knead with your hands until you have a smooth, nonsticky dough. Chill for 2 hours or overnight if more convenient.

3. Preheat the oven to 350º F. Grease 2 baking sheets or line with baking parchment.

4. Crush the nuts until they look like coarse crumbs. Whisk together the egg whites in a shallow bowl. Roll the dough into balls the size of a small walnut. Dip in the egg white, then roll in the crushed nuts. Place on the prepared baking sheets and flatten them slightly so they form 1 1/2-inch circles. Halve the cherries and place a half in the middle of each cookie. Bake for 20 minutes or until golden. Cool on wire racks. Makes 2 1/2–3 dozen cookies.

Mexican Wedding Cakes

These cookies get their melt-in-the-mouth quality from butter and walnuts and their Christmassy looks from a snowfall of confectioners' sugar. Sometimes they are called Russian Wedding Cakes, and Greek *kourambiedes* are a similar sugar-dusted shortbread. Whichever country invented them, they are justifiably popular.

2 cups chopped or halved walnuts
1 stick (4 ounces) butter, well softened
$^1/_3$ cup granulated sugar
1 teaspoon pure vanilla extract
2 cups all-purpose flour
1 teaspoon baking powder
$^1/_4$ teaspoon salt
$^1/_2$ cup confectioners' sugar

1. Preheat the oven to 325° F. Grease 2 baking sheets or line with baking parchment.

2. Crush the walnuts so they look like coarse crumbs, either by pulsing in a food processor or by putting in a plastic bag and beating with a rolling pin. Set aside.

3. Cream the butter with the granulated sugar and vanilla in a bowl, then beat for 2–3 minutes.

4. Mix together the flour, baking powder, and salt in a bowl. Add the flour mixture to the creamed mixture and mix into a stiff dough. Fold in the reserved walnuts.

5. Wet your hands with cold water. Form the dough into balls the size of small walnuts. Place on the prepared baking sheets and bake for 20–25 minutes or until golden. Remove from the oven and while they are still warm, shower them with $^1/_4$ cup of the confectioners' sugar. Store in an airtight container. Just before serving, shower the cookies with the remaining confectioners' sugar. Makes about 2 dozen.

Mincemeat Ice Cream

Mincemeat is a good standby, as this delicious ice cream proves. It's an alluring dessert after a hearty holiday meal, and you don't need an ice-cream maker to make it. Note, though, that the eggs remain uncooked, so this is best not served to toddlers and others who may not be able to resist the chance — statistically tiny though it is — that raw eggs may cause digestive upsets.

3 extra-large eggs
³/₄ cup granulated sugar
1 ¹/₂ cups heavy cream
¹/₄ teaspoon pure vanilla extract
2 tablespoons rum
12 red crystallized cherries
1 cup firmly packed homemade mincemeat (see recipe on page 161)

1. Beat the eggs for 5 minutes in a large bowl with an electric mixer or whisk 10 minutes by hand until they are bulky and pale in color. Add ¹/₄ cup of the sugar and vigorously beat in. Add another ¹/₄ cup of the sugar and beat in. Beat in the remaining sugar until the mixture is very pale and a noticeable "ribbon" or trail remains on the surface for several seconds when you let the mixture drip off the beater.

2. Beat the cream in another large bowl until it forms soft peaks. Add the vanilla and 1 tablespoon of the rum and beat in. Fold in one-fourth of the egg mixture using a rubber spatula. Gradually fold in the remaining egg mixture, a little at a time, until it is well blended. Put into the freezer for about 1 ¹/₂ hours or until frozen at the edges.

3. Remove the mixture and beat it hard, blending in the remaining rum. Replace in the freezer for 1 hour, then beat again.

4. Coarsely chop 6 cherries. Stir the chopped cherries and ¹/₂ cup of the mincemeat into the mixture. Beat thoroughly with an electric mixer. Transfer the mixture to a serving dish. Return it to the freezer for 1 hour or more until it is close to setting.

5. Now stir in the remaining mincemeat. (Adding the mincemeat in 2 portions, prevents it all from sinking to the bottom of the dish.) Smooth the top, then cover with plastic wrap or aluminum foil and freeze for at least 4 hours or until set.

6. Halve the remaining cherries and decorate the ice cream with them. Let stand for a few minutes to soften slightly before serving. Serves 6, as individual servings; serves 8, if served with pie.

Candied Orange Peel

Winter is the season for oranges. In earlier times, they appeared just in time for Christmas, so they were a bright symbol of the season, not to be treated casually, but tucked into the toes of Christmas stockings or piled in bowls as a centerpiece dessert. In order to waste nothing of this treat, the peel was often candied and rolled in sugar — a bittersweet confection that is easy to make.

Peel from 2 large washed oranges
1 ¹/₄ cups granulated sugar
³/₄ cup water
Juice of 1 small orange or tangerine (optional)

1. Cut the peel from the oranges by cutting it into fourths so you have 4 large pieces of peel. Using scissors, cut these pieces diagonally into 2 x ¹/₄-inch strips. Put the strips into a large saucepan, cover with water, and simmer for 5 minutes. Drain and repeat with fresh water two more times. Finally drain and set aside.

2. Put 1 cup of the sugar, the water, and the orange juice if you are using it, or an additional ¹/₄ cup of water if not into the saucepan. Stir over low heat until the sugar has dissolved. Return the reserved strips of peel to the pan and simmer for 15–20 minutes. Drain thoroughly.

3. Put the strips of peel onto a sheet of waxed paper or baking parchment, using a spatula or tongs to separate them so they do not touch. Sprinkle with the remaining sugar and let stand in a dry place exposed to the air until they are firm. Depending on the humidity and temperature, they may take from 1–3 days to dry. Turn them over occasionally to speed the process. Store in an airtight container. Serve with coffee.

To make Chocolate-Tipped Candied Orange Peel: *Candied orange peel swirled into melted chocolate tastes elegant, dramatic, and infinitely alluring — like a tango in your mouth. You will need 2 ounces of semisweet chocolate. Put it in a small bowl and melt it, either in a microwave or by standing it over, but not touching, simmering water. Have ready a dish filled with sugar to a depth of 1–2 inches. This is to stand the strips in while the chocolate cools — much better than cooling on a rack, which leaves marks. Dip one end of the candied peel in the chocolate so that you coat about 1 inch of the end. Stick the other end in the sugar so the strip is standing upright with its chocolate tip in the air. Let the chocolate firm up, then remove the strips from the sugar (which you can use for another purpose) and store them in an airtight container. But don't keep them too long; they are best served within a day or two of making.*

SELECT BIBLIOGRAPHY

Baron, Stanley. *Brewed in America: A History of Beer and Ale in the United States.* Boston: Little, Brown and Company, 1962.

Carr, Sister Frances A. *Shaker Your Plate: Of Shaker Cooks and Cooking.* United Society of Shakers: Sabbathday Lake, ME, 1985.

Child, Lydia Maria. *American Frugal Housewife.* (Boston: Carter, Hendee and Co., 1832) Bedford, MA: A Chapman Billies Reprint for Applewood Books, n.d.

Copage, Eric V. *Kwanzaa: An African-American Celebration of Culture and Cooking.* NY: William Morrow, 1991.

David, Elizabeth. *Harvest of the Cold Months: The Social History of Ice and Ices.* London: Michael Joseph, 1994.

Davidson, Alan. *North Atlantic Seafood.* NY: Harper & Row Publishers, 1989.

_____. *The Oxford Companion to Food.* Oxford: The Oxford University Press, 1999.

Farmer, Fannie Merritt. *The Boston Cooking-School Cookbook.* Boston: Little, Brown and Company, 1896.

Glasse, Hannah. *The Art of Cookery Made Plain and Easy (1747).* A Facsimile of the first Edition. London: Prospect Books, 1983.

Harris Brose, Nancy, Juliana McGovern Dupre, Wendy Tochler Kohler, and Jean McClure Mudge. *Emily Dickinson: Profile of the Poet as Cook.* Amherst, MA: 1976.

Hooker, Richard. *The Book of Chowder.* Boston: The Harvard Common Press, 1978.

Hornblower, Malabar. *The Plimoth Plantation New England Cookery Book.* Boston: The Harvard Common Press, n.d.

Kurlansky, Mark. *Cod A Biography of the Fish That Changed the World.* NY: Walker and Company, 1997.

Lee, N. K. M. (Published anonymously. Boston: Munroe and Francis, 1832) *The cook's own book: being a complete culinary encyclopedia.* NY: Arno Press, 1972.

Leslie, Eliza. *Miss Leslie's Directions for Cookery.* (Philadelphia: Carey and Hart, 1837). unabridged reprint of 1851 edition, introduced by Jan Langone. Mineola, NY: Dover Publications, Inc., 1999.

Lindsay, Eldress Bertha. ed. by Mary Rose Boswell. *Seasoned with Grace: My Generation of Shaker Cooking.* Woodstock, VT: The Countryman Press, 1987.

Mariani, John. *The Encyclopedia of American Food and Drink,* rev. ed. NY: Lebhar-Friedman Books, 1999.

Miller, Amy Bess, and Persis Fuller. *The Best of Shaker Cooking.* Hancock, MA: The Hancock Shaker Village, Inc., 1985.

Oliver, Sandra L. *Saltwater Foodways New Englanders and Their Food, at Sea and Ashore, in the Nineteenth Century.* Mystic, CT: Mystic Seaport Museum, Inc., 1995.

Phillips, Roger. *Mushrooms of North America.* Boston: Little, Brown and Company, 1991.

Several Ladies. *The Pocumtuc Housewife.* Originally published by the Deerfield Parish Guild, 1897; republished by Pocumtuck Valley Memorial Association, Deerfield MA, 1985.

Shapiro, Laura. *Perfection Salad: Women and Cooking at the Turn of the Century.* NY: Farrar, Straus and Giroux, 1986.

Simmons, Amelia. *American Cookery.* (Hartford: Hudson & Goodwin, 1796). NY: Dover edition of the 1958 Oxford University Press facsimile, 1984.

Thomas, Marguerite. *Wineries of the Eastern States,* 3rd ed. Lee, MA: Berkshire House Publishers, 1999.

White, Jasper. *Jasper White's Cooking From New England.* NY: Harper & Row Publishers, 1989.

Wilkie, Richard W., and Tager, Jack (eds.). *Historical Atlas of Massachusetts.* Amherst: Univerity of Massachusetts Press, 1991.

MAIL-ORDER RESOURCES

Atkins Farms Country Market
1150 West Street
Amherst, MA 01002
800-594-9537
www.atkinsfarms.com
Apples, cider, pears, jams, jellies, maple syrup,
gift baskets, cheeses

Boggy Meadow Farm
River Road
Walpole, NH 03608
603-756-3300
www.fannymasoncheese.com
Swiss-style cheese

Boyajian Inc.
349 Lenox Street
Norwood, MA 02062
800-964-0665
www.boyajianinc.com
Pure citrus oils, flavored olive oils and vinegars,
smoked salmon

Browne Trading Company
Merrill's Wharf
260 Commercial Street
Portland, ME 04101
800-944-7848
Smoked salmon, canned fiddleheads, Maine
specialties

Cabot Cheese
Main Street
Cabot, VT 05647
800-881-6334
www.cabotcheese.com
Vermont Cheddar cheese, maple syrup

Clark Farm
1647 Tadmer Road
Wells, VT 05774
802-325-3203
Maple syrup, maple pepper, other maple
products

Crowley Cheese
Healdville, VT 05758
800-683-2606
Vermont cheese

Davenport Maple Farm
111 Tower Road
Shelburne, MA 01370
413-625-2866
Maple syrup, maple sugar, candies, maple-
coated peanuts

Duck Trap River Fish Farm
57 Little River Drive
Belfast, ME 04915
800-828-3825
www.ducktrap.com
Wide range of smoked fish and shellfish,
including salmon and scallops

Harbor Fish Market
9 Custom House Wharf
Portland, ME 04101
800-370-1790
www.harborfish.com
Lobsters, shellfish

King Arthur Flour
The Baker's Catalogue
PO Box 876
Norwich, VT 05055
800-827-6836
www.KingArthurFlour.com
Unbleached all-purpose flour, specialty flours
and sugars, baking supplies

Stonewall Kitchens
Stonewall Lane
York, ME 03909
800-207-JAMS
www.stonewallkitchen.com
Jams, jellies, condiments, sauces

Vermont Butter and Cheese Company
PO Box 95
Pitman Road
Websterville, VT 05678
800-884-6287
www.vtbutterandcheeseco.com
Cultured butter, European-style cheeses

Vermont Shepherd
875 Patch Road
Putney, VT 05346
802-387-4473
www.vermontshepherd.com
Sheep cheese, maple syrup

INDEX